SUCCESS
THE **PSYCHOLOGY** OF **ACHIEVEMENT**

SUCCESS
THE PSYCHOLOGY OF ACHIEVEMENT

DEBORAH A. OLSON, PhD
WITH MEGAN KAYE

DK

DK | Penguin Random House

Senior Editors Hannah Bowen, Bob Bridle
Senior Art Editor Karen Constanti
Jacket Designer Nicola Powling
Senior Production Editor Tony Phipps
Senior Production Controller Luca Bazzoli
Managing Editors Dawn Henderson, Angela Wilkes
Managing Art Editor Marianne Markham
Art Director Maxine Pedliham
Publisher Mary-Clare Jerram
US Publisher Mike Sanders
US Editors Lori Hand, Michelle Melani
Special Sales Creative Project Manager Alison Donovan

Written by Megan Kaye
Illustrations Keith Hagan

This Paperback Edition 2022
First American Edition, 2017
Published in the United States by DK Publishing,
1745 Broadway, 20th Floor, New York, NY 10019

22 23 24 25 10 9 8 7 6 5 4 3
019–271734–Jan/2017

Published in Great Britain by Dorling Kindersley Limited

A catalog record for this book is available from the Library of Congress
ISBN 978-0-7440-8428-3

Printed and bound in China

For the curious
www.dk.com

MIX
Paper | Supporting responsible forestry
FSC™ C018179

This book was made with Forest Stewardship Council™ certified paper — one small step in DK's commitment to a sustainable future. For more information go to **www.dk.com/our-green-pledge**

CONSULTING PSYCHOLOGIST

Deborah Olson, PhD

Professor of Leadership and Management in the College of Business and Public Management at the University of La Verne, California, Dr. Olson specializes in the areas of strengths-based leadership development and mid/late career growth. She has received awards from the university for excellence in both teaching and scholarship, and has over 30 years of experience working in organizational development. In the 1980s, she worked at Chrysler Corporation in the Learning and Development department. She then worked as a consultant, and in 1995 became a partner at Hay Management Consultants, an international leadership development and human resource consulting firm. In 2001, she started her own consulting practice, which focuses on designing and implementing leadership development processes and strengths-based human capital management systems.

ACKNOWLEDGMENTS

Deborah Olson:

It is with deep gratitude that I acknowledge my husband and colleague, Dr. Kenneth Shultz, who through our three decades together has given me a clear understanding of what success means and how the concepts discussed in this book are demonstrated through the choices we make each day.

The publisher would like to thank:

Nicola Erdpresser for design assistance; Bob Saxton and Alice Horne for editorial assistance; Georgina Palffy for proofreading; Margaret McCormack for the index; and US editor Lori Hand, for her help and expertise.

CONTENTS

CHAPTER 3
HONE YOUR ATTITUDE
EXERCISE YOUR THINKING AND HARNESS YOUR SKILLS

CHAPTER 4
BASIC SKILLS FOR SUCCESS
AN EVERYDAY GUIDE TO EFFECTIVENESS

CHAPTER 5
IN YOUR SIGHTS
GOAL SETTING AND GOAL GETTING

CHAPTER 6
SUCCESS
A WHOLE-LIFE PROCESS

FOREWORD

Clarity is essential to create success and achieve goals that are important to us. For over 30 years, I have worked with managers, executives, and students to assist them in applying research-based practices to help them achieve their goals—both personal and professional. During this time, I have noticed a specific pattern: most of us can clearly describe what we *don't* like about our lives, work, and relationships, with the belief that if only we could *do this or change that*, we would be successful. However, when asked to describe what we *do* want for ourselves, the picture we conjure up tends to be blurry, for example: make more money, travel, be promoted at work, have a loving relationship, or start our own business.

In a digital age, the pervasiveness of social media and the frequency with which we "see" others succeed can make it more challenging to find clarity on what success means to each of us. With a continuous stream of images that show how other people *seem* to be succeeding, our lives, activities, vacations, relationships, and physical appearance can appear to be "less than" in comparison. If we are not yet clear about what we want to achieve, the images we see around us will only obscure our vision.

The ideas, tools, and approaches in the following pages summarize the research on success and achievement. Each chapter is designed to help bring your thinking into focus, enabling you to develop detailed and specific plans. This in turn will allow you to sustain your momentum, even in the face of tendencies to procrastinate, negative judgments from others about whether what you are doing is "right for you," a fear of failure, and concerns about what you may need to leave behind as you reach for whatever it is that you wish to achieve.

The material in this book is based on the psychological research and applied practices of positive psychology, which emphasizes the importance of building hope, resilience, and optimism. Chapter one explores the many ways of finding out what success means to each of us, while chapter two explains how you can harness the positive power of your beliefs to achieve success and fulfillment. Chapter three looks at the benefits of focusing on your strengths, and challenging self-limiting thoughts—such as, "I can't do that; I tried it before and it didn't work." To succeed and achieve, action is needed, and chapter four offers some essential, practical techniques for improving your effectiveness. As you move toward achieving your goals, chapter five discusses topics such as creative problem-solving, effective networking, and the psychology of influencing others. In the last chapter, the book looks at how nurturing our well-being and personal relationships is a vital element that contributes to our overall success in life.

You may find it useful to revisit these chapters as you refine your goals, new opportunities emerge, and your life circumstances change—when this happens, you can return with a fresh perspective. Your definition of success will evolve over time, and new goals will emerge and refocus your attention. This is a natural part of our development and growth.

Your picture of what success *looks like* is unique. Honor this, and know that comparing yourself with others isn't helpful. It's the journey of learning how to succeed and the process of continuing to reach for what *you* want that makes all the difference. Success is about making proactive and purposeful decisions each day about what is important to you, and creating goals that are linked to what you value and dream of achieving. This book will help you discover exactly what success means to you, and how to go about achieving it.

Deborah A. Olson, PhD

CHAPTER 1

A LIFE IN PROGRESS

THE MEANINGS OF SUCCESS AND FULFILLMENT

WHAT DOES SUCCESS LOOK LIKE?

THE DIVERSITY OF FULFILLMENT

A full life is more than the sum of its most obvious achievements. The first step toward living a more fruitful, engaged, and prosperous life means figuring out what success means to you.

There's probably a reason why you've picked up this book. Perhaps you're wondering what your next challenge will be, and you're looking for new ways to harness your ideas, energy, and ambition to get the best results. It could be that you already have a set of goals in mind, but you're not making sufficient progress toward them (or—somehow—not managing to achieve them at all). Or maybe you're stuck in a bit of a rut because your old plans are redundant, your usual habits aren't working any more, and you've lost direction.

Being realistic

Naturally, time pressures, as well as limitations on our multitasking skills and our stamina, prevent us from attaining excellence in every aspect of our lives. Compromise is inevitable. The important thing is that we don't agonize about what it would have been impossible for anyone in our circumstances to achieve. We can only play the cards we have been dealt.

Measuring achievement

The fact is that there is no single, simple measure of success. Although ambitions can relate to objective yardsticks such as wealth, status, and career, these benchmarks don't capture the whole picture. Indeed, objective criteria such as these often prompt people to make unhelpful comparisons between themselves and their peers; but these sorts of comparisons only make sense if the people concerned have ambitions in the same areas. Many people prioritize the private aspects of their lives, such as conducting a loving relationship with their partner over many years, rather than the public aspects, such as a successful career.

Changing ideas

Ideas within wider society as to what represents success change over time too. It could be argued that the idea of measuring success

HOW DO YOU DEFINE SUCCESS?

To achieve your goals you should first consider what it is that you want to accomplish. Start with these questions:

- What is most important to you?
- What do you think makes for a successful life?
- Is there anyone whom you admire? What is it about their life or life choices you wish to emulate?
- How much are you willing to commit to achieving your goals?
- How will you know when you've "succeeded"?

A SNAPSHOT IN TIME

In their book, *Co-Active Coaching*, Henry Kimsey-House, Karen Kimsey-House, Phillip Sandahl, and Laura Whitworth discuss the Wheel of Life, a tool to help you visualize the many aspects of your life. It functions as a snapshot of how you feel about your life at a particular moment in time.

Consider the different facets of your life, such as your career, personal relationships, physical health, financial position, and so on. (You can change the categories to make them more relevant to you.) Measure your level of satisfaction within each category on a scale of 1–10. One means "not satisfied at all," and 10 means "highly satisfied." Draw the lines in the wheel and link them up—as shown with the white line in the example here.

Have you got the "balance" right? Is the inner wheel you've created smooth and well-rounded, or is it "jagged" and uneven because some aspects of your life are being neglected? Use the wheel to help you identify where you could focus more time and energy from now on, showing you how a more balanced life might look. Take another "snapshot" further down the line and compare.

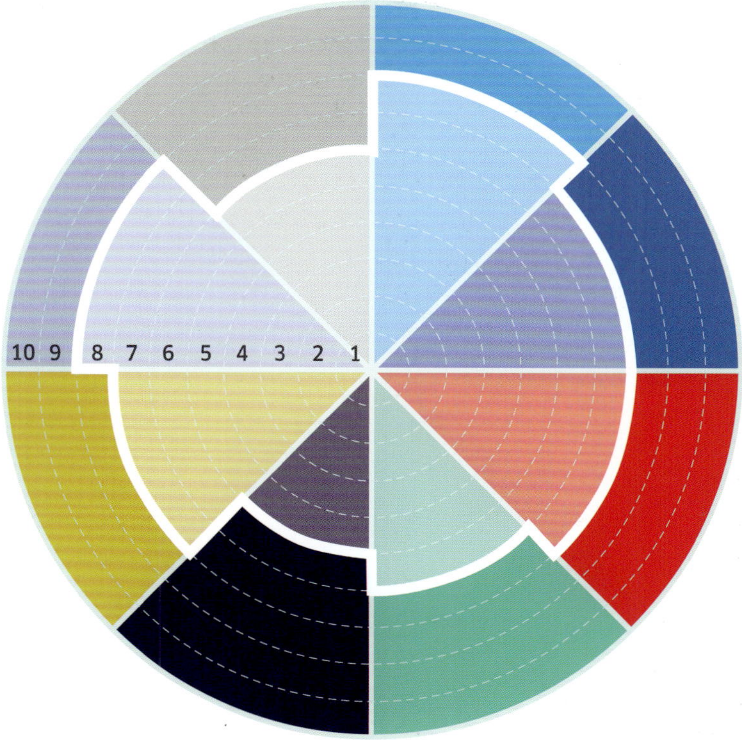

THE WHEEL OF LIFE

- Family
- Career
- Health
- Personal growth
- Friends and relationships
- Financial situation
- Leisure activities
- Home environment

in terms of public achievement has outlived its usefulness, not least because it may involve unacceptable sacrifices in other spheres, such as personal relationships, physical health, and psychological well-being. The material success that comes with a high-profile career may run the risk of clashing with the values of the "good life." And we must also take into account the cost to the individual and their family of work-related stress (see pp.96–101), a problem sharply on the rise in the Western world.

As will become increasingly clear throughout the course of this book, we each have our own ideas about what constitutes success, and how you define success will probably change as you progress through the different phases of your life.

> **Success** is liking yourself, **liking what you do**, and liking how you do it.
>
> **Maya Angelou**
> Novelist

A SUCCESS PINBOARD

STAR TRAITS OF A THRIVING PERSON

To be successful, you need to have a balance of qualities, and have clear ideas about what you want from life. You're likely to place greater value on flexibility than on trying to bend the world to your will.

Many people dream of a magic bullet that will make them more organized, productive, and successful. Indeed, highly effective people tend to observe a number of useful practices; perhaps the most obvious relates to good time management (see pp.124–125). For instance, be realistic about timing, and allow some slack to deal with the unforeseen. Work to a timeline to keep things on track. If you can, get up early—the sense of having the whole day ahead can make you feel energized and creative, and morning is often the best time for brainstorming. Alternatively, deal with your most tedious chores first so they don't hang over you all day.

Clear some space

A great way to mark a fresh start and clear your mind at the same time is to declutter. Apply it to your physical environment, or make time in your schedule to focus on one thing without any distractions. Whatever form it takes, decluttering can be a powerful tool, freeing you to focus on your true priorities.

> It requires a better type of mind to **seek out**... **the new** than to follow the worn paths of accepted success.
>
> **John D. Rockefeller**

GET ATTITUDE-SMART

Success can look very different in different fields, but the psychological habits that underpin it tend to look similar. Set your thinking right, and it can be the foundation of a more rewarding life.

Be passionate

Your level of emotional investment in any enterprise is often a principal driver of success. It provides you with the strength to overcome setbacks. Believing in a vision also gives you a compass to steer by.

Maintain perspective

Avoid focusing on the detail before you have the bigger picture in mind. The nitty-gritty is for later, once the outline of the wider plan has been formulated.

Take charge

Seize the initiative, knowing that you have sole responsibility for creating your own success.

Embrace failure

It's good practice to see failure as inevitable in any long-term project. Don't take it personally or let it diminish your enthusiasm.

Use your toolkit

Make the best use of the resources at your disposal. These may consist of time, money, objects—even people. Use them wisely, and wield them creatively.

Stay positive

An optimistic mindset will ensure an abundance of energy, which in turn will bring you constructive results. If ingrained in your attitude and habits, this positivity will give you the tenacity to triumph over any obstacles you may encounter.

Listen to yourself

Follow your inner voice. Do your best not to be swayed by peer pressure or naysayers.

MORE OR LESS SUCCESSFUL

SETTING YOUR SCALE OF ACHIEVEMENT

It is pleasing to feel passionate about our work; after all, that's what many of us spend most of our waking hours doing. Even if you don't have it now, meaningful work can be crafted by your actions and choices.

It's hard to be happy in a job you hate. While a good career doesn't guarantee happiness, the ideal is to find employment that at least doesn't undermine it. Well-being is the ultimate goal; the challenge is to find ways of creating it as we work. Indeed, research by the Gallup Organization finds that happy workers tend to earn more in later life, have better social lives, and be more supportive to their colleagues.

To fit, or to grow?

American psychologists Patricia Chen, Phoebe C. Ellsworth, and Norbert Schwarz argue that there are actually two different models for a meaningful career. In the first, we "find a fit," following our passion to a job that's perfect for us. This sounds great, but is tough to achieve when the job market isn't favorable or you aren't quite sure what your vocation may be. An alternative is to develop a passion for what you find yourself doing—in effect, cultivating your interest rather than bringing it to the job in advance. Is one better than the other?

We'd probably all rather find a "fit" if we could, but the psychologists' studies suggest that most of us feel we fit our jobs eventually in any case. If you can't find a job that matches your passions, you may still find meaning in it as time goes on.

Creating your own niche

If you don't feel that fitting into anyone else's business is your thing, have you ever considered starting your own? We certainly live in a society that admires

MONEY CAN'T BUY HAPPINESS

While poverty is miserable, it seems that wealth doesn't really make us happy. Over the last half-century, for instance, the US has grown increasingly rich as a nation, but people's life satisfaction has stayed pretty constant.

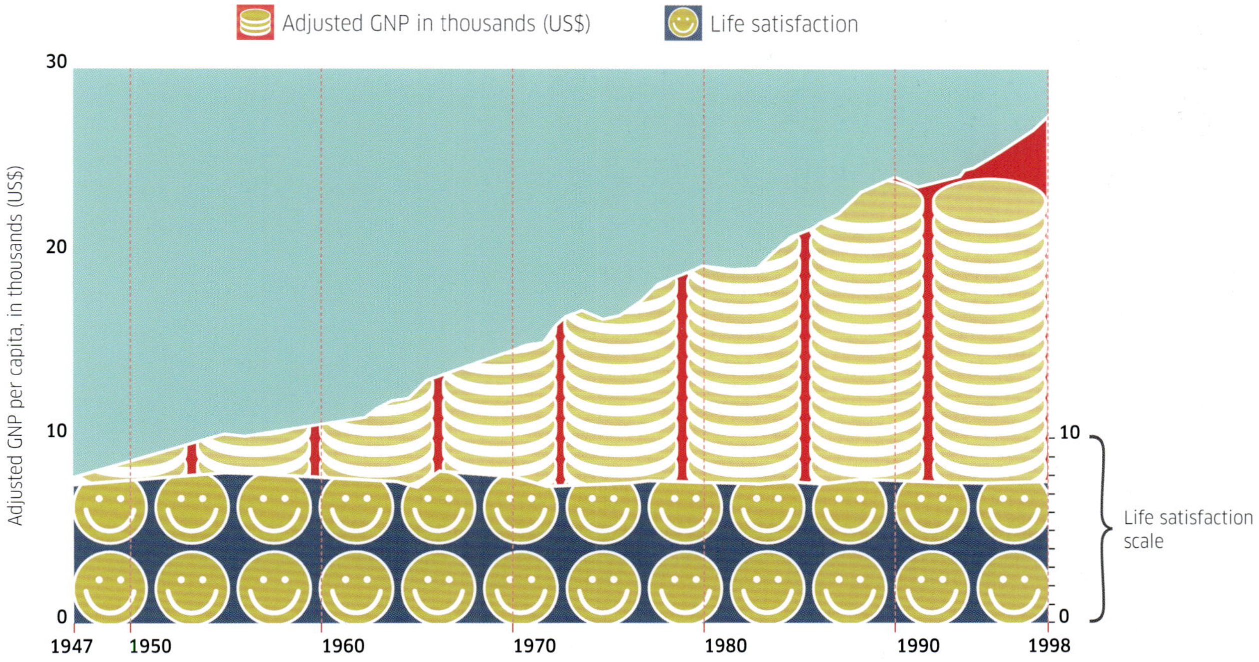

US GROSS NATIONAL PRODUCT (GNP) AND MEAN LIFE SATISFACTION FROM 1947 TO 1998

the image of the entrepreneur, but what is a life of freedom and challenge for some people might be a life of stress and misery for others. A 2011 Canadian study identified the two psychological qualities best suited to carving out your own place in the world:

- **Learning orientation:** How inclined you are to keep updating and expanding your knowledge.
- **Passion for work:** How rewarding you find working in itself.

While both these qualities are helpful, neither of them is a fixed character trait. Some people love to learn, but we can all up our game when circumstances demand; how much you enjoy work is liable to fluctuate throughout your life. So if you aren't quite sure what you want from a job, the best advice is to keep your mind open and never stop learning. There are many ways to be happy in what you do.

STARTING OUT PASSIONATE?
In 2015, American psychologists tested who felt best suited to their work: those who believed in doing what you love (the "fit" theory), or those who believed in loving what you do (the "develop" theory). "Fit" people often start out feeling better suited to the jobs they choose, but the good news is that "develop" people tend to catch up with them over time.

KNOW YOUR OWN MIND

THE SUCCESS THAT WORKS FOR YOU

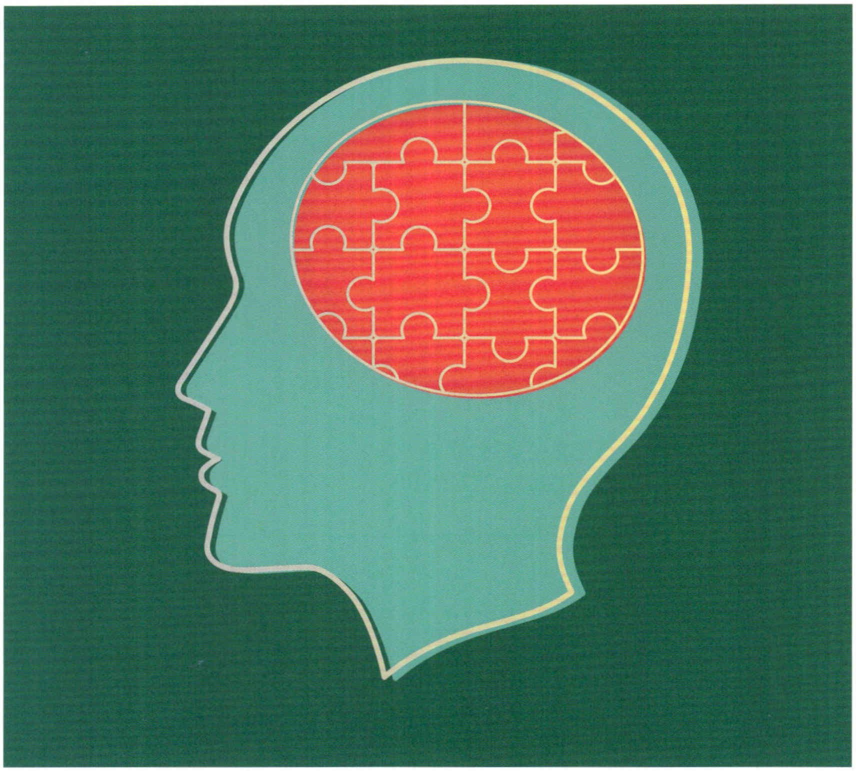

We may define success as achieving what we want or need, but does that one size really fit all? People want different things and, when considering your goals, it's also useful to consider your personal psychology.

We're all individuals, and your idea of success is probably different from your next-door neighbor's. Having an insight into your own personality can be helpful when planning what will work for you. When 75 advisory council members of Stanford Graduate School of Business were asked what was the most valuable quality for people to cultivate, their answer was, almost unanimously, self-awareness.

Five classic personality traits

Psychologists have a host of different theories about how to measure and classify personality dimensions, but most of them agree that the Big Five personality traits framework explains many aspects of our personality and behaviors. Research on this model began in 1949, and it has been expanded on many times since; one study found that these five traits applied to more than 50 cultures. With so much research behind it, there's some good evidence that this is a useful way of thinking about ourselves.

What are the Big Five? The broad categories are as follow:

1 **Extroversion/introversion.** Do you feel energized by social situations, or drained by them? Do you need quiet time to think through ideas and regain energy? Neither attitude is "better"—the issue is simply how to find ways of working that feel comfortable for you.

2 **Agreeableness.** Are you altruistic and affectionate, or contrary and cynical? Agreeable people tend to function well in

cooperative situations; less agreeable people may thrive in a more competitive environment.

3 **Conscientiousness.** Are you organized, detail-focused, and goal-directed? This is more manageable for some people than others. Of course, if you want to succeed you'll need a degree of conscientiousness, so even if you're not that strong in this area, it's something to work on.

4 **Neuroticism.** In this context, a "neurotic" person is someone who is easily upset, whereas a low "neuroticism" score suggests you're more resilient. Consider how much stress you can comfortably sustain and remember you can build your resilience and ability to manage your stress more effectively.

5 **Openness.** The more open someone is, the more willing they are to have adventures, expose themselves to new ideas, and find creative solutions. Less open people are more traditional, and may find abstract thinking challenging.

> People **trust you** when you are **genuine** and **authentic**, not a replica of someone else.
>
> **Bill George, Peter Sims, Andrew N. McLean, and Diana Mayer**
> *Harvard Business Review*, 2007

MOTIVATIONAL NEEDS

How do you think and what do you want? Psychologist David McClelland proposes three primary needs that success seekers are trying to satisfy; which of the following resonates most strongly with your sense of yourself?

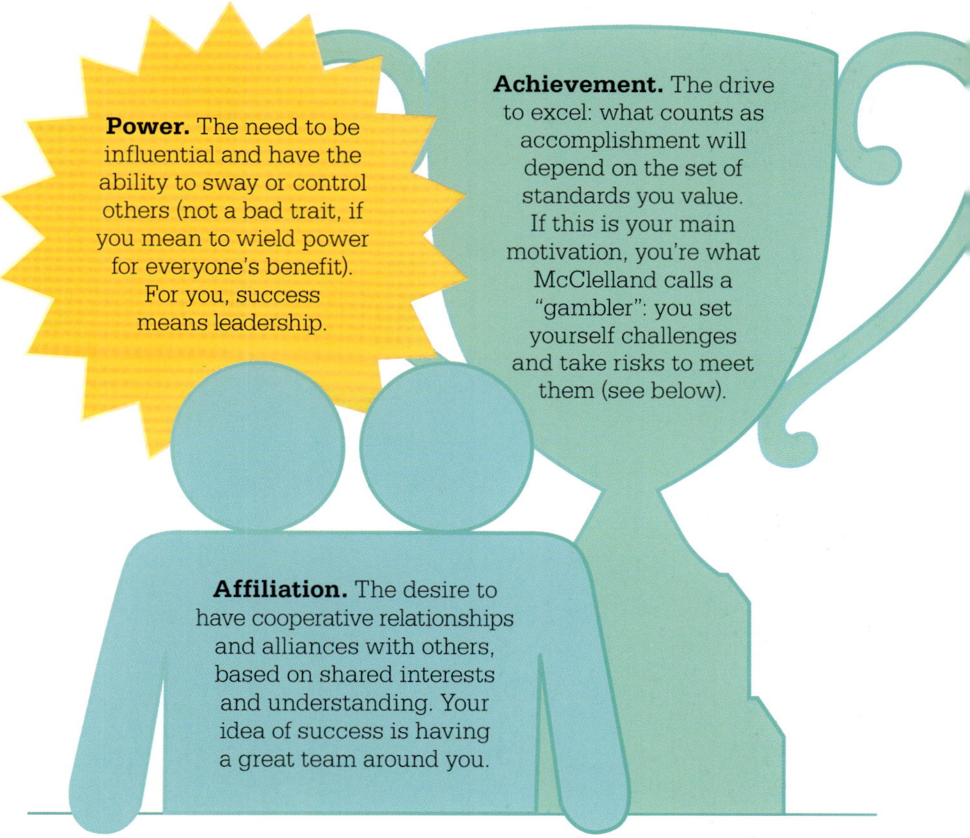

ARE YOU MOTIVATED BY ACHIEVEMENT?

If you're reading this book, the odds are that achievement motivates you. David McClelland identifies several key traits of such people:

- They care more about achievement than material rewards. Money only matters as a measure of success.
- Status and security aren't very important to them.
- They constantly look for ways to do things better.
- They look for jobs that allow them flexibility and the opportunity to set their own goals.
- They want feedback, not praise. The emotional reward comes from doing the task correctly, so they need to hear accurate assessments.
- They set realistic goals, following their interests and abilities, and thrive on a sense of accomplishment.

A LIFELONG JOURNEY

SUCCESS AS A CONTINUOUS PROCESS

When we imagine success, we often picture the external circumstances that go with it, such as profit and prestige. In fact, it's more helpful to picture a way of living, because circumstances can always change.

It's easy to look at successful people we admire or envy and think, "If I were in your position, I'd be set." The thing, of course, is that circumstances can change. Success is not so much a safe shore you can reach (and then put up your feet), but rather a course you should persistently chart.

Living the life?

Millionaire Richard St. John interviewed 500 successful people and identified eight principles that had helped them achieve (see "The secrets of success", opposite). St. John himself, though, considers his career a cautionary tale: at the beginning, he threw himself into it, but once he started succeeding, he began to think of himself as "this hotshot guy" for whom success was just the natural state of things. This led to a creative block, a falling-off of clients as he became more concerned with money than with service, and, finally, clinical depression. His career only started to recover when the near-collapse of his company meant he had to fight to save it: he was happier battling and striving than he had been coasting.

So it makes sense to think of success as a process rather than as a final goal; this approach is better for our emotional health as well as our careers. It is better to build up good habits and make a long-term effort to maintain them.

Overcoming reluctance

We have a natural resistance to changing set patterns: starting anything new means being a novice, and this can be daunting. In the *Harvard Business Review*, business expert Erika Andersen outlines four mental tools we can use to help ourselves along:

1 **Aspiration.** When a challenge comes along, most of us are quicker to see the pitfalls than the opportunities. Psychological research finds that if we can picture how good it will feel to achieve something, we're much more motivated to work on it.

2 **Self-awareness.** Nobody's perfect—indeed, it is human nature to have blind spots and failings. Foster an attitude of self-discovery (see pp.54–57); think about your strengths *and* your weaknesses, and how you can continue to grow and develop.

3 **Curiosity.** We're all born burning to learn, so try not to outgrow your youthful thirst for knowledge and new experiences.

4 **Vulnerability.** It's easy to stay in our comfort zone, but this is no way to improve. Be willing to try new things, make mistakes, and learn from them.

THE SECRETS OF SUCCESS

Success expert Richard St. John identifies the eight guiding principles that successful people live by:

Let passion be your guide
Do what you do because you care about it; remuneration comes second to natural enthusiasm.

Be industrious, yet playful
Work hard, but in a way that feels fun rather than dispiriting.

Develop expertise
Practice, learn, and hone your skills until you're really good at what you do.

Maintain focus
Give your work all the attention it needs.

Forge ahead
Push yourself, set yourself new challenges, and don't let self-doubt hold you back.

Aim to serve others
Don't do things for your own glory: do them to make something of value for other people.

Be inquisitive
Stay curious, observant, and interested in coming up with new ideas.

Remain persistent
Rejection, criticism, and setbacks are part of the game; don't let them stop you from doing what you believe in.

SITTING COMFORTABLY?

94%

A study by K. Patricia Cross, a scholar of educational research, found that 94 percent of professors reported that they were doing **"above-average work."** We're probably **more accurate** if we think of ourselves as always having **room to improve** and **learn new things**.

TELL YOURSELF A BETTER STORY

Circumstances can sometimes be discouraging, but this is often not the only factor at play. Expert Erika Andersen advises that we work on our "inner narrative": the self-talk that determines how we react to challenges.

Unsupportive self-talk
- I'm too old to start something new.
- This is too much hassle.
- I'm no good at this.
- I'll look stupid if I fail.

Supportive self-talk
- I can bring a lot of life experience to this.
- What will my life be like once I've achieved this?
- I'm still learning—I'll get the hang of it.
- I can gain valuable skills from this no matter how it turns out.

NAVIGATION SKILLS

FINDING YOUR SUCCESS PATH

Active and ambitious people often have more than one aspiration, and sometimes these can conflict with each other. What's the solution when it comes to deciding which options to choose?

You'd think everyone would have the same attitude toward personal ability, but in fact studies suggest that there are two opposing sets of beliefs at play:

The entity theory: the idea that our talents and competence are pretty much fixed. Some people are born good at things, others are not, and our abilities are just part of who we are.

The incremental theory: what we are capable of doing is something we can change and develop.

What these theories refer to is our perceived competence: how likely we think we are to succeed if we try something, either in terms of impressing others (performance goals), or in terms of learning how to do things (mastery goals).

The winner is...

Which of these theories should we give credence to? The encouraging news is that scientific research supports the incremental theory. A 2006 study published in the *Journal of Personality and Social Psychology* tested more than 450 people and found that the most solid predictor of success—even in supposedly objective measures like IQ tests—was how much a person believed in being able to change what they do. If you want to succeed, the first

> The person who **chases two** rabbits, **catches neither**.
>
> Proverb

step is to see yourself as someone who's capable of learning. Believing you can master new skills makes it significantly more likely you will do so—so let potential rather than current ability be your guide when making decisions.

Seek a positive environment

If you're considering moving on, approach any new workplace with an eye to the prevailing ethos and culture. Sustained stress and feelings of anxiety will limit your growth, so when selecting a new organization to join, it is better to select one where people focus on creating positive changes.

Positive Organizational Scholarship (POS)—an umbrella concept within organizational studies—has focused on the importance of creating cultures that facilitate the growth and development of people and ways of doing things to serve customers and sustainable change. POS emphasizes the importance of positive attributes, processes, and outcomes. One basic idea is that it's more effective for a leader or mentor to focus on someone's good points and build on them than it is to focus on their limitations. This creates a situation in which it's safe for them to experiment.

In short, when choosing your path, look for evidence that the organization seeks to grow and make a difference. You'll develop better and spot more opportunities if you see yourself as capable of learning, and you'll learn better with people who are more interested in what you *can* do than what you can't.

THE POSITIVE DEVELOPMENT CYCLE

Positive Organizational Scholarship (POS) argues that people learn most when they're taught to focus on their strengths rather than their weaknesses. This can create a virtuous circle:

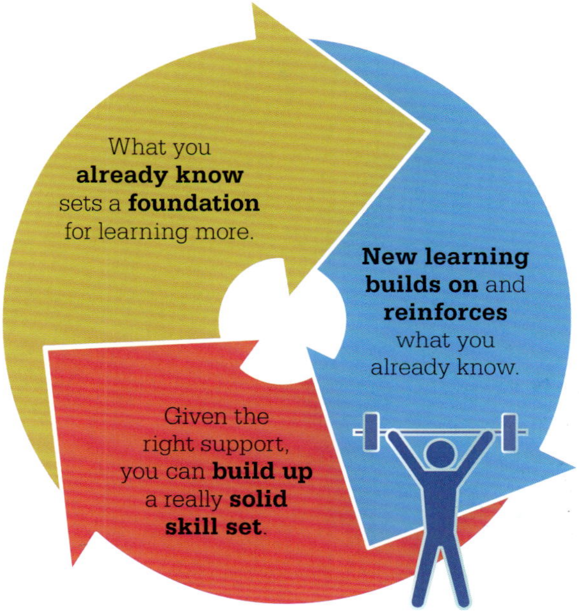

TROUBLE CHOOSING?

If it's proving hard to choose between your aspirations, try this technique, attributed to magnate Warren Buffett:

- Write a list of 25 things you'd like to accomplish over the next year. Include everything—personal life as well as work.
- Circle the five most important items on your list.
- Double-check that these five are the absolute top priority for you.
- Start formulating a plan for how to work toward these five goals, which resources you'll need to assemble, etc.
- Set aside the other 20 items. Once you've achieved your top five, you can reassess your goals, but until then the other 20 are distractions.

I WILL NOT FOLLOW WHERE THE PATH MAY LEAD, BUT I WILL GO WHERE THERE IS NO PATH, AND I WILL LEAVE A TRAIL.

MURIEL STRODE, POET AND AUTHOR

CLARIFYING YOUR AIMS

DETERMINING YOUR OBJECTIVES

Any strategy for success involves pruning: to focus on what you're doing, you have to decide what you *won't* be doing. When setting your priorities, don't overlook the less obvious consequences of your decisions.

Sometimes it can be difficult to know which priorities to focus on, and what the end result of our actions might be. Asking yourself specific questions can help focus your mind on what's important to you.

Avoiding pitfalls

American management consultant Fred Nickols, with input from his colleague Ray Forbes, has developed a set of questions you can ask yourself whenever you are trying to determine your objectives:

- What are you trying to achieve?
- What are you trying to preserve?
- What are you trying to avoid?
- What are you trying to eliminate?

The aim of these questions is to highlight the sometimes-complex interaction among our decisions, actions, and outcomes (see "Achieve, preserve, avoid, or eliminate?," opposite). The point is

FIXED OR GROWING?

Stanford University psychologist Carol Dweck proposes that there are two mindsets you can live by:

- **A fixed mindset:** you believe that intelligence, talent, and so on are traits that you either have or you don't.
- **A growth mindset:** you view yourself as a lifelong learner.

With a growth mindset, you aren't just more proactive: you're also less hard on yourself, because mistakes are part of the learning process. This makes setbacks easier to endure.

that you need to make choices to maintain an overall balance in your accomplishments by preserving what you have that you value, achieving in new areas, and avoiding any negative results.

You may have more goals than you think, and if you can factor in the "negative" goals as well as the positive ones, you're less likely to miss something important and end up short of where you started. When clarifying your goals, be clear about what you want—and consider the things you don't want to risk.

Maintaining momentum

If you have big plans and are starting from a less than ideal position, you're going to have to put in a lot of time and effort. There may be moments when you really don't feel like it: at that point, it may be time to double-check your priorities.

As Stuart Biddle, Professor of Active Living and Public Health at Victoria University in Australia, puts it, "Not having time is not a reality in most cases." If we have time to watch TV or take a break, that's time that we can, if we choose, decide to dedicate to a bigger project. The key here, as psychologist Carol Dweck explains, is to have a "growth mindset" rather than a "fixed mindset" (see "Fixed or growing?," opposite). Instead of being perfectionists who think we either can or can't do something, it helps to see learning as a process that continues throughout our lives. That relieves some of the pressure. You don't need to drive yourself to exhaustion; but when time is a limited resource, it's good to ask yourself whether you're really losing motivation, or if you're just tired.

We need to keep our spirits up as we push for success, and we also need to be aware that not jeopardizing what we already have can matter as much as gaining new things. The clearer you are on your priorities, the better off you'll be.

ACHIEVE, PRESERVE, AVOID, OR ELIMINATE?

Performance improvement expert Fred Nickols devised a set of questions to help establish and clarify priorities: sometimes "success" may be more about *preserving*, *avoiding*, or *eliminating* aspects of your life than it is about *achieving* something. Think about your different goals, and ask yourself these questions to see if your answers reveal any issues you may need to consider further:

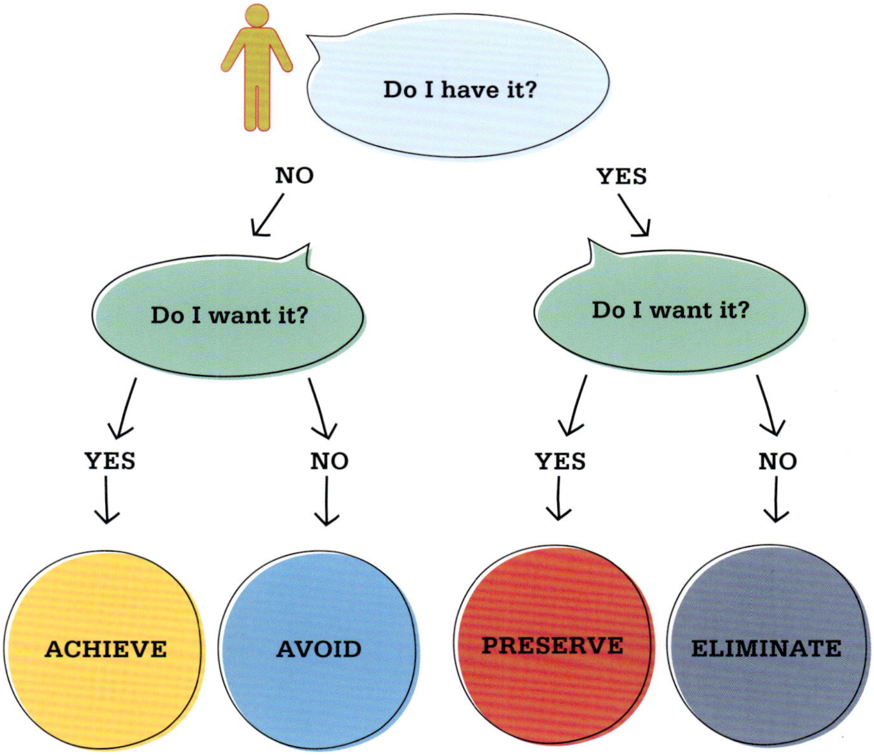

> There are **no solutions**; there are **only trade-offs**.
>
> **Thomas Sowell**
> Economist, social theorist, and political philosopher

WORK-LIFE BALANCE

HOW TO SORT OUT YOUR PRIORITIES

We're all under pressure to be multitaskers these days. The need to do so much at once undermines our sense of peace: it's hard to maintain your equilibrium if you constantly feel as if you're falling behind.

We hear the phrase "work-life balance" quite a lot these days, but it can feel like a bit of a mirage. There will probably never be a perfect balance between work and private life, but rather periods where one has to take priority and other times when the roles are reversed. How much work we have to do to keep on top of things is not, after all, entirely within our control. But we can all learn better habits to keep boundaries in place and our stress levels in check.

Eat your frogs early

There's a saying that if you get up in the morning and eat a live frog, you can spend the rest of the day safe in the knowledge that whatever else happens it can't possibly get any worse. Sometimes a "frog" is on your plate and it has to be eaten: your day will include some difficult tasks, and others that are more palatable. If you put off the tough ones, you will spend time feeling bad because there's a nasty task hanging over you, and eventually you'll still have to knuckle down

TIPPING THE SCALES

40%

According to a Mental Health Foundation survey, more than 40 percent of UK employees feel they are **neglecting other aspects of their life** because of **work**.

THE FOUR DOMAINS

According to Stewart Friedman, founding director of the Work/Life Integration Project at the Wharton School of the University of Pennsylvania, there are four spheres in your life you should consider when planning your priorities:

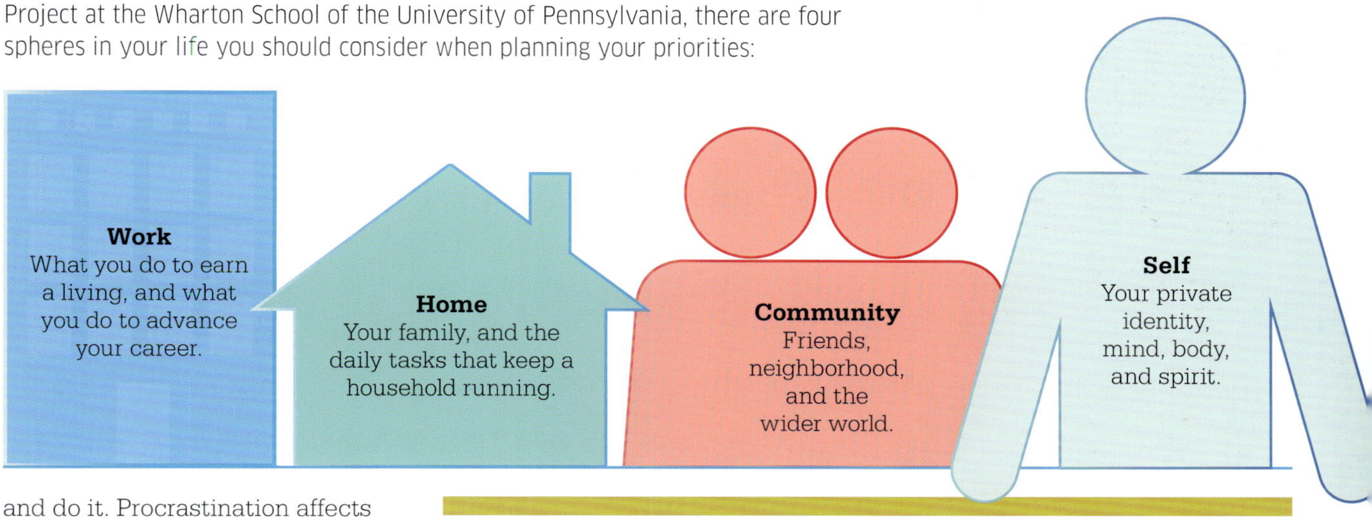

and do it. Procrastination affects all of us (see pp.156–159), but you'll suffer less if you get the frog out of the way early—so you can focus on other tasks with clarity and feel better knowing that you can check it off the list of things to do that day.

Take care of your mind

Let's be blunt: too much stress can have a negative impact on your psychological health and, over the long term, it impacts you physically as well. You'll notice if you come down with the flu, but do you pay attention to when your feelings of stress and anxiety are distorting your reactions and interactions with others? Mind, the UK mental health charity, estimates that one in four people experiences a mental health problem every year. Your mind is your motor, and it's in your best interest to keep it in good condition.

So, what can you do if your work-life balance has become too difficult? The Mental Health Foundation in the UK gives the following advice:

- Work smart, not long. Again, this is about priorities: eat your frogs, give yourself fixed times to complete tasks, and prioritize the essentials.
- Take breaks during the day, even if they are short.
- Draw a line between work and home. If you *have* to take work home, make sure you enjoy some totally work-free time.
- Time worrying about work adds to your stress just as much as time spent actually working.
- Friendships, exercise, and leisure activities keep you going. Don't cut them out: they're the oil that keeps your gears turning.

ALL EQUAL?

Gender roles can be a mixed blessing. A 2007 study by the Kenexa Research Institute in the US found that women tended to be more satisfied with their employers' flexibility about work-life balance than men.

The Mental Health Foundation in the UK, on the other hand, discovered that 42 percent of women were unhappy with the overall balance of their lives...

... compared to 29 percent of men. Employers seem more likely to acknowledge that women have family commitments, but this imbalance tends to leave women doing more than their fair share at home.

A WORKING LIFE

MANAGING CAREER UPS AND DOWNS

The idea of finding your place in early adulthood and rising through the ranks over a long, steady, and stable career is largely a thing of the past. In today's workplace, adaptability is the name of the game.

If you're on track but on a career path that doesn't feel particularly rewarding, or if you suffer a setback, feeling stuck and frustrated is natural given the energy you have invested. However, changing tack is normal, especially in the modern-day job market. The trick is to have the psychological skills to manage career transitions.

Think ahead

You may not be planning a change right this minute, but it's good to bear in mind that you may well want to at some point—so the best plan is to *keep learning*. A 2010 UK study found that the people least likely to get locked into a particular way of working were those who undertook "substantive upskilling or reskilling" every five to 10 years. This can sometimes be done on the job, but if you find yourself pigeonholed, the answer is to keep educating yourself outside work.

The researchers found that, in regard to both specific information and ways of thinking, it pays to

5 years

According to the US Bureau of Labor Statistics, **since 1983**, American workers **aged 25 or older** stay in **one job** for an average of **five years**.

DISRUPTIVE INNOVATION

Business consultant and scholar Clayton M. Christensen's concept of "disruptive innovation" is very influential nowadays. He argues that there are two ways to be innovative: "sustaining innovation," which means getting better at what you already do, and "disruptive innovation," where new markets are identified and old business models replaced. As an individual, how do you apply this thinking to your own life? Writing in the *Harvard Business Review*, management adviser Whitney Johnson outlines four tactics:

1 **Identify a need that could be better met.** Markets exist because people feel that products give them something they want, so look for opportunities to expand your career to meet these needs.

2 **Identify your own unique strengths.** Look for things you do well that most other people don't: they may not be your number-one skills, but if they are unusual, they're valuable.

3 **Be prepared to go sideways or even backward.** If you're trying something new, you may need to take a drop in status. If this opens up an opportunity to grow, though, this planned detour could be worthwhile.

4 **Be flexible.** Let your strategy emerge in response to feedback, so that you learn what untapped requirements are out there.

You may prefer steady growth to big risks, and you can succeed with either, but in both cases the key is to stay open to new experiences and opportunities (see pp.114–117). In a changing world, it pays to be adaptable.

stay informed. Concrete knowledge needs regular updating, and the experience of regular learning creates a mindset that stands people in good stead throughout their careers—in terms of curiosity, experience with a diverse range of people, a wider personal network, or greater confidence in their ability to master new skills.

Want to keep learning?
You're not alone. A 2012 survey for the HR journal *People & Strategy* found that the majority of professionals preferred the "contemporary" model of success: work that provides a sense of meaning, challenges, balance, and the chance to use their skills. "Traditional" rewards, such as status, money, and power, are losing popularity.

DEVELOPING ON THE JOB?

Your job may teach you how to do particular tasks, but it can also teach you transferable skills. A 2012 UK study identified four ways in which your experience gives you new skills:

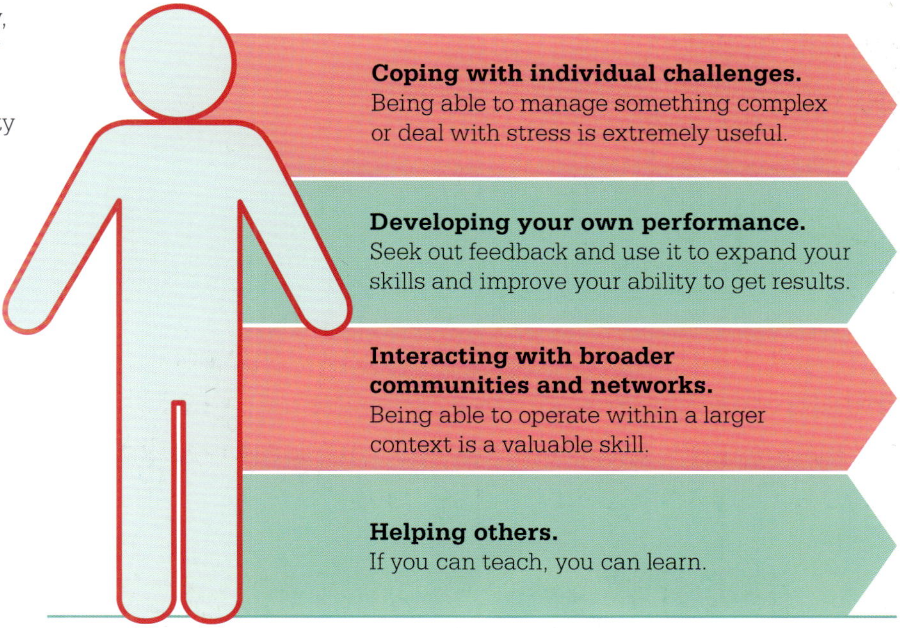

PEER PRESSURE

DOES THE SUPPORT OF OTHERS MATTER?

We all love a rebel, but must success mean being a rugged individualist? Actually, if you get it right, social influence can work in your favor. You're more likely to thrive if you have a positive group around you.

When we hear the words "peer pressure," we may think about experiences at school in which we felt pushed to do something we didn't want to do or that we knew was wrong. That feeling is something we never outgrow: people survive by working together, and it's natural to want to please those around us.

Resisting the negative

Sometimes peer pressure can make us act against our better judgment. What should we do in such situations? Sometimes we need to resist directly, but we can also resist more gently—by setting an example. You can turn people's natural conformity to your advantage: if you are openly tolerant and nonjudgmental, you create an environment in which accepting difference is the "normal" thing to do. Setting an example is less confrontational than arguing, and it may also be more effective.

OVERSHOOTING YOUR INFLUENCES

A 2015 US study found that social pressure can backfire. When a company tried to make employees sign up for a retirement plan by telling them that 75 percent of their colleagues had already done so, enrollments actually fell from 10 percent to 6.3 percent. The researchers concluded that people felt their colleagues must be so far ahead of them there was no point trying to compete. The lesson may be that when selecting your "peers," it is better to choose people you can realistically measure up to.

THREE DIFFERENT KINDS OF PRESSURE

Entrepreneur Sriram Bharatam identifies three kinds of peer pressure:

Direct peer pressure
This is the easiest kind to spot: it's when a friend or colleague tries to influence you to change your position.

Indirect peer pressure
This can happen without us even realizing. People are social animals, and we generally feel uncomfortable being out of sync with each other. If everyone is doing something a certain way, it can be easy to feel that we ought to be doing the same.

Individual peer pressure
Even in a friendly environment, we can end up putting peer pressure on ourselves. We all want to feel that we belong; sometimes we end up making decisions based on what everyone else seems to be thinking.

Good pressure

But is peer pressure always a bad thing? It can actually be turned to our advantage. For example, we can use our wish for group harmony for the greater good, or form a team to support each others' aims.

There's nothing like a public commitment to motivate us—even a small one makes a difference. A 2013 US study found that a public signup sheet made people join an energy-saving program more than a reward of $25 did. Although the cash raised the numbers of participants from 3 to 4 percent, the signup sheet increased the number from 3 to 9 percent. Feeling that your reputation may suffer if you opt out can be a greater impetus than money.

That's a negative incentive, but there are also some more positive ones. In 2011, the *St. Louis Business Journal* interviewed three women—Gail Taylor, Zundra Bryant, and Sarajeni Hammond—who'd taken part in a course by consultant Jan Torrisi-Mokwa. The results were impressive. The women had formed a group, written letters outlining their goals in specific terms, given themselves a narrow timeframe, and acted as a support network to each other. As a consequence, they met "audacious" goals. By holding a monthly "accountability meeting," they were able to provide each other with both support and positive pressure to keep their progress on track.

Of course we want to feel proud of ourselves, but don't be shy of looking to friends and allies for feedback and support. For these things, you need the right kind of peer: the path to success can sometimes be a team effort.

CLEAR PATH AHEAD?

According to organizational strategist Jan Torrisi-Mokwa, fewer than

16%

of people say they **have goals**.

Fewer than

4%

write those goals down.

And fewer than

1%

have **written goals** that they **regularly review**.

ACHIEVING EQUILIBRIUM

A BROADER SPECTRUM

It's one thing to choose a specific goal and go all out to achieve it. It's another thing to assume that a single goal will satisfy all your needs—chances are, you will be seeking to achieve multiple goals simultaneously.

Look around, and chances are you'll see the same story in a lot of places. This person has a highly lucrative career, but is bored and chafes against their "golden handcuffs"; that person has wonderful children but the nagging sense that they're not making any mark in the wider world; this person lives a freewheeling life with many great experiences, but can't stay anywhere long enough to find romance and feels lonely; that person works within the system and does a lot of practical good, but feels bad for compromising their youthful ideals. Sound familiar? We don't have a one-size-fits-all framework for success, so many people end up worrying whether they've succeeded at all.

Enduring success

Laura Nash and Howard Stevenson, authors of *Just Enough: Tools for Creating Success in Your Work and Life*, have developed a model they call "enduring success," which aims to guide people along a path that's emotionally renewing, not a source of constant stress. The key is to recognize that everyone, no matter how goal-driven, has their own idea of what success means, and that idea will change over time as they learn from new experiences. The research identified four key components essential to truly fulfilling and lasting success: happiness, achievement, significance, and legacy (see "Lasting success," opposite). This is what we'd all like; Nash and Stevenson found that if you took away a single component, people found their success rang hollow. People who tell you your problems are solved if you find work you love, they argue, are missing the point. Whatever your career path, you still have complex needs, and no job can satisfy all of them. You have to accept that there is more than one area in life that needs attention, and try to keep an eye on all of them.

Exactly what does a successful life feel like? It depends on you—but focusing your efforts on just one area of life is unlikely to lead to fulfillment.

> Pursuing success is like **shooting at** a series of **moving targets**.
>
> **Laura Nash and Howard Stevenson**

LASTING SUCCESS

Laura Nash and Howard Stevenson, academics at Harvard Business School who specialize in business ethics and entrepreneurship respectively, argue that to be truly successful we should be aiming for sustainable, enduring success throughout our lives across the four main spheres of self, family, work, and community. Within each of these spheres, we need to consider the four components of happiness, achievement, significance, and legacy:

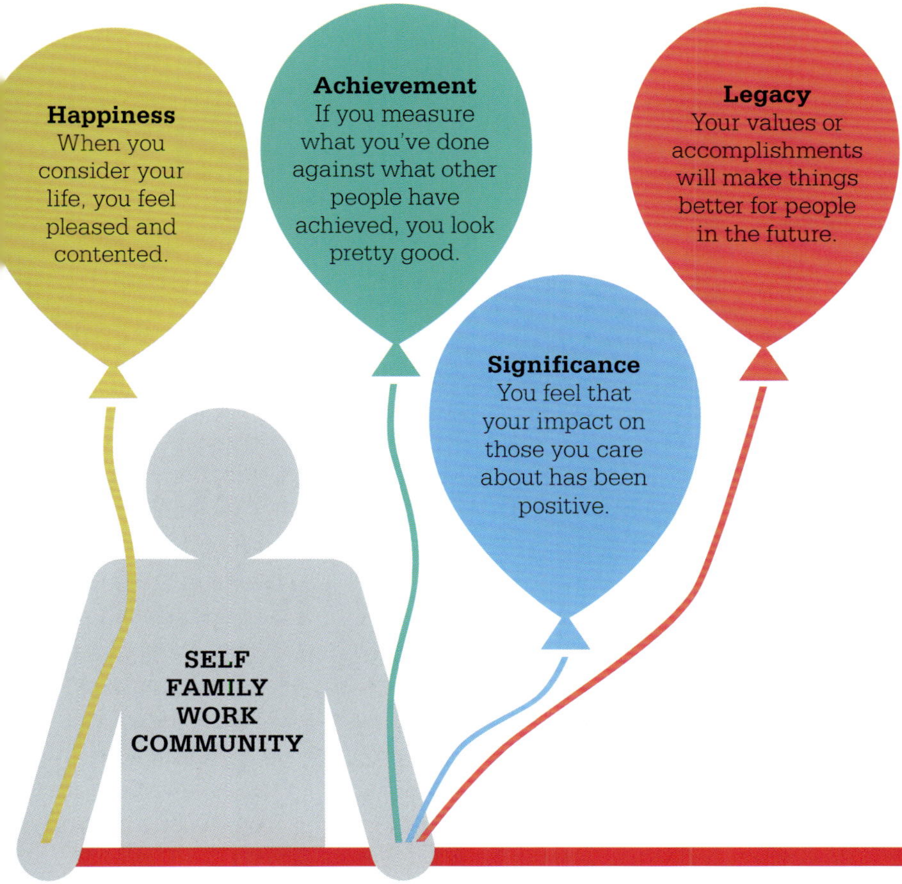

HAPPY HABITS

Since life is made up of days, one of the best tactics is to create a structure for each day that not only keeps us productive, but also includes a little space to check in with the nonwork aspects of our lives. Habit is a powerful motivator—much more powerful than we think. A 2007 study published in the *Psychological Review*, for instance, found that once we've established a goal, we're more motivated day-to-day by the habits we set up to reach the goal than we are by the goals themselves.

This doesn't mean we should forget our goals. A 2010 study found that people who regularly reflect on how they are progressing toward their goals and adjust their habits accordingly make better progress. It does, however, mean that when you're aiming for success, daily routines supported by regular reflection can really help.

MAKE IT CONCRETE

A study in the *European Journal of Social Psychology* found that people who are specific about their plans are more likely to act on them. Instead of simply deciding that you're going to do something, write down *when* and *how* you're going to make it happen.

People who relied solely on **mental resolutions**:

35% SUCCESS RATE

People who **clearly stated when** and **how** they'd act:

91% SUCCESS RATE

THE CHALLENGES OF GENDER

DIFFERENT ROLE EXPECTATIONS AT HOME AND WORK

Until we live in a perfect world, the reality is that most men and women will encounter different opportunities and expectations during the course of their lives. What does this mean for an ambitious woman?

The traditional workplace is built around the model of man-as-breadwinner, woman-as-homemaker, but these days few of us can afford to live that way. Even if we could, many people, both male and female, want to have a family, and workplaces are often not geared toward relieving the demands that places on parents. This usually falls heaviest on women. When you add the fact that many people, consciously or not, tend to read the same behavior as "confident" in men and "abrasive" in women, how can a woman with big ideas make her way in the world?

Patterns of employment

A 2012 study of several Western cultures found that women are more likely than men to change jobs, and to take part-time, casual, and temporary jobs to keep themselves going—particularly older women with families to support. This means women often have to manage multiple career transitions and also deal with less-secure employment conditions. Add to this any time taken out of the workforce for maternity leave, or time spent caring for sick family members, and it appears that women may sometimes have to swallow their pride and be less "choosy."

The sound of silence

When it comes to discussions, do women actually talk more than men? Australian feminist Dale Spender taped her students' discussions and asked whether they thought the men or women were talking more. The women's assessments tended to be accurate. The men thought the discussions were equal if the women talked 15 percent of the time, and dominated by the women if they talked 30 percent of the time. As Spender put it, "The talkativeness of women has been gauged in comparison not with men, but with silence."

Creating balance

For her book *When Work Doesn't Work Anymore: Women, Work, and Identity*, Elizabeth Perle McKenna interviewed hundreds of women. She found that women tend to want their lives to feel "whole," which means creating their own definition of success to include work and family goals.

DEALING WITH PROBLEMS

An international study published in 2012 picked out the "Five Cs," five ways in which women deal with obstacles:

- **Concern:** thinking ahead and planning to meet challenges.
- **Control:** being independent, trustworthy, and persistent; taking responsibility for dealing with difficulties.
- **Curiosity:** being observant, exploratory, informed, and willing to identify alternatives.
- **Cooperation:** both working with others, and being able to rely on a support network.
- **Confidence:** seeing themselves as capable, productive, and valuable.

> When a **man** is **successful**, he is **liked** by both men and women. When a **woman** is successful, people of **both genders like her less**.
>
> **Sheryl Sandberg**
> Business executive

COPING WITH THE CHALLENGES

A study carried out between 2010 and 2011 interviewed Sri Lankan women to find out how they saw their relationship with work. Eight themes kept recurring:

Adaptability. Women are expected to be more compliant; sometimes they have to put on a show of being accommodating to get ahead.

Compromising. Women don't always want to give up family time to attend company events; this can mean missing out on opportunities.

Manipulating. Women are expected to be likeable, and women who want to succeed learn that the hard way.

Deceiving. When work doesn't view your personal commitments as valid, you may need to tell the odd fib.

Explaining. Some bosses are more flexible if a woman can demonstrate that some things just aren't possible.

Networking. Good advice for everyone, but particularly good advice for women trying to compensate for a lack of opportunities to advance.

Resisting. You may need to dig your heels in. However, this approach can also get you fired; most women are justifiably cautious of this tactic.

Opting out. Some women decide it's not worth it, redefine their priorities, and look for a situation better suited to them.

SMALL STEPS

STAYING FOCUSED ON PROGRESS

The feeling of progress has a huge impact on your motivation: little victories can be just as important as big ones. Not only do they help you toward your goals; they can also give you the psychological boost you need.

If you have big aspirations, your ultimate goal may feel a long way off, with years or maybe even decades of hard work between you and your objective. That's not an encouraging feeling, and can leave you wondering if it's really all worthwhile. The trick is to learn how to enjoy the smaller triumphs—the stepping stones that take you toward your goal – in their own right.

The progress principle

There's a helpful theory, developed by psychologist Teresa Amabile, which is known as the "progress principle." The idea is that we all have "inner work lives," an ongoing stream of emotions and perceptions throughout the working day. Positive experiences, be they large or small, make people more committed, productive, creative, and favorable toward their coworkers.

What makes our inner work lives healthy? Over a decade of research, charting nearly 12,000 diary entries, Amabile and her colleagues found

5%

SLIM PICKINGS

In a 2011 US study, only 5 percent of **managers showed awareness** that the best way to **motivate employees** was through a **sense of progress**.

$300 billion

DISENGAGED DROP-OFF

The Gallup poll estimates the cost of **lost productivity** by **discouraged workers** in the US at $300 billion annually.

POSITIVE MOTIVATION

A feeling of progress can create a positive feedback loop, which leads to further progress being made:

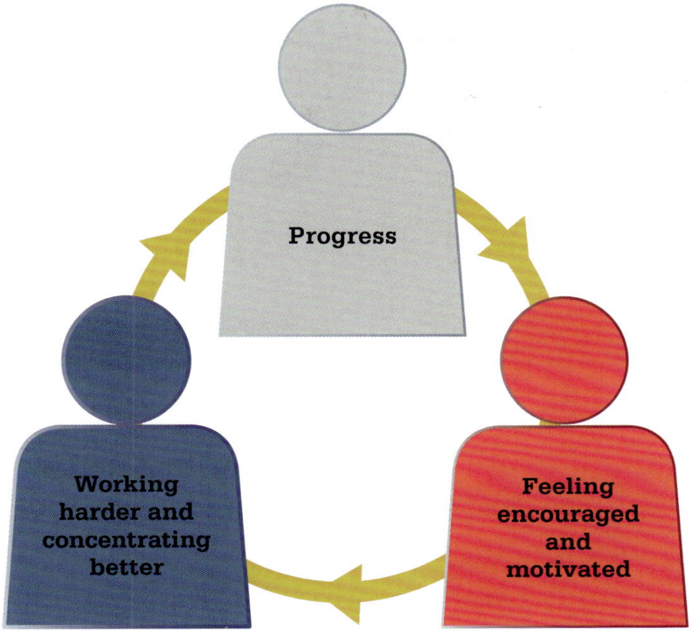

that by far the biggest motivator for people was feeling that they were making meaningful progress. The most interesting thing was, those moments of progress didn't have to be spectacular: just feeling that you were doing or providing something useful felt meaningful. Likewise, the progress didn't have to be an enormous breakthrough; just feeling that you were getting somewhere was reward enough.

Applying the lesson

In her work, Amabile focuses mainly on advising managers: her aim is to teach them how to be better leaders. If you are a manager yourself, or aim to rise to that level, the progress principle is useful: if you support a sense of progress, you're likely to develop a stellar team.

If you're still on the lower rungs, though, what should you do? It's hard to feel motivated if you're working under someone who micromanages, is grouchy, and never says "thank you." If this is the case, it's probably best to take stock: are you in a place where you are learning skills and/or making valuable connections? If the answer to either of these is "yes," you may need to find other ways to achieve a sense of progress: keep a journal of accomplishments, seek out sympathetic colleagues, set yourself a date by which you expect to have learned enough, and plan to move on after that. In the meantime, try to find ways of making progress in whatever free time you have outside work.

If the advantages don't outweigh the depressing atmosphere, however, it may be time to make your exit strategy your new measure of progress.

DAILY TRIGGERS

Harvard Business School professor Teresa Amabile identifies three kinds of "inner work life triggers" that keep us motivated or discourage us:

- **Progress versus setbacks**
- **Catalysts versus inhibitors:** actions that either directly support or hinder what we're trying to do
- **Nourishers versus toxins:** encouragement or criticism from other people

Whether we feel we're having a good or a bad day is often directly influenced by how many of these triggers we encounter.

SUSTAINING CLARITY

KEEPING YOUR FOCUS

When we're in it for the long haul, it can be hard to keep up the momentum. We all know that perseverance is crucial, but what's the best way to sustain it without burning ourselves out?

Achieving our goals is not easy, and there's no question that there will be times when you feel distracted or discouraged. It's all very well for people to tell us to stay focused, but what does that mean in practice?

Staying on track

Motivational speaker Chalene Johnson lists four pointers that can help keep you on track:

- **Set expectations.** Know what you want, and why you want it. In low moments, you'll have a clear picture of where you're going and can remind yourself why it's worthwhile.
- **Make a conscious decision.** You don't have to mentally shout "I DECIDE!" every 10 minutes, but you will benefit from telling yourself at regular intervals that you've chosen to do this, that you had good reasons for making this choice, and that consistency will help you get there.
- **Be accountable.** Write down your goals so that they're there in front of you and you can remember why you set them originally. As much as possible, break them down into smaller chunks, which will give you a feeling of progress. If possible, tell someone supportive about your goals so they can help you identify options or encourage you when you lose energy.
- **Don't be perfect.** There will be days where you're sick, have a crisis, or just can't face it. If you regard that as a failure, you'll give up; if you shrug, you can get back on track and you'll be fine.

The power of a true motive

From 2007 to 2014, Amy Wrzesniewski and Barry Schwartz tracked cadets at West Point military academy, a challenging course with a high dropout rate. Students reported both "internal" and "external" reasons for joining (an example of the former being wanting to get fit, and of the latter wanting to please their families). Cadets whose motivation was to "become an Army officer" were 20 percent more likely to make it through. Wanting something for its own sake has a significant impact on whether we stick with it.

> Unless **commitment** is made, there are only **promises** and **hopes**; but **no plans**.
>
> **Peter Drucker**
> Management guru

YOUR DAILY DIARY

Life is an accumulation of daily ups and downs, and there's nothing like concrete data for getting a good overview. Try keeping a journal, and, at the end of each day, ask yourself these questions:

Values	Successes	Obstacles
Progress	What do I feel that I've achieved?	Was there anything that undermined my productivity?
Meaning	What has my day's work contributed to the world?	Have I done anything that I regret?
Reputation	What have I done that I can use to increase my credit?	If I did anything that made me look bad, how can I fix it?
Feeling supported	Who has been a good mentor, ally, or help to me today?	Are there any relationships I need to manage better?
Supporting others	Have I treated people with respect, listened, and given help when asked?	Do I need to make amends to anyone?
Time	What did I do that proved time-efficient?	What did I do that wasted time?
Problem-solving	What challenges did I meet to my own satisfaction?	What problems do I need to put on my "to-do" list? (see pp.28–29)
Long-term priorities	What skills, connections, or resources have I gained today?	What do I need to do to develop, and how can I do that?
Personal life	What's happened outside work that helped me focus on my goals?	Are personal problems making it harder for me to concentrate?
Happiness	What did I enjoy today?	What should I have or do less of?

MAINTAINING YOUR ROUTINE

PAY ATTENTION TO WHAT YOU NEED

If you drive an animal to exhaustion, it'll collapse. No matter how clever we are, we're still living, breathing, earthbound creatures: never forget that you need to create a pace you can sustain.

We're all different, and some of us tire more easily than others. When gearing up for what you need to accomplish each day, don't forget to look after yourself, too.

Flexing your willpower

Resisting temptations, sticking to unpleasant tasks, and ignoring distractions is something we all need to manage, and if we have to do too many of these things at once, our willpower weakens. This is known as "ego depletion." Psychologist Roy Baumeister found that subjects asked to resist chocolate and eat radishes instead were quicker to give up when asked to solve impossible puzzles, and people told to suppress their emotions became worse at solving anagrams. Willpower seems to be a finite resource.

An exception to the rule...

Ego depletion theory does come with some caveats. Subsequent studies have found fault with the data, and other researchers have found that subjects' beliefs could influence their willpower: those who believed in ego depletion gave up quicker than those who didn't. Meanwhile, a 2012 study by psychologists Michael Inzlicht and Brandon J. Schmeichel found that subjects suffered less depletion when told the study would help develop therapies for Alzheimer's patients. So far, the evidence is controversial, but suggests that, if nothing else, motivation has a strong effect on our energy levels. If you have a tiring task to perform, your best strategy may be to find a reason to believe it will do some good.

THE FOUR DIMENSIONS OF ENERGY

Take a tip from productivity consultant David Allen and The Energy Project CEO Tony Schwartz: think of your energy in four dimensions. They add that it's risky to try and run ourselves like machines, fast and continually: human beings perform better when they have periods of activity followed by periods of rest. Working flat out is often less efficient than it looks.

Emotional
You need to cultivate positive emotions, and, as much as possible, encourage them in the people you work with, especially if you're in charge of them.

Mental
You need to be able to manage your attention, both in terms of focusing closely on what's in front of you and being able to shift comfortably from one task to another.

Physical
You need sleep, healthy nourishment, and rest. Different people need different amounts of these: be realistic and make time for them in your life.

Spiritual
You work best when you feel there's a real purpose to what you're doing—not necessarily a religious one, but something that feels meaningful.

KEEP ON THE LEVEL

There's a new slang word, "hangry," used to describe someone who is angry because they're hungry, and there's good science behind it. When our blood glucose falls too low, our systems release more adrenaline, the "fight or flight" hormone, and release more neuropeptide Y, which stimulates aggression. If you want good working relationships, don't skip breakfast!

HOW MUCH SLEEP DO YOU NEED?

Forget the superhumans who can supposedly get by on three hours a night; most of us need considerably more. The National Sleep Foundation recommends the following amounts–you may find you need more, or less:

Age	Recommended hours per night	Range that might be appropriate for you
14-17	8-10	7-11
18-25	7-9	6-11
26-64	7-9	6-10
65 and older	7-8	5-9

LEARNING FROM MISTAKES

KEEPING THINGS IN PERSPECTIVE

When success is important to you, you can take it badly if you get something wrong. To become truly proficient, though, we need to understand that mistakes are part of the process and to be expected.

We all make mistakes—indeed, it happens far more often than we realize. So why does it often take us by surprise when we find out that we're wrong about something?

Error blindness

Kathryn Schulz, author of *Being Wrong: Adventures in the Margin of Error*, has spent a lot of time pondering why our default assumption is that we are always right. She observes that from a young age we learn that people who get lots of things wrong didn't study for the test, aren't clever, and are troublemakers. They're the people we try our best not to be.

Schulz also points out that while discovering we're wrong feels bad, until we realize it, *it feels exactly like being right*. This is because when we're wrong, we usually don't *know* that we're wrong. Sometimes we're so focused on one thing that we miss something obvious (see "The selective attention test," opposite)—this is known as "error blindness."

In order to succeed and be happy, it's best if we shed the stereotype that only the "bad kid" ever makes mistakes. We all do: it's just that we

A work of art is **never finished**. It is **merely abandoned**.

Leonardo da Vinci
(also attributed to novelist E. M. Forster and poet Paul Valéry)

THE ARCHER'S PARADOX

To hit the target, aim dead-on? Not necessarily. Archery gives us a good example of why early misses can be crucial. Arrows flex, and this means their trajectory curves in mid-air. Archers have to factor in the stiffness of the arrow's shaft in order to judge how far its flight will deviate. This is the "archer's paradox": for a perfect shot, you have to aim slightly *away* from the bullseye.

Sometimes the only way to get a feel for things is to fire some arrows and see how they fly.

Think of your mistakes as test shots: look at where your efforts land, and that can tell you how to correct your aim next time.

often don't notice, or people are too polite to bring it to our attention. And it's not the end of the world: as Schulz contends, it's good to be reminded that we are imperfect—imperfection can even be a great source of creativity.

Success versus mastery

Would you say you are a perfectionist (see pp.160–161)? Sometimes we have to accept work that "will do," but which doesn't meet our standards—and this can be nearly as discouraging as an outright mistake. But do we need to feel bad about the odd mediocre moment? In a popular TED Talk, art historian Sarah Lewis describes watching archers practice over and over again to master the "archer's paradox" (see "The archer's paradox," above), whereby to hit a target, you have to aim slightly askew. This, she argues, is the difference between success and mastery: it's a success to hit the target, and mastery to be able to hit it more than once—but to reach that point, you have to miss many times.

Many great artists, Lewis adds, didn't much care for some of their artworks that others value greatly: the "near win" that doesn't please its maker is a part of learning. Being able to judge your work negatively should be taken as a sign of increasing mastery, as it means you are developing expertise (see pp.62–63).

Nobody likes to get things wrong, and nobody likes to feel they're doing less than their best. But go easy on yourself: the most accomplished people in the world make mistakes, too.

THE SELECTIVE ATTENTION TEST

In 1999, two psychologists at Harvard University, Christopher Chabris and Daniel Simons, showed volunteers a short video. In the footage, two teams of three people are milling around a small space: one team is wearing white T-shirts, the other team is wearing black T-shirts, and each team has a basketball.

The volunteers were told to count how many passes of the ball the players wearing white made between themselves in a minute of play. During the game, someone dressed in a gorilla suit entered from stage right, walked through the players, paused in the middle of the frame beating their chest, then exited the scene stage left.

Half of the volunteers were so focused on their task that they didn't notice the gorilla *at all*. This has become a classic example of selective attention: when we're set on a challenge, it is all too easy to miss something obvious.

CHAPTER 2

STARTING WITH YOU

POSITIVE PSYCHOLOGY AND THE POWER OF BELIEFS

FULFILLMENT IN THE ROUND

THE WHOLE-LIFE PICTURE

When we think of success, it's easy to focus too much on our careers. Enjoying our work can be part of it, but in the end, we need to think about our needs in a much broader sense.

What do we need to make us feel successful? It's likely that your first answer will include a lot of things you want to avoid: you don't want to struggle with money and finances, you don't want to end up lonely, you don't want to do boring and repetitive work that offers little opportunity for development. That's because we have a natural "negativity bias": we tend to pay more attention to and learn more from negative experiences and information than positive ones. This is how the human brain evolved to facilitate our basic survival: if you take no notice of a saber-toothed tiger, you probably won't live to have many descendents. This bias does not serve us well in the current world, though; more importantly, the negativity bias diminishes our ability to experience well-being.

Positive psychology

American psychologist Martin Seligman is a leading developer of the field of "positive psychology." Prior to the advent of positive psychology, the focus of research and practice in psychology was on areas related to dysfunction—depression, neurotic behavior, anxiety, and all forms of mental and behavioral tendencies that »

{ **Well-being** is everyone's **birthright**. }

Martin Seligman
Psychologist and founder of positive psychology

50–80

The people who are the **most satisfied** with their **romantic relationships** at the age of 50 turn out to be the **healthiest and happiest** at 80. This is a **better predictor of aging** than health indicators such as cholesterol levels.

REAL WELL-BEING

A useful touchstone in positive psychology is the "PERMA" model of well-being. Happiness, Martin Seligman argues, is not just one emotion; there are five factors that contribute to the experience of well-being:

P	**Positive emotions**	Optimism, enjoyment, love, contentment, amusement–any emotion that feels good or makes us kind.
E	**Engagement**	Getting into a state of "flow," where we're immersed in something that captures our full attention and focus.
R	**Relationships**	Loving, close, and trusting bonds with other people.
M	**Meaning**	Having a sense of purpose beyond mere personal gain; feeling part of something bigger.
A	**Accomplishment**	The satisfaction of achieving goals; even modest accomplishments help us feel good.

THE BENEFITS OF PERMA

The PERMA theory (see "Real well-being," above right) is a key principle. All of the five aspects of happiness are things we pursue for their own sakes: they are valuable in themselves, or "intrinsically" rewarding.

✔ **Positive emotions**, while by their nature fleeting, can make us more open, resilient, creative, and observant—even physically healthier.

✔ **Engagement** comes when we're feeling confident about our skills. It can be such a pleasant experience that we end up honing these skills for fun rather than as a duty. The better you know your strengths, the more you'll be able to get into the flow.

✔ **Relationships** are essential. This includes those with family, friends, romantic partners, colleagues, and your community. Without other people, successes ring hollow.

✔ **Meaning** makes us more satisfied, confident, and robust. Sometimes you're already doing something you consider meaningful, and sometimes you may need to work at finding the meaning, but this is something you can develop.

✔ **Accomplishment** is something all success-focused people care about. Positive psychology suggests that the key quality you need to succeed is perseverance, but actually all the other aspects of PERMA help to make this easier. If you're tired, isolated, or sad, it's hard to stick to challenges; if you're flourishing, it becomes a lot easier.

We all want to be successful because we think it'll make us happy. It's good to remember, though, that it can work the other way: being happy can also help us to succeed.

HOW HAPPY ARE YOU?

A 2014 Australian study asked student volunteers a series of questions to test their PERMA ratings. Try them and see how they come out for you. Life is fluid, so it's likely that you'll be able to give more positive answers in some areas than others, and a year from now you may find that the balance has changed. You're most likely to feel successful, though, if you have at least some good experiences in each aspect of PERMA, so if you have a nagging sense that something's missing, these questions might be useful to pinpoint what you need to develop:

Meaning

- Do you generally feel that what you do in your life is valuable and worthwhile?
- Do you feel your life has a purpose?

Relationships

Do you agree that…

- Your relationships are supportive and rewarding?
- You actively contribute to other people's happiness and well-being?
- When something good happens, you have people you like to share the news with?
- You have friends you really care about?
- There are people who really care about and love you?
- When you have a problem, someone will be there for you?

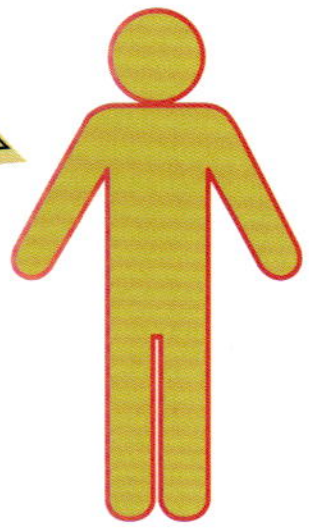

Positive emotions

- How often do you feel cheerful?
- How often do you feel energetic?
- How often do you feel delighted?
- How often do you feel calm?
- How often do you feel proud?
- How often do you feel daring?
- How often do you feel lively?

Engagement

- Do you lose track of time when you're reading or learning something new?
- Do you often get completely absorbed in what you're doing?
- When you see beautiful scenery, do you enjoy it so much you lose track of time?
- How often do you feel interested?
- How often do you feel alert?

Accomplishment

- Do you finish whatever you begin?
- When you have a plan, do you stick to it?
- Do you see yourself as a hard worker?
- Most days, do you feel a sense of having accomplished something?
- During the past two weeks, have you felt pleased about completing something that was difficult?

were causing the individual, their family, or the community "pain or suffering." Traditionally, psychology was more focused on how to eliminate suffering rather than what creates a life that is fulfilling and "worth living." Seligman focuses on what he calls "well-being": an overall sense of emotional health and happiness that makes a human being truly successful.

The value of accomplishment

If you're set on success, the "A" for "Accomplishment" in PERMA will likely mean a great deal to you (see also "Achievement versus accomplishment," below). The Positive Psychology Foundation observes that, along with a sense of pride, accomplishment can give us other things as well:

1 **Accomplishment creates a positive structure for our memories.** Days when nothing much happened tend to slip out of our memories, leaving little behind of that piece of our finite and precious lives. If we spend time working toward specific goals, on the other hand, then those days are part of a pattern that we can remember with satisfaction for years to come. Accomplishment is all about being able to look back and feel good, and this can help build a rich memory bank.

2 **Accomplishment encourages gratitude.** Very few of us can accomplish things entirely on our own. Research confirms that people who regularly feel grateful enjoy better mental health and quality of life. If you can look at what you've done and be thankful for everyone and everything that helped you get there, that's fuel for happiness.

3 **Accomplishment makes us more confident about the future.** There is always another challenge to face, and even the strongest and most cheerful of us have moments when we doubt we'll get through a difficult patch. Having had the experience of overcoming obstacles in the past is one of the best ways to build our confidence and the belief that we can handle obstacles as they arise in the future.

ACHIEVEMENT VERSUS ACCOMPLISHMENT

Who decides if you're a success? Positive psychologist Patty O'Grady identifies this key difference:

- **Achievement** is when we meet a standard imposed by others
- **Accomplishment** is when we reach a goal we personally value

A lot of contemporary society is focused on achievement: pass that exam, win that game, ace that interview. One reason is simply that these are easy to measure—you either get an "A," score a goal, get the job, or you don't. But precisely for this reason, such measures can feel reductive, and ultimately unsatisfying: they depend on other people's ideas of how to measure achievement, not your own. What's really rewarding is to do something because it will accomplish a goal you think is important, be it personal, professional, artistic, technical, or whatever seems significant to you. This often involves externally measurable successes, but the real reward is your own self-approbation, and the ability to thrive as a whole person. As O'Grady puts it, "Achievement is a by-product of accomplishment."

BETTER THAN OKAY

Positive psychology founder Martin Seligman argues that for most of its history, the discipline of psychology has focused on mental illness and unhappiness. Its goal has been to bring people up the "zero line" of simply not being sick. Positive psychology was developed with the aim of addressing the other side of the equation: what raises us *above* that base level to a state of true well-being? That is, how can we be actively flourishing, rather than just "all right"?

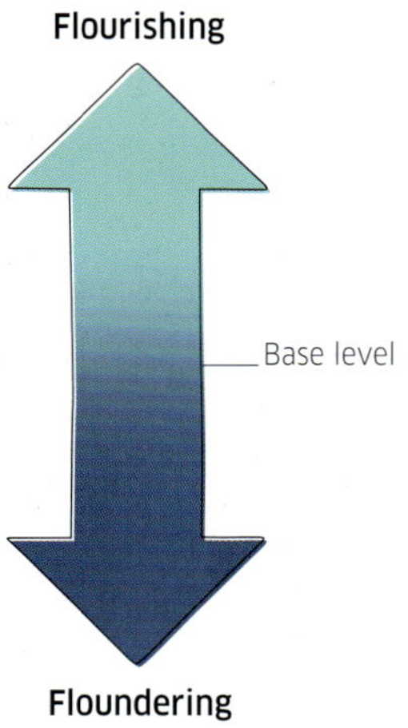

POSITIVE HABITS

WAYS OF THINKING AND BEING

Success, happiness, and feelings of accomplishment are all linked. What you think about and do make a difference: spur yourself on toward a more fulfilling life by cultivating positive mental attitudes and habits.

It is human nature to want to be happy, but what makes us so? What approaches can we use to create fulfillment and happiness, enabling us to achieve the goals that are important to us?

Possessions or experiences?
Contrary to what we may expect, given the emphasis in our culture on material possessions, "having things" doesn't make us happy (even if we feel "good" in the moment we buy something). According to a 20-year study by Cornell University psychologist Thomas D. Gilovich, material objects have drawbacks, because:

- **We get used to them.** Once the novelty wears off, we're still the same person with the same feelings, needs, and concerns.
- **Our expectations recalibrate.** Your new car is great compared with your old car, but in time you'll be comparing it to still *better* cars.
- **We compare ourselves to other people.** There is always someone who has shinier things than we do.

This is known as "adaptation": as circumstances change, we adjust to them. What doesn't lose its shine, however, is having experiences that are meaningful and memorable:

- **We don't compare in the same way.** You can set objects side by side, but comparing experiences seems pointless, which means their value has a sustained impact on our happiness.
- **Experiences become part of our identity,** both in how we see ourselves and how others see us.

FIVE WAYS TO IMPROVE WELL-BEING

In 2005, Martin Seligman and his team of researchers gave five different groups of people a task to perform over the course of a week. Each exercise was found to raise the participants' well-being:

At the end of each day, write down three good things that happened to you and reflect on what caused them.

Send a letter to someone you've never properly thanked.

Write about a time when you were at your best.

Identify and use your five signature strengths (see pp.76–77) more often.

Use one of your signature strengths in a new way.

- **We enjoy anticipating experiences.** Waiting to afford to buy something generally means feeling impatient; looking forward to a vacation or day out, on the other hand, is exciting.

The research shows that investing in experiences has a sustained impact on our short- and long-term happiness, as well as our feelings of success.

Train your brain

Neuroscience shows that our brains are "plastic," which means they are capable of being reshaped, even in adulthood. While it can be hard to shift your mental habits, consider the effort you make to change the way you think as similar to how you exercise to improve your body.

IT IS BETTER TO GIVE THAN TO RECEIVE

Psychologist Shawn Achor discovered that the greatest indicator of whether someone can sustain their levels of happiness during stressful periods is if they can count on good social support. Surprisingly, it is even *better* if they give support to others!

Workers who supported their colleagues were:

10x more likely to be **engaged in their jobs**

40% more likely to **get promoted**.

SIMPLE MOOD BOOSTERS

Happiness researcher Shawn Achor lists some ways to lift your mood:

- Write down three things you're grateful for
- Send a positive message to someone you care about
- Meditate for two minutes
- Exercise for ten minutes
- Spend two minutes writing about the most meaningful experience you've had in the last 24 hours
- Get in touch with someone in your social network.

This final activity has been shown to be the best of all for raising spirits, so never be "too busy" for time with friends, family, and close colleagues.

TRUE AND ACTUAL SELVES

THE IMPORTANCE OF LOOKING WITHIN

Our self-image goes right to the core of our being, and the path to success involves putting some thought into how we see ourselves. How can we cultivate a self-perception that's both accurate and helpful?

Self-image can help or hinder us: we judge our options based on how we see ourselves. Accurate self-awareness is a skill that develops with practice and it's something we need to refine over time through reflection.

Feeling good

There are benefits to being confident about our strengths and talents. A 2010 American study, for example, found that college students who were best at identifying and analyzing their strengths were also better at building on past successes and managing social support in general; they also tended to have greater well-being and higher self-esteem. Knowing what your strengths are, especially when they can be used in the service of your interests and passions, is a real advantage: it means you know what tools you have at your disposal.

The thing is, we're prone to be a bit blind to our own strengths. If we think that, for instance, courage is an important character trait, we may assume it's only right to be brave when circumstances demand. If we ourselves end up acting courageously at some point, we may think our behavior is only

> A man cannot be **comfortable** without *his own* **approval**.
>
> **Mark Twain**
> Novelist

TAKING STOCK

Consider the following questions. Your answers may reveal much about where your strengths lie:

- **When people have different strengths** from you, do you prefer to discount or learn from them? Are there "strengths" you don't admire? Are there qualities you don't particularly possess, but appreciate in others?
- **What energizes you**, and what exhausts and drains you?
- **Are there people in your life** who can help support you to make the most of your strengths?

"ordinary." What seems like "just what you should do" could in fact be a key to what's best in you.

What is a personal "strength"?
Positive psychology defines a strength as a combination of natural aptitude, knowledge, and skills, which creates a potential for excellence as long as these qualities are cultivated. Therefore, we need to identify our talents, integrate those talents into how we see ourselves, and modify our behavior accordingly.

Part of this change in behavior involves limiting how much we focus on the negative. When we're trying to accomplish something, it's easy to look at what we *don't* like about our lives and try to fix it, but there are studies that suggest it's more productive to focus on

IN THE WORKPLACE

Do you have a colleague whose opinion you trust? Ask them these questions, and see if their answers indicate ways you can improve:

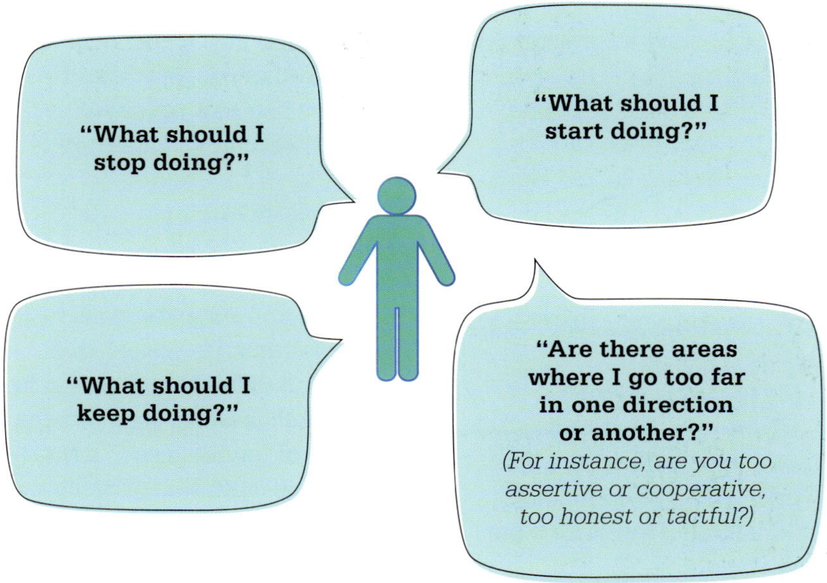

PLAYING IT RIGHT

It's good to have strengths, but you don't always have to use them at full strength. *The Journal of Positive Psychology* points out that it's more helpful to adjust ourselves to each situation, and to be aware of the context in which we are operating: we don't have to apply the same amount of force every time. When employing your strengths, ask yourself if you could use them more—or even, contrarily, underplay them—depending on what may be politically advantageous or in your best interests.

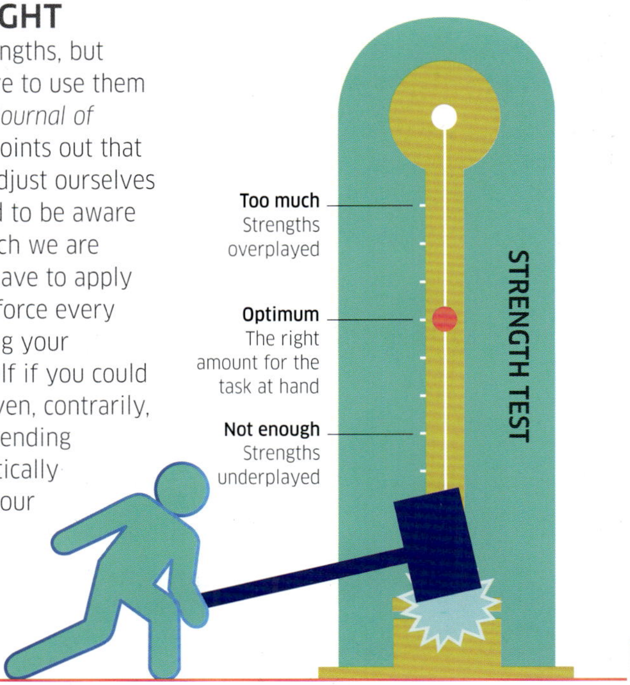

appreciating what we do well, and to do those particular things more often. People who try this approach feel more engaged and motivated.

Trusted friends and family can offer a candid appraisal, both from "inside" and "outside" our interests. We tend to gravitate toward people who share our passions, so friends can help us build on existing strengths; family who aren't automatically fascinated by our chosen field can provide loving reality checks.

WHAT IS MEDITATION?

Meditation can be a dynamic practice and a powerful tool. Two traditional words for it are:

- **bhävana** (Sanskrit), meaning "cultivate" or "cause to become"
- **sgoms** (Tibetan), meaning "the development of familiarity" (self-awareness and insight)

By meditating, you're training your mind and allowing yourself to become comfortable with mental states that will be beneficial to you.

Feeling good about ourselves is one of the biggest motivating factors available to us. Motivated people get things done and can sustain a productive pace for much longer than unhappy people. Work on appreciating what's good in you and what's good in other people too, and you may find that your path to success becomes a lot smoother.

Being mindful

Buddhists believe that it is limiting to have a fixed view of ourselves, and research supports the view that we have "multiple selves" that emerge in different contexts. A lot of research is being done into the efficacy of "mindfulness," a state of awareness cultivated in meditation (see pp.68–71). Mindfulness is based in the present moment, is nonjudgmental, and doesn't leap to react to every thought and experience that passes over you.

Psychologists speak of the "S-ART" framework, which stands for self-awareness, self-regulation, and self-transcendence. What this means is that with practice we can develop a state of self-awareness that helps us manage our emotions and rise above our self-focused needs to see the bigger picture and relate better to others.

Mindfulness has four key aspects:

- Balanced and focused effort
- Discerning things clearly
- Mindful awareness
- Equanimity: observing things impartially, rather than letting our desires and discontents dominate us.

A MINDFUL APPROACH

If you're too rigid in your idea of what kind of a person you are, you can sometimes talk yourself out of broadening your horizons.

NEGATIVE THOUGHT PROCESS

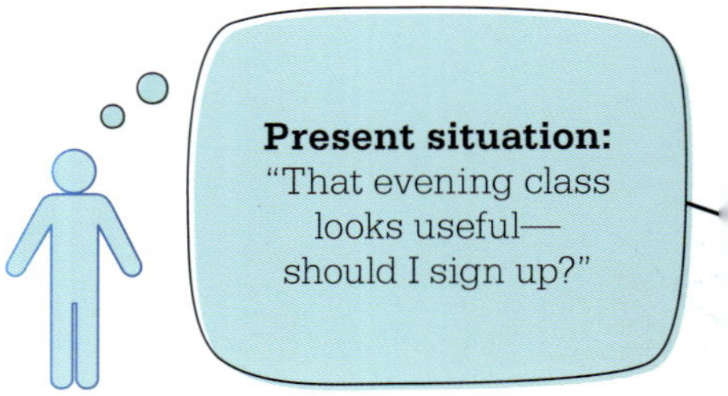

POSITIVE THOUGHT PROCESS

In other words, to be mindful, we need to focus on the present moment, see it for what it is, be aware of how we feel, and accept that this moment is what it is and stay with it, instead of racing back to memories or ahead to thoughts of the future.

Uncomfortable emotions

How does this affect us? How we see ourselves can limit our ability to act—and the more we put labels on events, interactions, and outcomes, the more vulnerable we become to

By staying in the present moment and acknowledging how you feel, you can stay "on topic" and remain constructive.

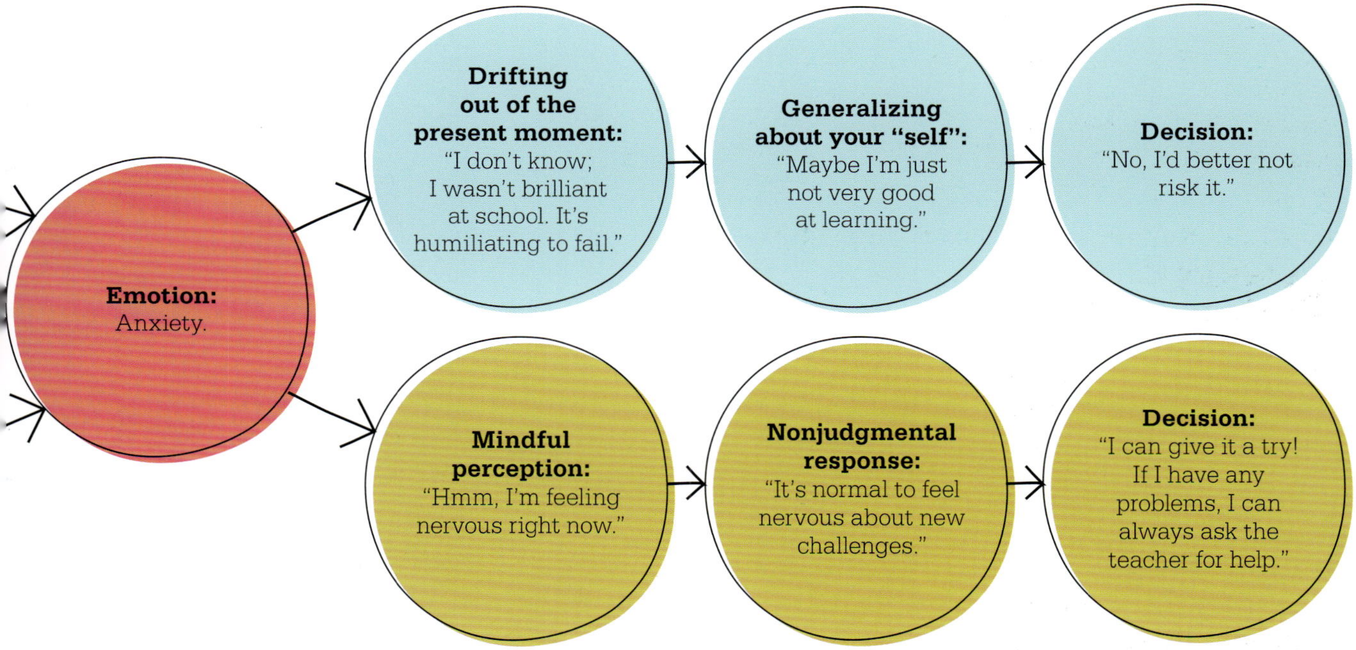

biases. Memories of how we used to be can interfere with what we feel capable of now; generalizing from our experiences can limit our ideas of what we're capable of.

We've all had the experience of an unpleasant occurrence bringing up uncomfortable associations, and the natural response is to try to push those feelings away. But this doesn't help: the less self-aware we are, the more likely we are to succumb to mistaken beliefs. Memory is associative, and if we're feeling a negative emotion, our mind naturally starts bringing up other negative experiences we've had, and we can end up in a downward spiral. It's more helpful to acknowledge that we're feeling something negative, and let it be what it is: an uncomfortable moment that will pass in its own time, which doesn't have to mean anything more.

The consistency principle

We have a great psychological need to see ourselves as stable, rational beings. This can lead to problems if we do or say something that doesn't match our self-image; the temptation is to rationalize it away, so that we can feel consistent with our beliefs and past actions. It is better to accept that inconsistency is part of human nature, and to acknowledge these "aberrations" instead of brushing them aside.

The more you're clear on your good points, and the more able you are to be gentle and patient with your mistakes, the more comfortable you'll be taking the steps that lead you to new heights.

EMOTIONAL INTELLIGENCE

THINKING WITH YOUR FEELINGS

Trying to succeed without knowing what we really feel is like trying to find our way in the dark. Achievement in all aspects of our life depends on understanding our own feelings and those of the people around us.

Sometimes it's easy to get focused on the "externals" of success: what are my qualifications, who are my contacts, what do I have to show for myself? If we want to manage these skillfully, though, we need to understand ourselves and the feelings of the people we come into contact with.

Emotional insight

The concept of "emotional intelligence" has become increasingly influential since it was first put forward in the 1990s. Psychologist Daniel Goleman defines emotional intelligence as being able to:

- Monitor your own and other people's feelings
- Label those feelings accurately
- Use this information to guide your thoughts and actions.

This means we need to be attuned to our own feelings and the emotional content of our interactions with other people, and be able to make sound judgments based on these insights. This comes more easily to some of us than others. The good news is that emotional intelligence is something we're able to learn.

38%

In American high schools that implemented a **program** to **teach emotional intelligence**, 38 percent of students **improved** their GPA (grade-point average).

Enhanced effectiveness

Developing your emotional intelligence can make you highly attractive to employers. Teacher and positive psychology trainer Ronen Habib reports that, at a conference involving top HR executives from high-profile employers such as Google and Facebook, the following skills were listed as being highly sought after: working well with others; creativity; basic knowledge of the subject matter; perseverance through adversity; and time management.

These qualities, they observed, are actually difficult to find. Children are not taught them in school, and we have to learn them for ourselves. If you can do these things, it puts you well ahead of the competition. Working adeptly with others, for example, requires well-developed emotional intelligence skills.

Cultivating your awareness

Practice looking within to see how your feelings, thoughts, and beliefs are affecting your actions and

TRANSFERABLE SKILLS

According to psychologist Daniel Goleman, people with strong emotional intelligence are better able to do the following:

- **Tolerate uncertainty**
- **Handle conflicts**
- **Communicate effectively**
- **Motivate others**
- **Cope with the inevitable ups and downs of life**
- **Help other people feel less stressed**
- **Build long-lasting relationships**

choices. This may not be easy, especially if it confronts you with new ideas: studies suggest that when confronted with unfamiliar situations or concepts, we tend to feel anxious and rely on past experiences instead of working to create new ones. Try to avoid falling back on old habits, though, because changes for the better mean learning new skills and responses.

Difficult emotions exist, and it's best to acknowledge that instead of ignoring or avoiding them. Instead, try doing one thing differently each time. It may be uncomfortable in the short term, but if we cultivate our emotional awareness, it can pay off handsomely.

ACHIEVING EMOTIONAL EQUILIBRIUM

According to psychologists Daniel Goleman and David McClelland, self-awareness involves both recognizing our emotions and regulating our responses. This can help us as an individual and when we're operating as a member of a group:

SELF-AWARENESS

BENEFITS TO YOURSELF

Recognition
Self-knowledge and confidence

Regulation
Self-control, integrity, adaptability, and initiative

BENEFITS WITHIN A GROUP

Recognition
Empathy and cooperativeness

Regulation
Influence, alliance building, and leadership

THE SIDEWAYS MIRROR

SEEING YOURSELF AS OTHERS SEE YOU

Self-awareness is essential to your continued growth and success. The best way to understand how you're coming across to others is simply to ask and listen—and that can be an advanced skill in itself.

When it comes to how we're performing, there's no substitute for feedback. This can call for some robustness on your part, because that feedback isn't always delivered with perfect tact or sensitivity. Other people, after all, have their own emotions, biases, fears, assumptions, and expectations, and, what's more, their actions are then filtered through our own perceptions. A 2010 Canadian study found that we listen less to feedback that clashes with our self-image, and we're better able to hear it if it doesn't undercut our confidence. When looking for people to give you an honest opinion, find those who can balance candor with support.

Learning to listen

Should we just try to be rational about this? Actually it's not that simple: research has found that when it comes to taking feedback, our reactions can be led astray by two broad categories of influence: "hot cognition" and "cold cognition" (see "Hot and cold thinking," opposite). The former is caused by emotions, and can cause problems when we're too caught up in our feelings to listen. The latter is more to do with the ways in which our attention, memory, and judgment can sway our logic, an example being confirmation bias (see p.75).

It isn't always comfortable to receive feedback, but it is useful. The science says to seek out people who present it helpfully, and to try to be aware of our own reactions—which are never as clear-sighted as we might wish.

HOT AND COLD THINKING

We're prone to both "hot" (emotional) and "cold" (logical) thinking: this is known as hot cognition and cold cognition. When listening to others, it's helpful to be aware that both emotion *and* logic can trip us up:

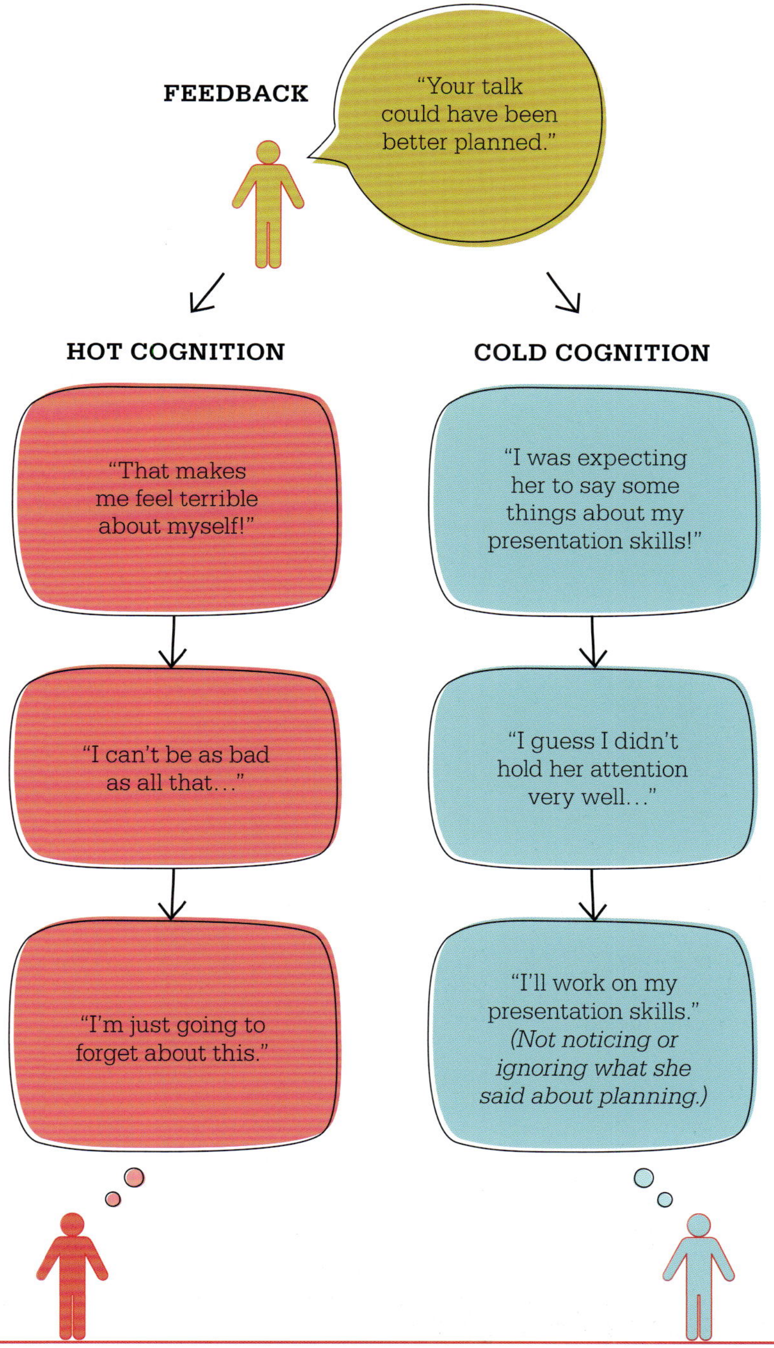

THE INFLUENTIAL YOU

We know we're coming across well when we start influencing other people. This means that we're communicating clearly; those around us can see what we're about and are learning in turn. Positive psychology author Travis Bradberry identifies the hallmarks of influential people:

1 They think for themselves and go by facts rather than trends.

2 They question the status quo, challenging convention without being antagonistic.

3 They inspire discussion: they're so interested in exploring new ideas that other people catch the mood.

4 They freely make and foster connections, sharing information and introducing people to each other.

5 They focus on the main point, and communicate it to others.

6 They know they're not infallible, and welcome disagreement.

7 They're proactive; they see what's coming and let others know so that they can prepare, too.

8 They respond rather than react—which is to say, they don't behave in a knee-jerk fashion, but try to preserve relationships even if they're being criticized.

9 They believe in the power of people to change things.

DELVE DEEP

UNDERSTANDING THE INNER YOU

Self-knowledge is one of the most important things in life, but also one of the most difficult. We're all prone to blind spots, but the good news is that there are many ways to deepen our self-awareness.

You'd think that you'd be the best judge of your own abilities—after all, you're the only person who witnesses everything you do. In practice it's a little more complicated. The evidence suggests that we're not terribly accurate, and the reason for this is that we tend to judge ourselves by our intentions, while others only see our actions and the resulting impact.

Blind to our blind spots

In 1999, American psychologists Justin Kruger and David Dunning published a paper describing what is now known as the "Dunning–Kruger effect." Put simply, their finding was this: the understanding you need to be good at something, and the understanding you need to assess your own abilities in that area, are basically the same. This means that if you have a poor grasp of something, *you probably don't realize it*. In fact, below a certain level of competence, people often drastically overestimate their abilities, because they're too incompetent to understand how incompetent they are (see "The Dunning–Kruger effect," opposite). This isn't necessarily arrogance: it's just that when we're learning something new, we probably don't know how complex it is yet.

Do we want accuracy?

When it comes to self-knowledge, we usually want conflicting things. On the one hand, we want to have an accurate assessment of ourselves. With that in mind we often fall back on objective measures, such as how we do on tests and in performance reviews, how we compare to our peers, how we've performed in the past, and so on. On the other hand, we also want to have a positive assessment of ourselves. Studies suggest that people who have slightly exaggerated views of how great they are tend to be happier and more popular. So, for most of us, there's a tension between wanting the cold, hard facts and wanting to feel that others respect us and can see that our intentions are good.

CRITICAL MEMORY

4:1

We **respond better to praise**—but we **remember criticism longer**. Studies show that when asked to remember important emotional events, people recall **four unhappy memories** for every **positive one**.

THE DUNNING–KRUGER EFFECT

In a seminal paper David Dunning and Justin Kruger investigated the limits of our self-knowledge. They showed that people who don't understand a skill generally don't *know* that they don't understand it, because they don't realize what understanding would involve. In the study, the participants were asked to assess their capabilities, and then undergo a series of tests:

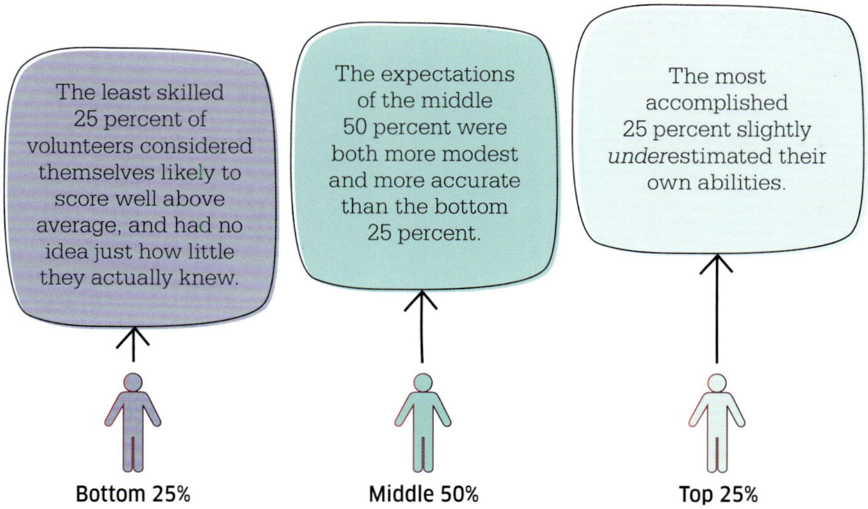

Dunning and Kruger speculated that the skills required to do something and the skills required to judge your own performance have a lot of overlap, and so able people are the most likely to be self-critical.

FINDING YOUR THEMES

When collating other people's feedback (see "Gathering useful feedback," right), look for comments that corroborate similar attributes or behaviors. The information might look something like the example below. In this case, the theme is "level-headedness":

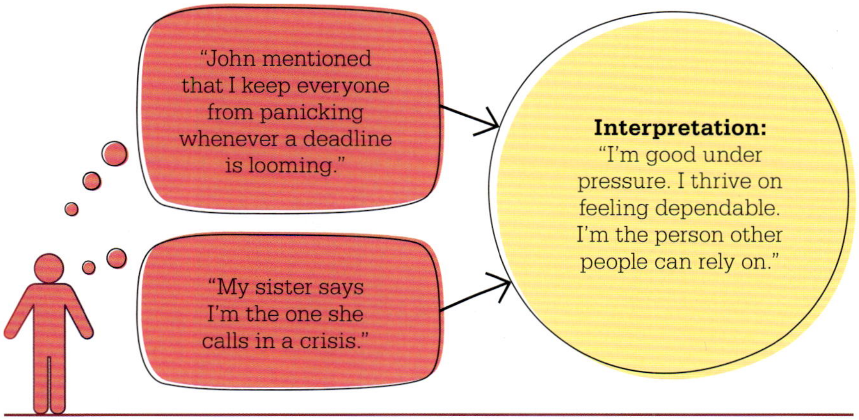

GATHERING USEFUL FEEDBACK

When assessing ourselves, we need to be as specific and concrete as possible. We're better at assessing ourselves when a challenge is:

- **Objective.** There's a clear answer that can be stated and understood.
- **Familiar.** If testing a skill, it helps to have some prior understanding and knowledge.
- **Low in complexity.** Keep it simple: if necessary, break it down into smaller tasks.

Seek appraisals from others (but positive ones, since we tend to overemphasize criticism). A 2005 study in the *Harvard Business Review* suggests the following:

- **Identify some trusted people**, including colleagues, friends, and teachers if possible, and ask them for an honest assessment of your strengths. Asking via email is a good way to keep the information on record and easy to organize.
- **Recognize patterns.** Look for themes that keep coming up in different ways.
- **Create a self-portrait.** Combine what people have said with how you see yourself, and see if this shows a clearer picture of you at your strongest.
- **Adapt your plans/job** to build on your strengths.

THE POWER OF GRIT

DEVELOPING RESILIENCE

There will be days when we're tired and discouraged, and at such times it's a challenge to follow through on what we have committed to do. Achievement is a blend of short-term and long-term decisions and actions.

Have you ever heard someone described as having "grit"? It's a colloquial phrase, but it's also a concept that psychologists have found to be linked to the way that some people sustain their effort over time, even when obstacles slow them down.

The science of sticking to it

What is resilience? Psychologist Carol Dweck, pioneer of the "growth mindset" (see p.26), describes it as any constructive response, be it in behavior, attitude, or emotion, to a challenge. Resilient people are confronted by obstacles the same as everyone else, but they see the situation as a challenge, not as a defeat, and become aware of what they could do differently next time. In a 2002 study a team of researchers (correctly) told undergraduate students at Stanford University that the brain is malleable and develops new connections when presented with fresh challenges. These students went on to significantly outperform their peers, who had been told that intelligence is fixed by early childhood and cannot be expanded.

Dweck suggests that a view of yourself as able to develop and learn tends to make people better able to survive social embarrassment, manage conflict, get the help they need, and master new things. If you encounter misfortune, don't forget that the experience has given you an opportunity to discover something new about yourself or the situation itself.

No matter what happens, finding ways to adapt and maintain your confidence is essential for success.

Finding your grit

A major researcher in the area of "grit" is American psychologist Angela Lee Duckworth. The qualities she studies are partly about staying on your path despite setbacks, and resisting distractions: adaptability is good, but if you change your interests so often that nothing gets finished, you're not really advancing. As she observes, you may need to be flexible, but "you also have to be good at something." That something needs to be a "long-term passion" to be rewarding; if you find it, your focus will keep you motivated.

To stay resilient, you need a positive mindset ("I can learn, I can improve") combined with a clear, long-term goal. Focus on something you care about, and then your quest to gather more knowledge about what you find most interesting will contribute to your success.

THE CABBIE'S DAY

Angela Lee Duckworth, author of *Grit*, found that taxi drivers tend to drive least on the most profitable days. People take more cabs when it rains, but cabbies usually go home *early* on rainy days. This is because they've picked up more fares, made their usual day's earnings, and decided to call it quits. If you're aiming for something big, look out for the "rainy" periods: those are the times to power forward, not take your foot off the pedal.

"WHAT I DID" VERSUS "WHAT I AM"

People who bounce back are able to take responsibility, but they don't take disappointments to heart. Consider these two different attitudes:

IN ORDER TO SUCCEED, PEOPLE NEED A SENSE OF SELF-EFFICACY, TO STRUGGLE TOGETHER WITH RESILIENCE TO MEET THE INEVITABLE OBSTACLES AND INEQUITIES OF LIFE.

ALBERT BANDURA, PSYCHOLOGIST AND ORIGINATOR OF SOCIAL COGNITIVE THEORY

AT EASE WITH YOUR MIND

MINDFULNESS, MEDITATION, CLARITY, AND CONFIDENCE

When you're committed to a certain path, you need to feel good about what you're doing—and also why you're doing it. If you cultivate mindfulness, you may find that the "why" becomes easier to see.

Mindfulness has long been a tradition in various religions and spiritual practices, but new research is finding that it has good scientific support as well. Mindfulness is a skill we can use at any time, but one of the best ways to practice it is through meditation, which you can incorporate into your routine.

What does meditation have to do with success? An increasing body of research suggests that it can have considerable power in helping us develop self-awareness, self-esteem, and the ability to cope with and recover from the inevitable knocks of life. Doctors and psychologists are increasingly interested in what the World Health Organization calls "a state of complete physical, mental, and social well-being, and not merely the absence of disease and infirmity"—and in that model, meditation is considered a "health behavior."

Choose the practice for you

There are many different meditation practices; we'll explain two of the most common here (see "Mindfulness meditation" and "Loving-kindness meditation," opposite). You may like to experiment with different kinds of meditation: if sitting still or finding time is a problem, for instance, walking meditations may be easier to fit into your daily routine. If you choose to explore further, the internet has a wide variety of exercises, visualizations, and practices you can search through and adapt to suit. Try them and see which practice works best for you.

MINDFULNESS MEDITATION

Mindfulness is a relaxed and nonjudgmental state of mind that allows us to observe calmly and accurately, which can make all the difference when we're facing a tough decision or coping with a setback. This is a classic meditation to help you develop the skill:

1 Choose somewhere where you won't be interrupted, and sit in a comfortable position. You don't need absolute silence; part of the practice is to let yourself be untroubled by background noise.

2 Close your eyes, relax, and let yourself feel your body. Notice how your feet feel in your shoes, how your body feels against the chair, the temperature of the air on your skin. Just notice these things; you don't have to do anything about them.

3 Don't worry if your mind wanders: it *will* wander, and it doesn't mean you're doing it wrong. If thoughts start popping up, just notice they're there. Don't follow these thoughts, don't fight them; let them come and go. This is one of the key experiences of mindfulness: by letting yourself experience thoughts and feelings without leaping to react to them, you're cultivating emotional awareness and resilience.

4 Notice your breathing. Can you feel your breath cooling and warming under your nose, the rise and fall of your chest, the passage of air down your throat? Focus on this, letting distractions happen and pass. You don't have to change the rhythm of your breathing if you don't want to: just notice it.

5 Sit like this for 5 to 10 minutes. When you're ready, bring your attention back to your whole body; this will recenter you, and make you more aware when you open your eyes again.

6 Finish your meditation, and congratulate yourself. There's no "right" way to do it: whether you were focused or distracted, it was still a successful exercise.

> Mindfulness practice means that we **commit fully** in each moment to be present... with the intention to embody the best we can an orientation of **calmness**, **mindfulness**, and **equanimity** right here and **right now**.
>
> **Jon Kabat-Zinn**
> Scientist, writer, and meditation teacher

LOVING-KINDNESS MEDITATION

Life inevitably holds moments of frustration, and conflicts with other people often hold us back. To help cultivate a more positive attitude, try this traditional meditation:

1 Sit yourself comfortably, relax, and experience the sensations in your body. Focus particularly on your "heart center," the area around your chest and solar plexus.

2 Cultivate a feeling of kindness and compassion, and direct it toward yourself. Silently repeat phrases such as, "May I be well," "May I be happy," "May I be healthy and well," and "May I live in joy and peace."

3 Next, think of someone you like or admire. Direct your feelings of kindness toward them, and wish that they may also be well, happy, healthy, and joyful.

4 Direct your loving-kindness to someone to whom you have no strong feelings. Wish them the same joy.

5 Think of someone you have difficulty liking (but not someone you absolutely hate, as this will distract you), and direct your loving-kindness toward them.

6 Expand your sense of well-wishing out toward everyone in the world.

FINDING TIME TO MEDITATE

We live busy lives these days, so how do we fit meditation in? First, we needn't do it for too long–20 minutes is ample, and if that's not possible, a shorter meditation is still better than none. Second, we can optimize our time. Health psychologist Linda Wasmer Andrews recommends the following times of day:

First thing in the morning
If you wake up with a lot on your mind, starting the day by calming yourself might be just what you need.

During your lunch hour
It's a good time to get a break from your routine, and can make you more relaxed and creative for the rest of the day.

At the end of the working day
This draws a line between your daily tasks and leisure time, helping you get the most out of your life.

In moments of particular stress
Even if you feel pressed for time, a few minutes to settle yourself may make you more productive afterward.

Zzz...
Just before bed is *not* recommended, as your brain can start confusing meditation with sleep.

The four principles

A 2013 study for *The Journal of Positive Psychology* found that people who meditate had strong self-esteem if they developed the four key facets of mindfulness, which are as follows:

1 **Nonreactivity.** You feel what you feel, but you don't jump to act on that feeling.

2 **Awareness.** You know what you feel; these feelings are not suppressed.

3 **Labeling and expressing.** You're able to describe your feelings accurately.

4 **Nonjudging of experience.** You know what is happening, but you don't have to call it "good" or "bad": it just is what it is.

Mindfulness at work

The benefits of meditation aren't merely personal. A 2008 study for the Academy of Management found that people who practiced mindfulness experienced many positive benefits in the workplace. These people were:

- More aware of what was happening on the job, picking up on details and subtle social cues
- Better able to get along with their colleagues
- More flexible and spontaneous
- More at ease
- More realistic in their goals
- More empathic and responsive to others; less self-centered
- Less focused on material gain
- Less dependent on validation from others
- Better able to derive their sense of meaning in life from more sources than just their job
- More level-headed under stress
- Enjoying their work more
- More adaptable

50%

WIDER GOODWILL

A study at Harvard University found that **people who meditated regularly** showed **kindness and compassion to others** 50 percent more often than people who didn't.

HEALTH BENEFITS

Studies find that meditation can support our physical health. It can:

- Help us maintain good exercise habits
- Reduce risky behaviors, such as excessive drinking and drug-taking
- Enhance the functioning of the immune system
- Improve our ability to manage pain
- Reduce inflammation at a cellular level
- Develop our self-control
- Improve cortical thickness in the areas of the brain related to attention and focus.

- More likely to feel that new situations presented a challenge, not a threat.

The evidence is that mindful people are healthier, happier, and better collaborators—all great advantages in your quest for success.

BARRIERS TO PRACTICING MINDFULNESS

If you don't feel like trying mindfulness, can you identify a strong reason why not? A 2011 study listed the most common objections:

I can't stop my thoughts.

I am uncomfortable with silence.

I can't sit still long enough to meditate.

I prefer to be accomplishing something.

Meditation might be boring.

It is a waste of time to sit and do nothing.

I don't know much about meditation.

Prayer is my form of meditation.

There is no quiet place where I can meditate.

I don't have time.

There is never a time when I can be alone.

I wouldn't know if I were doing it right.

I'm concerned meditation will conflict with my religion.

My family would think it was unusual.

I would feel odd meditating.

I don't believe meditation can help me.

I wonder if meditation might harm me.

The researchers found that these barriers were rather effective at discouraging people. If you want to give meditation a try but feel uncomfortable, consider which of these objections sound familiar. If you can suspend your belief in them, even briefly, it might make space in your life to experiment.

FINDING YOUR PASSION

ENGAGEMENT, PURPOSE, AND MEANING

What, to you, is really worth doing in life? We all have our own ideas about what is important, but to feel fully satisfied we need to channel our energy and passions into something that is productive and meaningful to us.

When we are doing something meaningful, it holds our attention and engages our interest, keeping us focused and persistent over time. Motivation gives us energy, and passion focuses that energy. But what really motivates us?

Extrinsic versus intrinsic

A series of seminal experiments by psychologist Sam Glucksberg offers a counterintuitive result. Building on Karl Duncker's "candle problem" (see "How our expectations can limit us," opposite), Glucksberg tried the same test on two groups. He told one group that the purpose of the research was to establish how long it took people to solve the problem. The other group was told that if they solved it faster than their peers, they'd get a cash reward. The group with the cash incentive solved it faster, *if* the tacks were left out of the box; but if the tacks were *inside* the box and the problem required lateral thinking, they took 3½ minutes longer than the group who thought they were trying to discover something interesting. This is a good example of the difference between extrinsic

A THOUGHT EXPERIMENT

Ask yourself: "If I won the lottery, would I keep doing what I'm doing right now?" If the answer is "yes," it is probably because you enjoy what you are doing and view it as important. If "no," it highlights that at this point you may not be pursuing your true passion.

HOW OUR EXPECTATIONS CAN LIMIT US

The findings of German psychologist Karl Duncker's most famous experiment, the "candle problem," were published in 1945. In this research, each volunteer was left alone in a room with a candle, a book of matches, and a box of thumbtacks. Their task was to find a way to attach the candle to the wall so that the wax wouldn't drip on the table.

Tacking the candle to the wall didn't work, and neither did trying to melt it on. In the end, most people realized that they needed to use the box, too: they tacked the box to the wall and placed the candle in it.

If the tacks were presented *outside* the box, they reached the solution quickly, but if the tacks were *in* the box, it took longer for them to find the solution. This is due to a cognitive bias known as "functional fixedness." The box's apparent function–holding the tacks–blinded people to the fact that it could be used to solve the problem.

The lesson? Solving a problem often relies on thinking about your resources and opportunities in new ways. Doing so creates long-term success and builds your confidence when finding solutions and making difficult decisions.

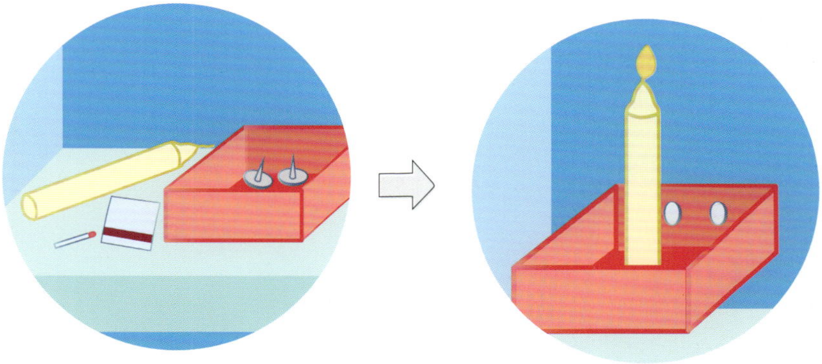

Problem

Solution

and intrinsic motivation: extrinsic rewards prompt us to solve simple tasks, but if we want to do well on complex ones, we need to be inspired by its intrinsic worth. Engagement, meaning, and purpose all sustain our intrinsic motivation.

Pinpointing your motivation

How do we apply this in real life? "Live Your Legend" online community founder Scott Dinsmore recommends that you:

- Figure out what your unique strengths are (see pp.76–77).
- Consider what motivates you: for example, recognition, a sense of mastery, or connection to others?
- Think about what you love doing, and what you hate doing.

Add all these together, and you have concrete information to act upon.

JOB CRAFTING

What if you're in a job that doesn't motivate you but you're not in a position to leave? Psychologists Amy Wrzesniewski, Justin M. Berg, and Jane E. Dutton recommend a process called "job crafting": stay where you are, but start to manage things differently. They identify three key ways in which you can do this:

- **Tasks**. What do you want to do more of? Suppose you like teaching: take younger colleagues under your wing and volunteer for more mentoring. This way, you're showcasing and developing your teaching skills.
- **Relationships**. Think about the people in your workplace who can help you establish the skills you're trying to cultivate. Look for mentors, allies, and people you can learn from.
- **Perceptions**. Mentally reframe the different elements of your job to allow you to focus on the most meaningful elements.

Our jobs shape us, but we can also shape our jobs (at least to some extent) if we're proactive. Be clear about how you want to develop, and set about creating situations where these opportunities for growth become possible.

WHEN DISAGREEMENTS ARISE

THE HARMONY OF CONFLICT

However passionate you are about your vision, you're likely to meet people who simply won't see things your way. Before you get frustrated, stop and reflect: another perspective might reveal a great opportunity.

It's undoubtedly true that we thrive on support and encouragement: too much criticism discourages the best of us (see pp.62–63). That said, there's a difference between criticism and disagreement. The former can be hurtful, but the latter, in the right context, can help us to excel.

Finding the truth

Some of the best work in human history has come from active and ongoing disagreement. The key is an atmosphere in which nobody takes disagreement personally: you aren't focused on *who's* right, but on *what's* right. By taking opposite positions and challenging each other to prove every point, you are working together to reach the right conclusion. This way, disagreement can be pure collaboration.

Business consultant Margaret Heffernan tells a story of constructive disagreement. In the 1950s, a dreadful problem faced British society—more and more children were being diagnosed with cancer. Scientist Alice Stewart collected extensive data and came to the

85%

of **European and American executives** have **concerns at work** that they don't raise for **fear of conflict**.

conclusion that the cancer was caused by the children having been X-rayed in utero. Conventional medical thinking at the time was very resistant to this idea. Stewart, though, found her perfect collaborator in statistician George Kneale. His standpoint was: "My job is to prove Dr. Stewart wrong." Because Kneale worked tirelessly to find weak points in Stewart's theory, together they were able to prove just how strong it was—thus saving hundreds of lives.

Confirmation bias

An important psychological concept to remember here is "confirmation bias," in which we test our ideas by looking for evidence that supports them and forget to look for evidence that might contradict them. While we can be even-handed weighing evidence about a neutral subject, when we're emotionally invested in something, we're liable to:

- **Overvalue evidence** that supports what we already believe and undervalue evidence to the contrary.
- **Look only** (or primarily) for evidence that supports our beliefs, rather than evidence that might refute it.
- **See what we're looking for**, even finding patterns that aren't actually there.

We all do this sometimes. If you can find partners to counterbalance you, and remind yourself to focus on what you can learn and improving your ideas, relationships, and work practices, then disagreement can help you succeed in ways you hadn't thought of before.

CREATING POSITIVE CONFLICT

Disagreement doesn't have to be antagonistic. When we're invested in our ideas, it's easy to take criticism personally—but it's worth remembering that someone criticizing your idea isn't criticizing *you*. When it happens again, reframe what was said, and ask yourself the following questions:

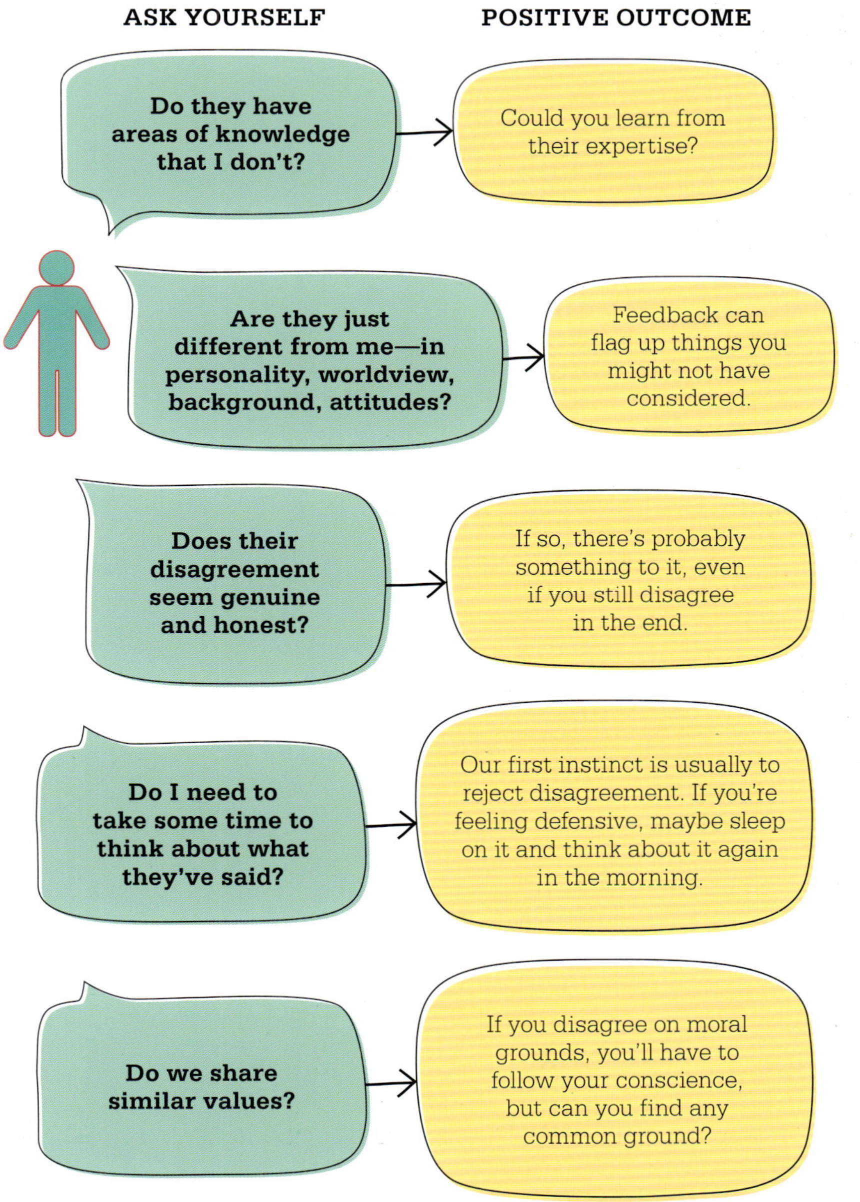

TAKING STOCK OF YOUR STRENGTHS

UNDERSTANDING YOUR UNIQUE ADVANTAGES

Knowing who you are is essential when seeking success, but what sort of person are you? Recent research has created a system that clarifies the pattern of strengths that makes each of us unique.

To achieve success you need to understand the unique combination of strengths that are the essence of your character. This is a concept that psychologists have started studying in more detail.

The VIA classification system

In the early 2000s, a three-year study involving 55 distinguished scientists at the nonprofit VIA Institute on Character examined positive traits of character: the result is the "VIA classification of character strengths and virtues." Much has been written about this system since; notably, in 2004, positive psychologists Christopher Peterson and Martin Seligman published a book called *Character Strengths and Virtues: A Handbook and Classification*. This system identifies 24 key traits, organized into six broad categories, that are universally deemed to be morally good. We each possess our own distinct combination of these strengths and virtues; we are stronger in some qualities, and weaker in others, and they all contribute to our unique character. If you can identify your strengths and use them to fulfill your goals, there's a better chance you'll feel like you're pursuing a "calling," not just a job or other pursuit.

Test yourself

If you want to analyze yourself in detail, try the VIA Institute on Character's Survey (see p.215). In the meantime, take a look at the traits themselves (see "The VIA classification of character strengths," opposite). Which of these do you most identify with, and which do you most admire in others?

KEEP YOUR VIRTUES IN MIND

Being our best selves can take some discipline. Tiffany Shlain of The Moxie Institute, a film studio that makes films about social awareness and change, adheres to the following process. When you're about to take action, pause for a moment and ask yourself:

- Does this reflect who I am?
- Does this reflect who I want to be?

64%

WORK YOUR STRENGTHS

According to a 2015 VIA Institute on Character study, almost two-thirds of **workers in the US** think that **success depends on building on their strengths**, rather than focusing on their weaknesses.

THE VIA CLASSIFICATION OF CHARACTER STRENGTHS

The VIA Institute on Character has devised a framework to help people identify their best qualities. Approaches vary, but your top five or six traits are likely to be your "signature strengths." The VIA system can be a good way of identifying them when you're trying to decide what your core qualities and aspirations are, as well as a way to identify both like-minded allies and people whose differences balance you out:

JUSTICE

Teamwork. Being loyal; pulling your weight; good citizenship.

Fairness. Giving everyone a chance; acting without bias; treating everyone fairly.

Leadership. Getting things done; encouraging others; maintaining good group relationships.

HUMANITY

Love. Valuing other people and being close to them; caring and sharing.

Kindness. Being generous, nurturing, helpful, and compassionate.

Social intelligence. Being aware of others' feelings and knowing how to get along with people.

TEMPERANCE

Forgiveness. Accepting that nobody is perfect; forgoing vengeance.

Humility. Letting your work speak for itself; not setting yourself above others.

Prudence. Being careful; thinking ahead; not doing things you might later regret.

Self-regulation. Having discipline and controlling your feelings and desires.

WISDOM AND KNOWLEDGE

Creativity. Being ingenious and original.

Curiosity. Being open to new things; taking an interest in the world.

Judgment. Being able to think critically, weigh things fairly, and consider without prejudice.

Love of learning. Being curious, but also being systematic in how you add to your knowledge and skills.

Perspective. Giving sound advice; being able to make sense of things.

TRANSCENDENCE

Appreciation of beauty and excellence. Being able to marvel at the wonderful, wherever you find it.

Gratitude. Taking time to be thankful.

Hope. Being optimistic and working to bring about a better future.

Humor. Being playful, seeing the funny side, and liking to make people laugh.

Spirituality. Having a sense of purpose about how you fit into the grander scheme of life.

COURAGE

Valor. Being brave in the face of threats, challenges, and suffering; speaking up for what's right.

Perseverance. Working hard and finishing what you start.

Honesty. Being authentic and sincere; acting with integrity and responsibility.

Zest. Living life to the fullest; approaching things with energy and enthusiasm.

NATURE VERSUS NURTURE

ARE PEOPLE BORN TO SUCCEED?

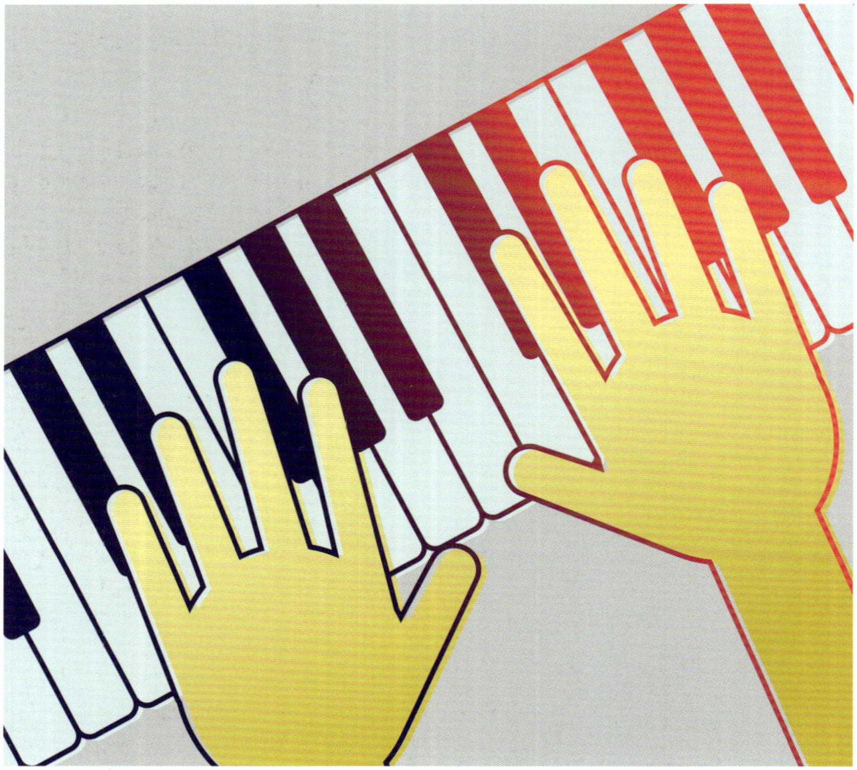

Psychologists talk about cultivating your strengths; leaders talk about working hard. Where do we find the balance between natural ability and self-improvement? The best course is to appreciate the value of both.

The phrase "practice makes perfect" is a good starting point on the path to success. But what can we realistically expect from ourselves when it comes to natural talent versus hard work?

10,000 hours?

You may be familiar with the theory that to get good at anything you need to put in 10,000 hours of practice. First proposed by Swedish psychologist K. Anders Ericsson, the idea was popularized by Malcolm Gladwell's 2008 book *Outliers*. In fact, the data suggests it's a bit more complicated.

Ericsson himself stated in 2012 that he didn't intend to deny that genetics may also play a part, only to say that the evidence hadn't been found yet. He also stressed that 10,000 is only an average, and that the practice has to be dedicated, intensive, and systematic. In the meantime, other studies have queried his findings. A 2014 analysis of a number of independent studies found that practice, on average, accounted for as little as 12 percent of skill mastery and later success.

> Overall, our **intelligence** and **academic performance** have a great deal to do with our **social background**.
>
> **Oliver James**
> Psychologist

Musical twins

A 2014 study by Swedish neuroscientist Miriam Mosey found that, when it came to musical ability—one of the key abilities Ericsson was testing—of over 1,000 pairs of identical twins, practice made surprisingly little difference to basics such as a sense of pitch and rhythm. (One twin had practiced over 20,000 hours more than his brother, without dramatic difference.) She added that practice could improve a person's technical skills, but that the twin studies suggested that both nature and nurture impact musical acumen.

The power of flow

How do we get good at things? Neither genes nor practice are the whole story: on their own, neither will take us all the way. What may be more productive is to find a mental space where we can experience a sense of "flow."

"Flow" is part of the "PERMA" scheme of happiness (see pp.48–51). A 2013 American study draws an interesting distinction between "pleasure" and "engagement." When seeking pleasure, we look to gratify ourselves, whereas when we're engaged, we lose ourselves because we're so absorbed in what we're doing: that's "flow." It's also a key to success: the study found that people who pursued pleasure more than engagement were more likely to get distracted, while people who pursued engagement had more "grit" (see pp.64–65), were more persistent, and were moving toward greater accomplishments.

BORN TO BE HAPPY?

Positive psychologist Martin Seligman posits that our general level of happiness—an important part of fulfilling our potential—can be encapsulated by this equation:

$$H = S + C + V$$

H stands for happiness: your enduring level of happiness, which is impacted by a combination of three factors.

S is your "set range": your biological disposition toward positive or negative moods, which accounts for about 40 to 50 percent of your happiness level and seems to operate as an "emotional steersman." Your choices influence whether positive or negative emotional states take control.

C stands for "circumstances": whether you live in a wealthy democracy, have a strong social support network, and are able to avoid or keep to a minimum negative situations and feelings.

V indicates the actions under your voluntary control: the actions, choices, and decisions you make each day that affect your level of happiness.

Positive psychologist Martin Seligman estimates that talent and practice account fairly equally for our ability, but he also draws a distinction between "talent," inborn and involuntary, and "strengths," healthy ways of thinking that we are able learn. Practice may never make us perfect at something for which we have no aptitude; in such cases, one answer may be to find trusted collaborators who are able to counterbalance us (see pp.74–75). When setting out to achieve results that are important to you, engaging in your passion and finding flow will make a difference and enable you to sustain momentum. In so doing, you give your abilities the chance to develop to the fullest.

TESTING YOUR STRENGTHS

Strengths have many elements that define them. With your strengths, you:

- **Feel authentic**—"This is what I really love." You don't have to be good at what you're doing to begin with: you yearn to keep improving.
- **Feel excited** when you make even small advances. Do you study people who already do this particular thing well, so you can build your skills in this area too?
- **Seek out feedback.** When you're focused on making progress, you ask for feedback from others whenever you get the opportunity.
- **Feel energized** and enthusiastic when making use of your abilities.

CHAPTER 3

HONE YOUR ATTITUDE

EXERCISE YOUR THINKING AND HARNESS YOUR SKILLS

BEATING NEGATIVE THINKING

THE POWER OF OPTIMISM

Can we "think" our way to success? Of course hard work, skill, and luck play their part as well, but the evidence shows that positive mental habits are essential, and our attitude does make a difference.

The path toward success can be emotionally tough: there may be knocks and frustrations as well as moments of excitement and satisfaction. A positive attitude can sustain you through unpredictable times, and studies on physical well-being show that optimistic people have stronger immune systems and live longer. Psychologists also find that optimists tend to be happier, better at coping, and more persistent, have a wider network of friends, and are more successful in general. The good news is that optimism can, with practice, be cultivated.

Five steps to optimism

Over the past 20 years, positive psychology researchers have formulated a five-point plan that educators use to teach students a positive outlook. If you're working on improving your optimism, try these approaches:

1 **Identify and prioritize your top goals.** Look at the big picture. Some will be "micro" goals and some "macro" goals, so settle in your own mind which are the most important.

2 **Break them down into steps.** This is especially helpful with long-term goals. The idea is not to achieve everything at one stroke: you need a series of milestones, which you can celebrate as successes as you reach them.

3 **Appreciate that there's more than one way to reach a goal.** Studies show that pessimistic students have difficulty problem-solving their way past obstacles, so flexibility is a key skill.

COGNITIVE DISTORTIONS

Cognitive Behavioral Therapy tells us we're vulnerable to "cognitive distortions," as shown here, which undermine our optimism. Combat such thinking by identifying and questioning such thoughts when they occur (see "Clear your mind," below):

Overgeneralization
Assuming that if something happens to you once, that's how things will always be.

Personalization
Blaming yourself when things go wrong.

All-or-nothing thinking
If you aren't always perfect, then you must be hopeless.

Emotional reasoning
Taking your feelings for facts.

Mental filter
Focusing on a negative detail, screening out the broader (and more positive) context.

Disqualifying the positive
Finding ways to write off good news and positive feedback.

Labeling and mislabeling
Thinking that one action sums a person up.

Maximizing and minimizing
If it's bad news, you "catastrophize"; if it's good news, it's no big deal.

Jumping to conclusions
Particularly "mind reading" (assuming you know what others think) and "fortune telling" (predicting disaster).

"Should" statements
Making up rules to motivate yourself, and ending up feeling worse.

4 **Tell your success stories, and hear other people's.** Seek out opportunities to remind yourself that adversity can be overcome.

5 **Stay light and positive.** Self-pity is the death of optimism, so keep your self-talk positive, find the funny side of your mistakes, and enjoy yourself as much as you can.

Clear your mind

Cognitive Behavioral Therapy teaches ways to build optimism when you find yourself thinking negatively (see "Cognitive distortions," above). If you find yourself caught in such thinking, try the following:

- Identify the thought that is bothering you.
- Ask yourself how much you believe it. Assign a hypothetical percentage to reflect the amount.
- Ask yourself if there are any cognitive distortions at play.
- Consider alternative explanations. You don't have to fully believe them; just try them on for size.
- Look at the evidence as calmly as possible. Does it support your troublesome thought? Is any evidence more encouraging?
- Ask yourself again how much you believe the negative thought. The answer doesn't have to be "not at all"; if you've dropped from, say, 85 to 45 percent, that's a significant improvement.

The benefits of this strategy over the long term can be great, from improved mental health to better focus and resilience—all of which support a more successful life.

LEARNING TO TRUST YOURSELF

CONFIDENCE-BUILDING TECHNIQUES

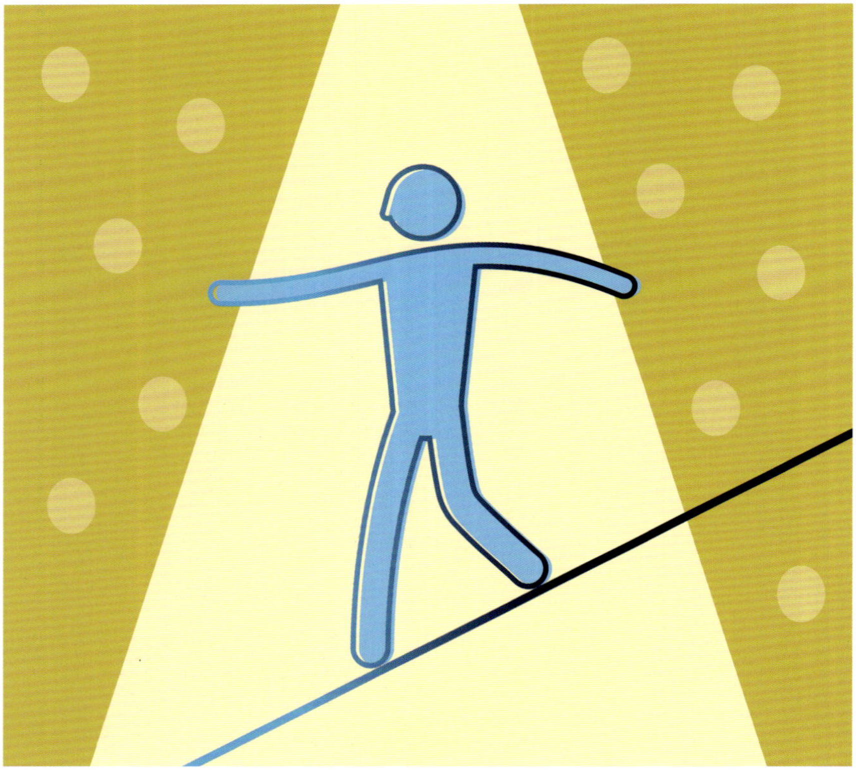

It sometimes seems that confident people stand a better chance in life. It's a self-fulfilling prophecy: being self-assured and having faith in yourself encourages other people to believe in you, too.

It may be true that some people have more natural confidence than others, but that's no reason to despair if you're subject to self-doubt. Instead, regard confidence as a necessary component in your plans to succeed, and give yourself permission to build it up.

Practice, practice, practice

Begin by cultivating an awareness of how you "talk" to yourself. Do you spend a lot of time dwelling on worries or self-criticism? If so, work on nipping these thoughts in the bud: replace negative self-talk with positive self-talk. Successful sports coach Ivan Joseph, for example, recommends writing yourself a letter listing all your accomplishments, and reading it regularly. The key is repetition: it's easy to forget your good points if you only think of them occasionally.

At the same time, practice doing things that make you nervous. Pushing past your comfort zone

Health is the greatest possession. **Contentment** is the greatest treasure. **Confidence** is the **greatest friend**.

Laozi (Lao Tzu)
Daoist philosopher

is something that only gets easier with familiarity. Start with low stakes; picture yourself like a tightrope walker beginning with a rope only a few feet off the ground. That vertiginous sense of anxiety is still going to be there, because we all fear falling, but once you've learned with a relatively safe "drop," you'll be better balanced when you try something more daring.

Start small and build up

Trying to feel confident about everything all of the time can feel like a big task. If you're not sure how to build yourself up, try breaking it down: make a list of things that you'd like to be more confident *about*. This will give you a more detailed picture: imagine specific situations that push your comfort zone (but not too much), and then go and do them—every day, if you can. Start small and work on it regularly, and you may find that over time confidence comes more naturally than it did before.

IMPROVING YOUR SELF-CONFIDENCE

Grab a piece of paper and note your thoughts on the following:

1. Ask yourself what your deepest fears are. Abandonment? Humiliation? Dependence? Think about what they are, and how they enter the picture when it comes to your plans for success.
2. Make a list of why these fears are understandable. Your life experiences have shaped you, including the bad ones, and these fears are a product of those experiences. Don't get too invested in blaming others, or yourself: the aim is to make peace with the past and move on.
3. Think about positive experiences that have helped you in your life, such as any support you've received, pride you've felt in your own actions, or new skills you've mastered.
4. Create a plan for using these techniques to help build yourself up in the future.
5. Anticipate ways in which this might be difficult—setbacks that may discourage you, particular demons that are hard to shake. Remind yourself that this is all part of the process, and consider ways to keep your compassion for yourself in view in those moments.

POSE FOR POISE

Social psychologist Amy Cuddy asked volunteers to sit or stand in a certain way, not revealing that these were "high-power" or "low-power" poses. After two minutes, each group showed changes in their hormone levels, of both testosterone (a hormone that increases with confidence in both men and women) and cortisol (the "stress" hormone). Her message? "Fake it 'til you make it."

HIGH-POWER POSE

20%
increase in testosterone

25%
decrease in cortisol

Result:
Calmer; primed to assert yourself

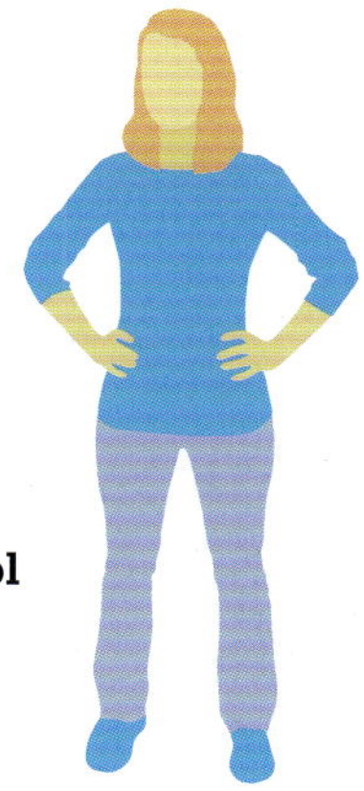

LOW-POWER POSE

10%
decrease in testosterone

15%
increase in cortisol

Result:
More nervous; less able to speak up

THE VALUE OF LEISURE

STAYING REFRESHED AND INVIGORATED

To sustain your focus on achieving long-term goals, balance is essential. The evidence suggests that a healthy amount of hobbies and vacations increases your resilience, making you more likely to succeed.

If your goals in life require hard work to reach them, ensuring that you actively schedule downtime into your plans is essential to sustaining your energy over time. As you focus on what you want to achieve, don't make the mistake of neglecting yourself, your family and friends, and the leisure activities you enjoy. A substantial amount of research suggests that a good use of free time makes a significant difference in how healthy you are, both mentally and physically.

What counts as leisure?

Is it leisure time when you just don't happen to be working? That's one way to view it; psychologists call this the residual definition of leisure—something that, in a pressured economy, is not always in abundant supply. This is one reason why so many of us are anxious to succeed on our own terms: if we have to work this hard, we'd like to enjoy it.

But there are other ways to categorize the things we do with our time off: some researchers distinguish between active and passive leisure, and others between serious and unserious leisure. There is a difference between watching television and playing tennis or joining an art group: some pastimes allow us to switch off, while others require more engagement. On the whole, the research indicates that we benefit most when we participate in leisure that gets us actively involved. We all need a rest sometimes, but active pursuits can

THE BENEFITS OF LEISURE

Leisure time is not just fun—it can be therapeutic, too. American psychologist Linda Caldwell identifies a number of ways in which leisure helps us, by:

- Being meaningful or interesting to us, and perhaps providing a good personal challenge.
- Putting us in touch with social support and friendships.
- Increasing our sense of self-efficacy (see pp.102–103) and competence.
- Giving us a sense of personal control and choice.
- Helping us relax or forget our daily troubles.

These elements support our mental health, which means that when we get back to focusing on our goals, we're better able to stick at them. Recreation makes you more stable and well-adjusted, so enjoy it with a clear conscience—and be mindful about what you do with your leisure time, to make sure it gives you the energy to keep moving forward.

have further benefits as well: they give us a sense of achievement and mastery, which boosts our mood.

Leisure can encompass a wide range of activities; the key element is what psychologists sum up as "perceived freedom"—which is to say, whether tranquil and relaxed or active and exciting, it feels like a rest because the choice is yours.

ALL THE WORLD LOVES...

A 2013 study across 33 countries found that certain activities proved universally good at boosting happiness. The researchers found that people were most fulfilled by activities that either helped them be the person they were, or strengthened their relationships with others. The top choices were:

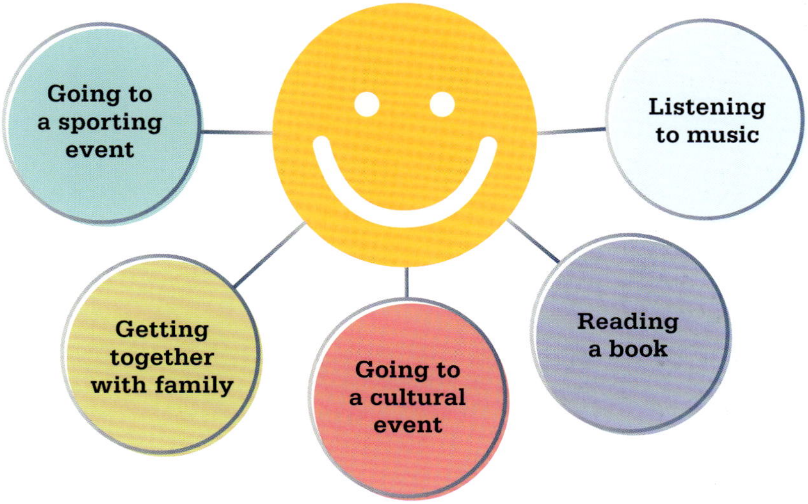

COMPELLING EXPERIENCES

Most of us watch films and TV, read books, listen to the radio, and play games in our time off–but what do we get out of it? One theory, based on video games but applicable to other cultural forms, was proposed in 2004 by American researchers Robin Hunicke, Marc LeBlanc, and Robert Zubek. They argued that there are eight ways of enjoying something, and that we find certain experiences compelling for different reasons. Why do you enjoy your favorite pastimes? Your answers may give you some interesting insights:

- **Discovery.** Exploring new territory.
- **Sensation.** Enjoying a spectacle or the mechanics of the gameplay.
- **Fantasy.** Make-believe; the joy of stepping into someone else's shoes.
- **Narrative.** The pleasure of following a story.
- **Challenge.** The satisfaction of overcoming obstacles.
- **Fellowship.** The fun of playing with others.
- **Expression.** Self-discovery and identity.
- **Submission/abnegation.** Sitting back and switching off.

AT EASE WITH YOURSELF

THE IMPORTANCE OF A HEALTHY BODY IMAGE

A healthy body image is one dimension of feeling successful. Being comfortable in your own skin makes for a better quality of life, and is likely to make you more attractive and impressive to others as well.

However accomplished you are, it's hard to feel like a success if you're not entirely happy with your physical appearance. Of course, you can exercise and be more careful about what you eat and drink, but it's also a good idea to begin by accepting and learning to enjoy your body here and now, whatever it looks like. When we think of the body beyond mere appearance, there's a lot it can teach us.

Positive body image

Research finds that a positive body image tends to support a variety of healthy behaviors, including:

- Higher levels of psychological and social well-being
- Better coping skills
- Improved sex life
- Intuitive eating (that is, eating appropriate quantities when hungry, rather than comfort eating or starving yourself)

If you can become more relaxed with how you feel about your body, the evidence suggests that you become better able to read its signals—and this in turn leads to more positive behaviors.

Dress for success

Getting dressed can sometimes be a fraught issue if you're not wholly confident about how you look. The concept of "enclothed cognition" may come in handy here.

A series of experiments at Northwestern University in Illinois, published in the *Journal of Experimental Social Psychology* in 2012, found that the clothes we

LET'S DANCE!

Israeli health psychologist Tal Shafir observes that our physical stance gives our brains feedback that can translate into emotions. Hence, assuming a downcast posture tends to make us "feel" sad, while a confident posture picks us up–so, for instance, dancing has been proven to improve mood more than hunching over an exercise bike. Shafir's research identifies key movements that cheer us up:

- **Expanding the body upward and horizontally,** such as stretching, jumping, and arm-raising.
- **Lightness.** Walking or moving with a spring in your step.
- **Repetitive movements**–dancing is particularly good for this.

> I've never wanted to look like models on the cover of magazines. I **represent** the **majority of women** and I'm **proud** of that.
>
> **Adele**
> Singer-songwriter

wear have a symbolic meaning, and can make a difference in our level of achievement when completing a task. Preliminary research found that a white lab coat, as typically worn by scientists and doctors, is associated with being attentive and careful. In the experiment, volunteers were shown a white lab coat and given the option of putting it on or not—but first, some volunteers were told it was a doctor's coat, while others were told that it was an artist's coat. After making their choice, the volunteers took part in a test. Those wearing the "doctor's coat" outperformed everyone else: the image of a doctor's precision and intellect had heightened their concentration. (Attention levels did not increase among those whose coats had been described as belonging to an artist.) The researchers concluded that the influence of clothing depends on the symbolic meaning attached to an outfit and the act of wearing it.

Certain outfits can bring out in us the positive qualities we associate with their role. When choosing our clothes, perhaps the key is to worry less about how we'll look, and think of it more as choosing a costume for who we want to feel like.

Being in the world

In a society full of images of impossible physical perfection, it's easy to feel we're lacking. Instead of thinking of your body as an accessory, though, it's healthier to think of it as a tool: however it looks, your body can carry you toward your goals. Confidence, dynamism, and action are more than skin deep, and these are the qualities that will help you to succeed.

LOVE YOUR BODY

Positive psychologist Kate Hefferon points out that people who feel comfortable with their bodies tend to be physically and emotionally healthier. She suggests a combined set of techniques to encourage us in the right direction:

Physical activity: Focus on how exercise and eating good food make you feel rather than how they make you look.

Media literacy: Be familiar with how advertisers feed our insecurities in order to make us more suggestible consumers.

The beauty myth: Appreciate how unrealistic ideals limit both men and women in today's society.

Improved self-esteem: Work on liking and accepting yourself as a valuable person, no matter how you look.

WILD HORSES

DEALING WITH YOUR EMOTIONS

Chasing your dreams can be an emotional business, and passions can ignite many feelings, ranging from excitement about the possibilities to frustrations with obstacles that get in your way.

Our emotions give us energy and are a crucial source of information that needs to be attended to and understood. Research on emotional intelligence clearly demonstrates the link between awareness about one's own and other people's emotions and the ability to successfully achieve goals. Understanding and managing our emotions is the key to success and effectiveness.

Creating a balance

We generally prefer to avoid uncomfortable feelings, but in fact, that's not the most productive or effective way of dealing with them. Life will frustrate and upset us at times, no matter how successful we are, and we need to learn how to cope with the inevitable ups and downs. If you are experiencing a painful emotion, it's better to "sit with it," as popular author and founder of the *Tiny Buddha* blog Lori Deschene puts it—that is, to accept that it hurts right now, while also knowing that this feeling will pass. Meanwhile, we can "create situations for positive feelings": if there's something that makes you happy, make opportunities to do it regularly. We need a place in our life for both.

Managing our emotions

Much as we'd like to consider ourselves objective, our brains are rather good at shaping reality to our expectations. Take, for instance, the

THE EMOTION DECODER

Having trouble identifying your emotions? Psychologist Darlene Mininni, author of *The Emotional Toolkit*, recommends that you examine what you're experiencing, and ask yourself what message your feelings are trying to send you.

Emotion	Sensation	Ask yourself
Anxiety	Tight muscles, racing heart	"What am I afraid of?"
Sadness	Tired, heavy, possibly tearful	"What have I lost?"
Anger	Tension, teeth clenching, changes in body temperature	"How have I, or the values I hold dear, been attacked?"
Happiness	Lightness, laughter, smiles	"What have I gained?"

emotion of loneliness. A 2000 study among 2,500 students at Ohio State University found that there were really no differences in social capital between students who called themselves lonely and students who didn't: their socio-economic status, looks, and academic achievements were pretty much the same, and they belonged to as many groups and lived with as many roommates. The difference was in how they would "construe their self in relation to others": they were more likely to blame other people for problems in relationships, and more likely to see themselves as victims who were already doing their best.

The study didn't look into whether this affected how other people felt about them—though it's quite possible that people would act less warmly toward someone who always blamed them for any conflict—but it's a useful warning. How we label ourselves and our interactions can become reality, even if the external evidence doesn't initially seem to support it.

Ways to move forward

What can you do if you're faced with an emotionally complex situation? First, be sure you know what it is that you're feeling (see "The emotion decoder," opposite). Second, consider the possible responses and choices you can make (see "Taking charge," right). Our emotions are our own, and while it can sometimes be difficult, the more we are able to take responsibility for them, the better off we'll be.

TAKING CHARGE

Can we be more proactive in how we deal with our emotions? According to James Gross, who specializes in emotional regulation at Stanford University, we can view our emotional responses as part of a process: if we make good decisions early on, we can achieve better outcomes. In any scenario, there are opportunities where we can change our actions, the focus of our attention, our framing of a situation, and our response to it. Suppose you've been invited to a short film festival, which would be good for making connections—but one of the films is by a former collaborator with whom you've fallen out. What are your options?

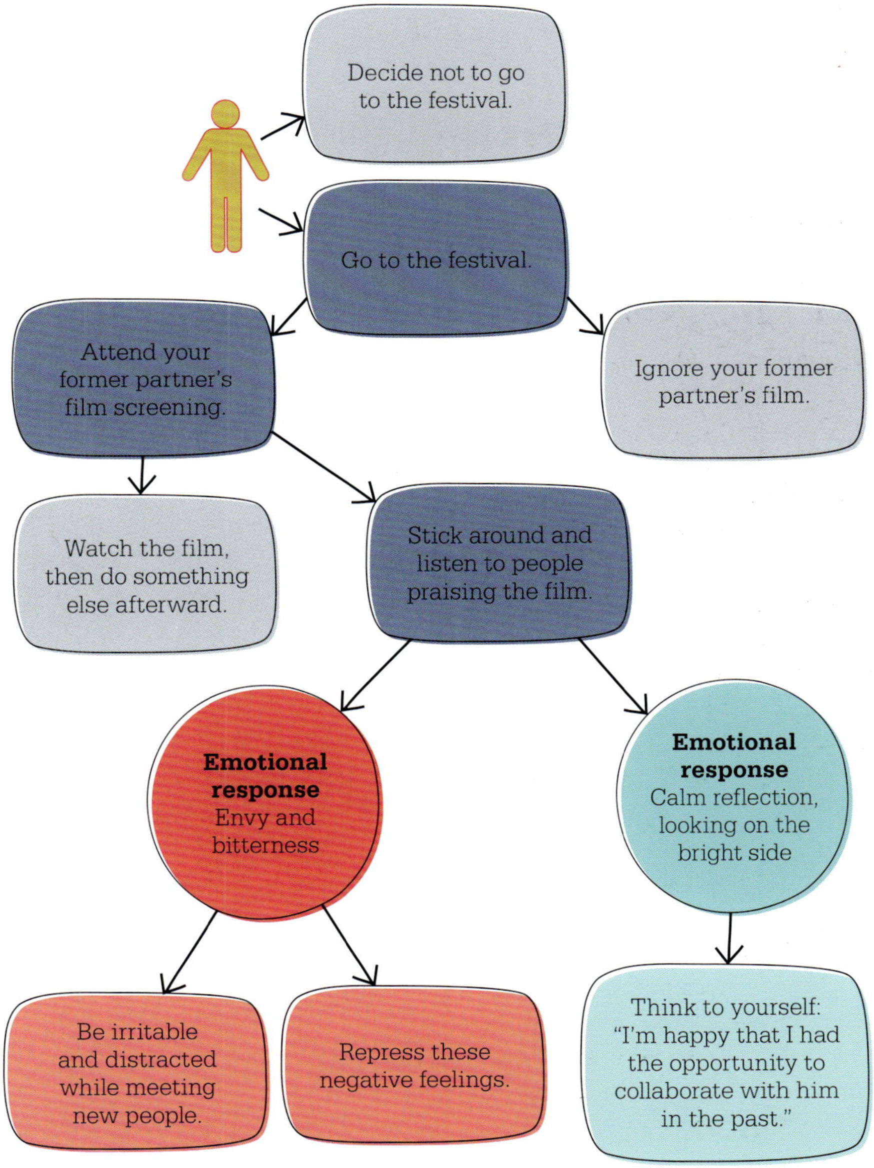

ONE CAN CHOOSE TO GO BACK TOWARD SAFETY OR FORWARD TOWARD GROWTH. GROWTH MUST BE CHOSEN AGAIN AND AGAIN; FEAR MUST BE OVERCOME AGAIN AND AGAIN.

ABRAHAM MASLOW, PSYCHOLOGIST BEST KNOWN FOR HIS THEORIES ON SELF-ACTUALIZATION

THE ART OF SELF-CONTROL

HOLDING OUT AGAINST TEMPTATION

Achieving long-term goals takes persistence, which often means you need to delay short-term gratification. How can you learn to say "no" to immediate rewards if they conflict with your bigger plans?

We all have multiple goals that we seek to fulfill, and which give us the feeling of being successful. Unfortunately, many distractions can cause us to focus on short-term good feelings ("I want to buy a new car") rather than on the longer-term goal ("I want to pay off my student loans so I can save more and buy a house"). The feelings triggered by the desire to fulfill both the short-term desire (driving a nice car) and the long-term desire (getting on the property ladder) can evoke powerful, compelling feelings that impact our choices.

The struggle comes when our long-term priorities come into conflict with other desires which, while less important to us overall, are easier to undertake and more fun in the short term.

Making choices

A 2014 study by American psychologists Angela Lee Duckworth and James Gross argues it's partly a matter of hierarchy. We don't just have one goal: we have big, overarching goals, and then smaller goals that tend to be more practical and action-oriented. Problems arise when these clash. At that point, we need to go back and decide which of the long-term goals is most important (see "The hierarchy of goals," opposite). When we have to make a choice, it's helpful to be able to distinguish between what are competing priorities and what are everyday short-term temptations.

Resisting that marshmallow

The "marshmallow test" was performed by Walter Mischel at Stanford University in the 1960s. In this test, a group of four-year-olds were offered a marshmallow and left alone in a room, having been promised that if they resisted eating it until the experimenter returned 15 minutes later, they could have the marshmallow *and* a second one as well. This longitudinal study followed these children over many years and found that those who had resisted the marshmallow turned out, in later life, to be doing better academically, health-wise, and indeed in life in general. The findings of this research sparked a series of studies that focused on understanding the dynamics of self-control and how people respond in different situations.

Testing the marshmallow test

In 2013, a further experiment was done by a group of American researchers to test the original marshmallow theory. In the second test, children were given the same choice of one marshmallow immediately, and, if they could resist eating it, a second one later too—but with a twist. Before the marshmallows came promises about crayons and stickers. The children were told that if they waited before they started using the crayons and stickers, the experimenters would return with better crayons and stickers. With some children, the better supplies did appear; with others, the experimenters came back empty-handed.

The result? The "reliable environment" group resisted the marshmallow *four times longer* than children who had experienced an "unreliable environment." The researchers surmised that the marshmallow test is more a measure of how much trust a child has in their circumstances: for children who had reason to believe a promise, resisting that marshmallow was much easier.

Perhaps the key to self-control is directly related to emotional intelligence (see pp.58–59) and the ability to understand how your emotions are impacting your responses and behaviors. Psychologist Daniel Goleman identifies self-regulation as one of the elements of emotional intelligence: this means you don't make decisions on impulse, and you are able to delay gratification. Next time you need to strengthen your resolve, listen to what's going on in your head and heart.

> If we have the **skills** to allow us to **make discriminations** about when we do or don't do something... and when we do and when we don't **wait** for something, we are no longer **victims** of our **desires**.
>
> **Walter Mischel**
> Psychologist and creator of the "marshmallow test"

THE HIERARCHY OF GOALS

Even if you have a particular aspiration that outshines all the others, it's helpful to think in terms of multiple goals. One approach is to consider them as long-term, medium-term, and short-term: that way, your long-term goal or goals can be as broad as you need, and you can keep your short-term goals practical. Draw up a chart, and see if any of your short-term goals conflict with each other—for instance, does networking with clients at a conference conflict with time spent socializing with friends and family? If you can lay it out in this way, it may be easier to decide which short- and medium-term goals best support your long-term goals, and prioritize your decisions accordingly.

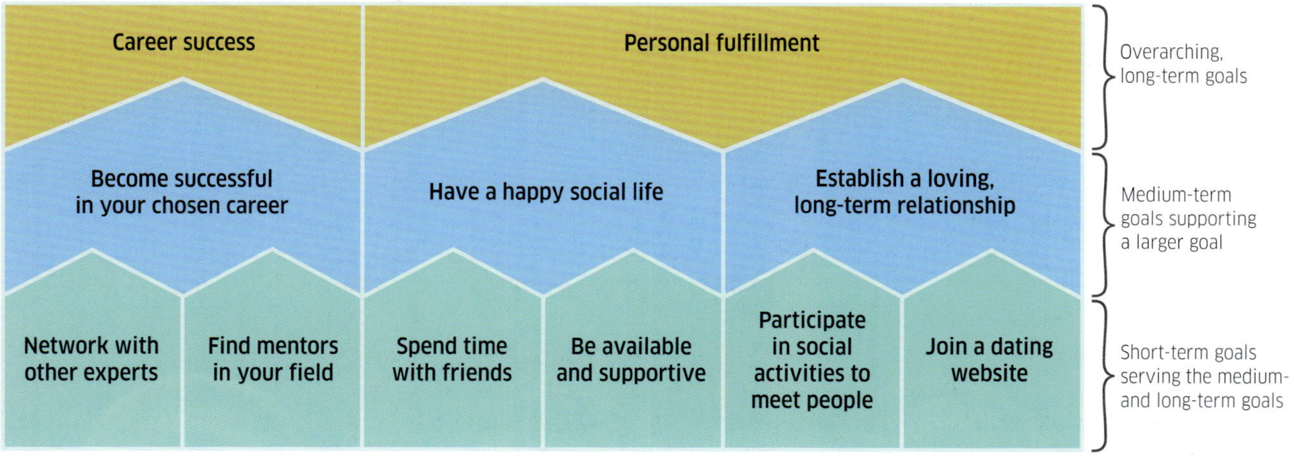

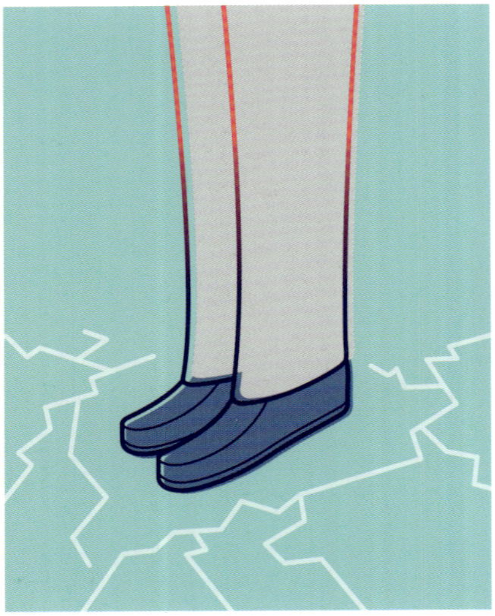

THE WARP FACTOR

HOW STRESS CAN UNDERMINE SUCCESS

Motivating yourself to keep going despite obstacles helps, but pushing yourself to the limit does not. You may need to be careful: chronic stress can hurt you—and perhaps your chances of success as well.

Stress is what happens when you perceive, or at least feel, that the demands life is placing on you are greater than your ability to cope. Sometimes stress can be helpful, giving you the impetus and focus to achieve (see pp.100–101). But stress can also be a trade-off: are you toughing it out because you know the short-term strain will be worth the long-term benefits, or has the short-term harm started to become a long-term liability? In short: how much stress is too much?

The dangers of stress

We all know stress is an uncomfortable sensation; what we don't always realize is that it can be damaging. There are many ways in which the brain's chemistry, structure, and even physical size can be adversely affected by chronic tension (see "How stress affects the brain," opposite). Chronic stress doesn't just increase your risk of physical illness (though it does that, too); it also makes you less motivated and, literally, less intelligent. Our bodies are designed to respond automatically in times of threat: this makes sense if you're fleeing a bear, since you act faster when you're operating on instinct, but if you've ever found yourself freezing in an interview or getting stuck during a presentation, you'll know there are times when it undermines you. Severe stress simply makes you do worse at the tasks you'll need to perform well to succeed. When you consider that it also increases your chances of mental illness—something that can incapacitate the most talented—you'll know that it's something you need to keep in check.

72%

MONEY WORRIES

According to the American Psychological Association's 2014 "Stress in America" survey, 72 percent of people say they are **stressed about money** at least some of the time.

What can you do?

The important question is this: when you feel you can't cope, where does that feeling come from—the situation, or your faith in your coping abilities? Both are possible, and neither is "wrong," but each answer calls for a different solution. If you're in a chronically stressful situation, you may need to revise your plans:

STRESS ON THE JOB

A 2014 survey by Towers Watson, a global HR and risk management professional services firm, found that:

57%

of **highly stressed workers** said they felt **disengaged from their jobs**, as opposed to only

10%

of workers with **low stress**.

a stressful period that will definitely end may be endurable, but you can't succeed if you burn yourself out.

If you feel you have to stick with the situation, there are ways you can at least moderate your stress levels (see pp.98–99). None of these suggestions represents a magic bullet, but try them out and see what works for you.

A successful life includes a level of stress you can tolerate over the long term. You may be stronger than you believe—but it is also sensible to listen to your instincts, and to take action when necessary.

HOW STRESS AFFECTS THE BRAIN

Stress physically changes your brain in a variety of ways:

- Too much "white matter" (myelin) develops. In a healthy brain, this provides an insulating electrical sheath enabling nerves to send their signals efficiently. In excess, it overinsulates, slowing down connectivity between different parts of the brain
- The protein BDNF (brain-derived neurotrophic factor) is slowed down. Because BDNF is responsible for the development and differentiation of new brain cells, this impedes the brain's functioning and can increase the risk of mental illness, dementia, and Alzheimer's
- Levels of dopamine and serotonin, hormones associated with happiness and well-being, drop. In mild cases this leads to a habitually lowered mood; in more extreme cases, it increases the risk of mental illness and addiction
- The brain's immune cells (microglia) get overactivated, risking brain inflammation
- The thalamus, which helps create the fear response, becomes habitually overactive
- The sensory cortex sends stronger fear signals to the body, creating physical symptoms such as muscle tension, stomach upsets, and restlessness
- The hippocampus shrinks, reducing self-control, memory functioning, and emotional regulation
- The pituitary gland stimulates the adrenal glands in the torso, releasing more of the "stress hormone" cortisol.

Your brain is a physical organ, so take care of it. If you're really stressed, remember that it's not a sign of weakness to take a rest: it's sound medical sense, and much better for you in the long run.

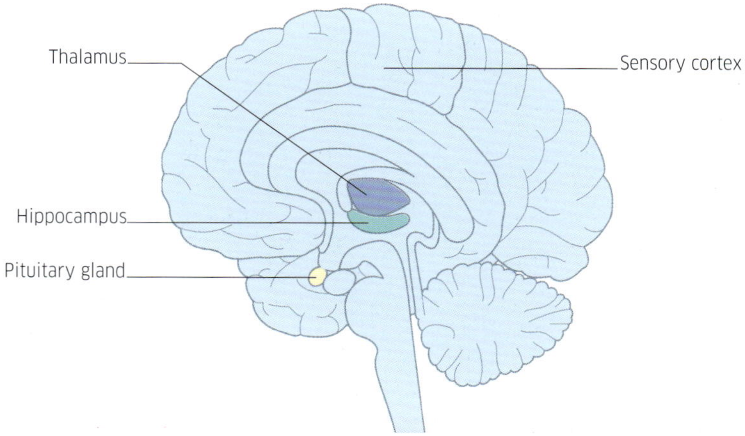

MANAGING STRESS

RESPONDING PRODUCTIVELY TO PRESSURE

Success involves hard work and high stakes. To keep yourself on the right track when the pressure is on, make sure your habits—both mental and physical—enable you to stay composed and in control.

Stress in life is inevitable. A moderate amount of stress can be good for us (see pp.100–101), but the key lies in how we respond to each situation we face, as this is what will determine if it is something we can handle or if it ends up getting the better of us.

Orderly thinking

It's tempting to overgeneralize and think "My whole life is stressful!" and sometimes it can certainly feel that way. Instead of giving in to the sensation of being overwhelmed, however, try to identify and monitor the things that cause you the most anxiety: keep your focus as specific as you can. Make a list and see where you might be able to reduce or eliminate certain sources of stress in your life.

Next, formulate a plan to address situations and people you know trigger a stress response in you. This will facilitate your ability to react effectively when these circumstances arise. Remember, you always have a choice as to how you respond.

A good way to manage day-to-day pressure is to make lists. Prioritize the most important or pressing items, and enjoy the satisfaction of crossing them off when they're done. If you consistently feel that you're falling behind on the things you need to do, employ time-management techniques to help boost your efficiency (see pp.124–125).

> The **greatest weapon** against stress is our ability to **choose one thought** over another.
>
> **William James**
> Psychologist

Accept the inevitable

What *can't* you control? Being proactive about things you can change will help you, but trying to change things that are fixed creates a sense of what psychologists call "learned helplessness." Trying to do what can't be done has been shown in studies of both humans and animals to reduce initiative and cause depression. So, don't train yourself to expect failure: focus instead on what you *can* influence and change.

The power of nature

Even if you have to stay inside most of the time, most days, it's a good idea to spend at least some time outside. Pleasant environments

COMMON WAYS TO ALLEVIATE STRESS

The Australian Psychological Society's "Stress and Wellbeing" survey of 2015 revealed the various ways people deal with stress. The "prevalence" column shows the percentage of respondents who undertook each activity, while the "effectiveness" column indicates their estimations of how successful they found these activities to be–offering good insights for when you're considering how best to alleviate your own stress levels:

Way of managing stress	Prevalence	Effectiveness
Watch television or a film	85%	73%
Focus on the positives	81%	79%
Spend time with friends and/or family	81%	83%
Listen to music	80%	80%
Read	75%	78%
Adjust expectations	73%	75%
Do something active	69%	81%
Avoid stressful people and/or situations	65%	70%
Spend time doing a hobby	64%	80%
Go shopping	57%	64%
Sleep more	54%	60%
Visit social networking sites	46%	52%
Play video games	32%	67%
Do something spiritual	30%	78%

such as parks and green spaces can help distract us from our worries, and exposure to sunlight helps our bodies to manufacture vitamin D. This isn't just good for our physical health; research suggests that it can raise our levels of serotonin, the "feel-good" hormone. A walk in the park might cheer you up on a biochemical level.

Brightening up your environment indoors can make a difference too. According to a study conducted at Washington State University in 1996, volunteers working in a computer lab displayed a lowered stress response when plants were introduced to the workspace—they were more productive and their blood pressure fell. Even a little indoor greenery can help you relax.

EMOTIONAL SUPPORT

If you have friends or family willing to support you, don't be afraid to turn to them. A 2015 American survey found that while people who lacked emotional support rated their stress levels at 6.2 on a scale of 1 to 10, people who *did* get support rated their stress at only 4.8. They were also twice as likely to feel able to make positive lifestyle changes.

People without emotional support:

STRESS LEVEL

6.2/10

21% did not make positive lifestyle changes because they were too stressed.

People with emotional support:

STRESS LEVEL

4.8/10

10% did not make positive lifestyle changes because they were too stressed.

IN THE ZONE

MAKING STRESS WORK FOR YOU

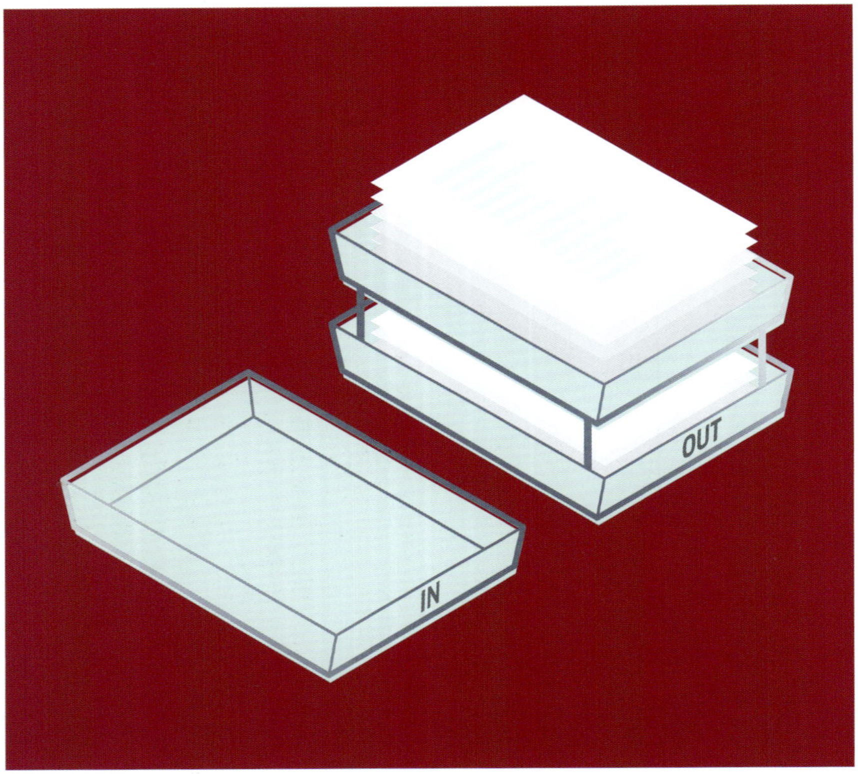

Chronic stress is bad for your health and performance, but if you want to get things done, a moderate amount helps you focus and perform at an optimum level. The ideal state is when you're both engaged and productive.

It is detrimental to suffer from constant pressure and stress (see pp.96–97). However, an eight-year study of 30,000 American adults found that, while stress shortened lifespans, it did so only in the cases where the individuals had described stress as harmful to their health. People whose stress made them miserable were damaged by it, but people who were stressed—but not *distressed*—were able to survive it much better. What does this mean?

Recasting stress

The "misattribution of arousal" may provide an answer (see "Is it stress you're feeling?" opposite). Emotions produce physical sensations, but we experience similar sensations for a variety of emotions, and the feelings we experience can be easily confused. What for one person is painfully stressful can be, for another, exciting and challenging.

A study by Alison Wood Brooks published in 2014 in the *Journal of Experimental Psychology* showed that, instead of trying to remain calm in stressful situations, people perform better when they recast their stress as excitement instead. This can be achieved with positive self-talk (for example, saying "I'm excited!" out loud to yourself), and by viewing the situation as an opportunity rather than as a threat.

Hitting the sweet spot

Some kinds of stress are just too much, no matter how positive your attitude. But exactly how much, according to what psychology calls

OPTIMUM PERFORMANCE

The Yerkes–Dodson law of arousal suggests that there's an optimum stress level at which we perform at our best–when we are "in the zone" and functioning productively. As a general rule, purely physical activities call for higher levels of arousal, because stress sets our bodies to "fight or flight" mode–necessary for when we are, for instance, competing in a sprint race. For a purely intellectual activity, such as reading a book, our stress level would need to be on the low side to place us "in the zone." The graph below shows the "zone" for an activity that combines physical and intellectual performance, such as an orienteering challenge. Here a medium level of stress sets us on the right track. When deciding how much stress is too much, think about what kind of task you're undertaking and monitor your stress level accordingly.

STRIKING A PRODUCTIVE BALANCE

IS IT STRESS YOU'RE FEELING?

An experiment performed in Canada in 1974 by psychologists Donald Dutton and Arthur Aron showed how we can misinterpret the sources of our stress. Male passersby who had walked over either a safe, steady bridge or a shaky bridge were approached by a female researcher on the other side, asked to fill out a questionnaire, and then given her number and told that they could call her if they had any questions. The men who'd walked across the less stable bridge were more likely to call the woman. Why? They'd noticed their trembling knees, rapid breathing, and butterfly-filled stomachs, but had attributed them to their attraction toward the woman, not the terrors of the bridge. This "misattribution of arousal" occurs when we misidentify the true source of our feelings. Make a habit of asking yourself whether what you are feeling is fear, stress, or excitement, so you can react appropriately as circumstances demand.

"the Yerkes–Dodson law of arousal" (see "Optimum performance", above), varies from challenge to challenge:

- **If you're not stressed at all,** you won't be alert enough to perform well.
- **If you're under the right amount of pressure,** you're "in the zone," performing at your peak.
- **If you're too stressed,** your performance will start to suffer.

Instead of eliminating stress altogether, what you need to do is avoid *excessive* stress.

Preventing avoidable stress

How do we circumvent inordinate levels of stress? Neuroscientist Daniel Levitin recommends a "pre-mortem": consider what might go wrong in any given situation, and prevent, minimize, or think about what you can ahead of time. Stress strains the hippocampus, the part of the brain associated with memory, which means you can become muddled. Levitin advises storing important information in places you can always access (such as digitally, or in "the cloud") so you don't have to rely solely on your memory. Anticipation won't fix everything, but it can make a difference when you're in a pressurized situation.

THE ENEMY WITHIN

COMBATING SELF-DEFEATING ATTITUDES

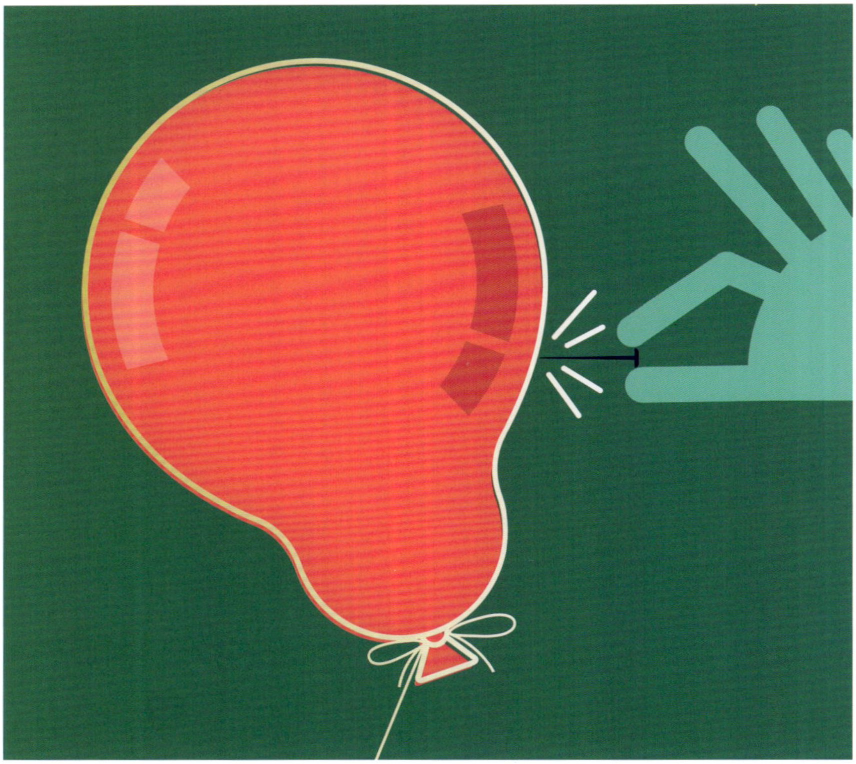

Many of us have heard our inner voice telling us we're no good, we'll never achieve what we want, and that nothing we have achieved is worth anything. It's time to challenge these thoughts and remove their sting.

If our inner voice is often negative, undermining our self-confidence, it can create roadblocks that stop us from taking action to build our skills and mastery, and so hinder us when we want to move forward.

View yourself as capable

To defuse these unhelpful thoughts we need to develop a strong sense of "self-efficacy"—the belief that we are capable and competent, and can develop new skills and approaches that contribute to our ability to achieve our goals (see "Self-efficacy," opposite). Self-efficacy isn't an all-encompassing trait, as very few of us feel equally capable in every area. If you're pursuing your passion, though, you do need to build up a sense of self-efficacy in the areas that apply to it.

Reframe your responses

If you have a tendency to underrate yourself, pay attention to how you "frame" events—that is, the way you explain them to yourself. If you're not feeling competent, work on reframing your responses. For instance, if you feel that a meeting went badly, view it as a learning experience by identifying what you missed during your preparation for the meeting and what you will do differently at the next meeting. This kind of thinking can become habitual, so cultivate the habit of framing events positively and improve your sense of self-efficacy by focusing on what you are learning and the skills you are developing.

FORGIVING YOURSELF

Almost nobody is suave, athletic, or criticism-proof in every situation. If you're feeling glum about yourself, bear these points in mind:

- **Don't make odious comparisons.** Put down the celebrity magazine; stop brooding on your "superior" friends. You're on your own journey, and that's what is important.
- **Accept your vulnerabilities.** Focus on the progress you have made and the goals that are important to you. Forgive your flaws and foibles: have compassion for yourself.
- **Please yourself first.** We all seek approval from others, but prioritize your own conscience and standards: they're key to your sense of self.

ALL IN THE MIND?

Social cognitive theory proposes that three things contribute to negative thoughts–personal, behavioral, and environmental factors–and that they all interact. You have some power over your personal and behavioral issues, but if your wider circumstances are discouraging, you may need to direct your efforts toward making some changes.

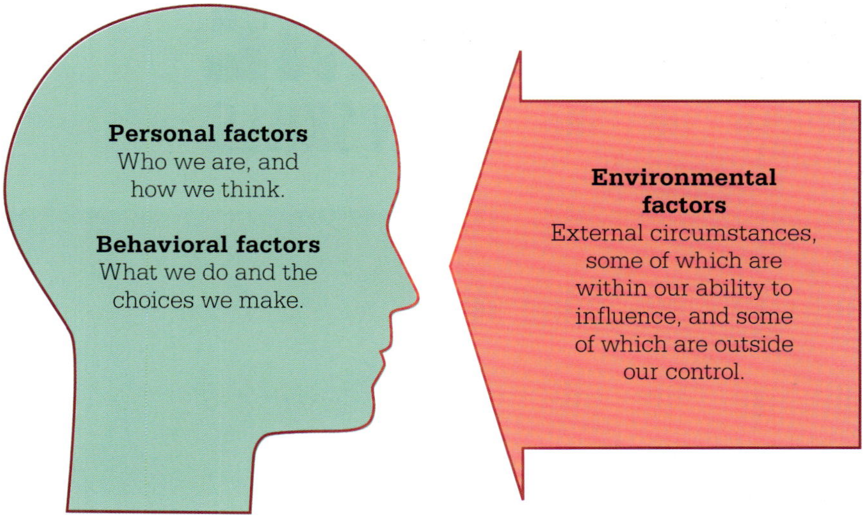

SELF-EFFICACY

When psychologists talk of "self-efficacy," they mean our belief that we're capable people who can accomplish what we set out to do. There are four main factors that shape this:

1 **Mastery experiences.** Working hard and accomplishing a specific result helps us to build skills and fuels our belief that we can achieve the goals we set for ourselves. Our faith in ourselves is stronger if we've experienced times when it took effort and persistence to overcome obstacles.

2 **Social modeling.** We're influenced by what we see around us. Watching and learning from others who are able to show us how to approach a problem or respond to a difficult situation is important. Understanding that we sometimes need to "see" others handle a problem that is similar to the one we are dealing with helps us to develop new skills and approaches that we had not considered before.

3 **Social persuasion.** Seeking out feedback and insight into how we are doing contributes to our self-efficacy. The perspective of others can help us calibrate what we are doing well and where we need to improve, rather than us over- or underestimating our abilities in a specific situation.

4 **Choice processes.** In each situation, be optimistic about the fact that you can learn and improve *or* that you can choose a different option in order to continue to move toward your goals and the results you are seeking. Remember that you can modify or change your goals at any point.

IMPOSTOR SYNDROME

ACCEPTING YOUR OWN SKILLS

Have you ever sat in a room full of successful people and thought to yourself: "I don't belong here. They'll find out soon, and where will I be then?" If so, the truth is you're far from alone in having those feelings.

Many successful people have high standards, which means we may judge ourselves harshly if we come up short. When our standards are high and our self-esteem is less than solid, we can experience "impostor syndrome," feeling like our successes must be due to pure chance and that sooner or later, other people—real experts, unlike ourselves—will find us out.

Who suffers?

Ironically, the people most vulnerable to impostor syndrome tend to be qualified, skilled, and at least reasonably successful. Logically, we have to reach a certain level before we start to worry we've exceeded ourselves, and the higher we climb, the more we may fear the fall.

The experience was first studied as a female phenomenon. The first use of the term was in a paper published by Pauline Clance and Suzanne Imes in 1978 in the journal *Psychotherapy: Theory, Research and Practice*, entitled "The Impostor Phenomenon in High Achieving Women." In a culture in which women can sometimes be judged for being too talkative or not compliant enough (see pp.36–37),

> At any time I still expect that the **no-talent police** will come and **arrest me**.
>
> **Mike Myers**
> Actor and comedian

it's not surprising that many women might feel unprepared to assert that, yes, they're sure they have the skills and talent required for a high-stakes position.

Men, too, are far from immune. Impostor syndrome expert Valerie Young observes that men have attended her workshops in increasing numbers in recent years, and that among graduate students surveyed as to whether they were prone to feelings of impostorism, the male to female ratio stood at 50:50.

For all of us, focusing on the fact that we always have more to learn is essential—in which case, it is only to be expected if someone finds out that we don't know everything yet. This means that we don't need to pretend we *do* know everything, and centers our attention instead on how we can develop and grow.

DO YOU EVER FEEL LIKE A FRAUD?

How much do you agree with the statements listed below? The more you can relate to them, the more likely you are to be susceptible to impostor syndrome. It may be reassuring to reflect that even highly talented and successful people often feel the same way!

	✔	✖
■ I admire people who have achieved what I aspire to, but I don't think I belong in their ranks.	☐	☐
■ I feel like a lot of my successes were a matter of luck.	☐	☐
■ I feel foolish or uncomfortable describing my achievements.	☐	☐
■ When I'm around other people in my field, I tend to feel they deserve their place in it more than I do.	☐	☐
■ I worry that people will realize how little I know.	☐	☐
■ When people praise me, I feel like I'm getting away with something.	☐	☐
■ I can't believe that my successes will last.	☐	☐
■ I feel like my successes don't really prove anything.	☐	☐

BANISHING YOUR DOUBTS

Don't compare your insides with other people's outsides. When we experience impostor syndrome, we are comparing our anxious feelings to other people's apparently composed facades. In so doing, we overlook the fact that everyone else may feel just as uncomfortable as we do—and that they may even be worrying about measuring up to us just as much as we are about matching up to them.

Remember no one is perfect. The right mentor can help us a great deal, but if we see them as unreachably brilliant, we can end up feeling worse because we think we'll never meet the same high standard. A study by American sociologists Jessica L. Collett and Jade Avelis found that a significant number of female students felt they could never match up to their female mentors, while economist Kate Bahn observed in *The Chronicle of Higher Education* that even reading advice from the "hyper-successful" can leave those of us who are "moderately successful" feeling inadequate. Role models can be helpful, but only as long as we see them as people like ourselves.

Mistakes happen. If you haven't made any mistakes, you might not have been taking risks to try new approaches or do things differently. Stretch yourself and look for ways to do "experiments" that may result in mistakes so that you can learn from them.

WANT TO WIN OR SCARED TO LOSE?

WHEN FEAR OF FAILURE IS HOLDING YOU BACK

The fear of doing poorly can have a significant impact on our actions and choices, hindering us from making progress. The first step toward overcoming your fears is to reframe how you think about failure itself.

Nobody wants to fail. There's a difference, though, between fearing failure because it means the frustration of our plans, and fearing failure for its own sake. Sometimes our motivations are active: we do something because we want to, or because we want to bring about a result. Sometimes, however, our motivations are avoidant: we do something because we fear what will happen if we don't.

Using fear to your advantage

Fear of failure isn't always a bad thing. A 2015 Dutch–American study published in the *Journal of Business Venturing* found that many successful entrepreneurs cited fear of failure as one of their strongest incentives. The difference appeared to be what psychologists called an "internal yardstick" for success: the people galvanized by fear were the most ambitious. Afraid to "fail" by not making further progress in their endeavors, they harnessed this fear and used it to spur themselves on.

What about those of us who freeze at the thought of being found lacking? It's one thing to decide not to take a risk because failure seems likely. It's a problem, though, if fear of failure *increases* our chances of it happening. The trouble is, we're prone to undermine ourselves if we're anxious. A 2010 Canadian study found that students who were especially afraid of failure were also particularly likely to procrastinate. Other research has found that we can make ourselves ill with worry: if you keep getting headaches or stomach upsets, or find it harder to focus the more stressed you are, it's time to examine what you're really afraid of.

> You **build on failure**. You use it as a **stepping stone**.
>
> **Johnny Cash**
> Musician

Learn not to take it personally

If something falls apart, it's normal to feel sad or disappointed—even angry. But the key to success is understanding and accepting that these are subjective reactions to an event, not objective measures of what kind of person you are. Disappointment and frustration eventually pass, and if you can keep yourself from getting too caught up in these feelings at the time, they're likely to pass sooner. It's normal to feel bad if something fails—but it doesn't mean that *you* are bad.

WHAT SCARES YOU?

Fear of failure can be experienced in a variety of ways. A 2016 international study published in the *Journal of Business Venturing* identified several main themes to how we express our worries. Do you recognize any of these concerns or coping mechanisms in your own thinking? If so, fear of failure might be inhibiting your behavior:

MENTAL ANXIETIES

Personal ability
"Do I have what it takes?"

Social esteem
"Will my reputation suffer?"

Opportunity costs
"Can I still have a decent work-life balance?"

EMOTIONAL TENSION

Feeling unhappy
"This is stressful!"

BEHAVIORAL RESPONSES

Inhibition
"I have to be cautious."

Motivation
"I'll just have to try harder."

Repression
"I can't think about this right now."

If the idea of failure holds a particular terror for you, it may be a sign that you need to bolster your self-acceptance. Everyone fails sometimes; you'll make more progress if you learn from the experience and figure out how to do things differently in the future.

NIGGLING SELF-DOUBTS

Does the fear of failure dominate your thinking? We all have moments of doubt, but keep an eye out for certain assumptions. If you find yourself dwelling on any of the ideas in the left-hand column below, remind yourself that there are other, more productive ways of considering things:

If I fail, I'm afraid that...	Instead, try thinking:
"It'll show I'm not smart, capable, or good enough."	"My ability is only part of the picture. Even the smartest and most competent people have setbacks." (Remind yourself of personal heroes who worked through difficult periods.)
"I'll ruin my chances and face an uncertain future."	"'Uncertain' isn't the same thing as 'doomed.' I may have to adapt, but there's always more than one chance in life."
"People won't respect me or love me."	"If anyone thinks differently about me because I failed at something, I can focus on my true friends instead."
"I'll let down the people I care about."	"It's good that I'm a responsible person, and that's a virtue I'll still possess even if I fail."
"I'll look ridiculous for having wanted it in the first place."	"I'm a worthwhile person, and there's nothing absurd about me wanting to do something difficult."
"I won't be able to cope."	"I can't know what it will be like until I get there. I'll cross those bridges when I come to them."

COPING WITH FAILURE

CHANGING YOUR OUTLOOK

No matter how talented you are and how hard you try, sometimes you will fail. Recognize that if you aren't taking risks and failing, you may not be stretching yourself in ways that will enhance your success.

If you aim high, you inevitably run the risk of falling short, perhaps over and over again. Almost nobody reaches a peak of success on their first attempt, and while we do all know this on some level, it doesn't stop us from being disappointed, frustrated, embarrassed, and discouraged when it happens to us. How much can we experience these feelings and still focus on and learn from what is important each time we fail?

What's in the frame?

We're familiar with the "glass half full or half empty" paradigm: psychologists refer to this as a "gain frame" (half full) or a "loss frame" (half empty). The thing is, it appears that humans are hardwired to pay more attention to negative information (loss frames) than positive information (gain frames). For instance, social psychologist Alison Ledgerwood has found that our brains have to work harder to see the positive rather than the negative side of things (see "Counting the cost," opposite).

In addition, it is easier to change a gain frame to a loss frame than the other way around. To test this theory, Ledgerwood presented two groups of people with the same information, differently framed: one team was told a surgical procedure had a 70 percent rate of success, and the other that it had a 30 percent rate of failure. As you might expect, the first group rated the procedure positively and the second assessed it negatively—but when they were told to look at things the other way around, their responses differed. The first group, reminded that 70 percent success meant 30 percent failure, changed their minds and rated the surgery negatively. The second group, reminded that 30 percent failure meant 70 percent success, stuck to their original negative evaluation.

Ledgerwood's conclusion is that we need to make an effort to balance out our focus; for example, we should talk more about positive experiences, and cut back on any unnecessary negativity.

Embracing vulnerability

You might assume that successful people are tough. According to researcher Brené Brown, however, it's the opposite: to lead a fulfilling life, we need to accept that vulnerability is part of who we are. We're all afraid of being rejected for not being good enough, and this fear can hold us back. Interviewing thousands of people over six years, Brown found the people living the happier, more successful lives were those who were, in her words, "wholehearted": they embraced vulnerability as a necessary part of life. As our brains are designed to process losses better than gains, we can find it hard to see failures as positive learning opportunities. But, as Brown points out, vulnerability is the foundation of innovation and creativity: if we don't risk looking foolish, nothing changes. In her words, we need the "courage to be imperfect"—to accept that vulnerability is a part of being human and that, despite our failings, we're still worthy of love, acceptance, and success.

COUNTING THE COST

Social psychologist Alison Ledgerwood led an experiment in which participants were asked to imagine a disease with 600 victims, and then asked one of two questions. Those asked, "If 100 lives are saved, how many will be lost?" took 7 seconds, on average, to answer. Those asked, "If 100 lives are lost, how many will be saved?" took longer—around 11 seconds—to figure it out. This supported the hypothesis that we are naturally biased toward negative information, or loss frames, rather than positive information, or gain frames.

Loss frame calculation time:
7 seconds

Gain frame calculation time:
11 seconds

UNCOMFORTABLY NUMB

Researcher Brené Brown argues that, for fear of feeling vulnerable, we can numb our emotions: unfortunately, this affects *all* our emotions, not just the ones we want to eliminate, creating a spiral we need to break—as shown below. Letting ourselves feel the bad times is the flipside to enjoying the good.

THE TERRIFIED WINNER

DEALING WITH THE FEAR OF SUCCESS

Do you ever find yourself worrying about what might happen if you actually reach your goal? If so, it's worth considering what success means to you, and what might be at the root of your fears.

You may be completely committed to achieving the goals that you value and still feel nervous about it. Our aspirations are subject to change and chance, and as we get close to accomplishing outcomes that we feel passionate about, we can start to feel apprehensive.

Exciting... or stressful?

The "misattribution of arousal" (see pp.100–101) can be a problem if you've been used to worrying about whether you will reach your goal. As we come close to the realization of a goal, our systems start to feel "aroused," which is to say, alert and stimulated. Ideally, we should recognize this feeling as one of excitement, but if you've had a history of negative stresses or disappointments, your mind might attribute that keyed-up feeling to fear or tension. If you find yourself getting nervous when a good thing approaches, remind yourself that even if you're not used to success yet, the jittery feeling is probably a positive sign (see "Telling the difference," opposite).

Old expectations

Many of us want to be accepted by our community; that's a natural and healthy wish. But communities carry expectations, and those expectations aren't always the best fit for our personal ambitions. The more your goals make you different from people around you, the more of a social price you'll anticipate, and the harder you'll have to focus on satisfying yourself rather than pleasing others.

DO YOU FEAR SUCCESS?

In 2001, American psychologists Dawn Deeter-Schmelz and Rosemary Ramsey set out to study the fear of success. They gave a collection of statements to volunteers, and found that certain assertions were clear indicators of whether or not the person feared success. Which of the two groups of statements shown below sounds more like what you believe?

AFRAID OF SUCCESS

- "Often the cost of success is greater than the reward."
- "A person who is at the top faces a constant struggle to stay there."
- "A successful person is often considered by others to be both aloof and arrogant."
- "People's behavior changes for the worse after they become successful."

UNAFRAID OF SUCCESS

- "I expect other people to fully appreciate my potential."
- "Achievement commands respect."
- "When you're at the top, everyone looks up to you."
- "When you're the best, all doors are open."

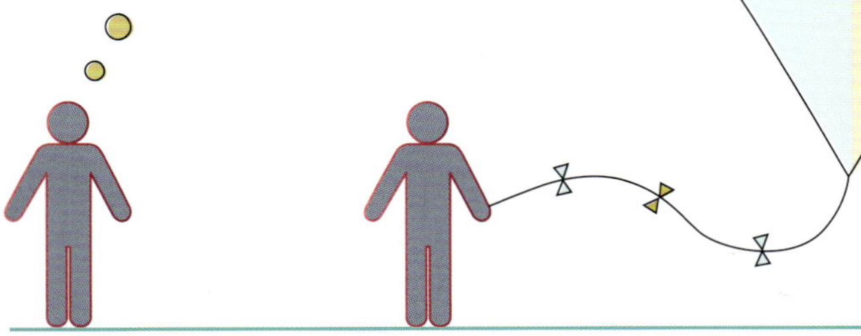

Psychologists have found that fear of success tends to inhibit our initiative and creativity much like the fear of failure (see pp.106–107). Many of us have heard the saying "It's lonely at the top," and we don't want to be isolated and alone—we're afraid of flying in the face of other peoples' expectations and being rejected in some way as a result. But at the same time, holding back is also a loss: as esteemed American basketball coach John Wooden observed, success is the peace of mind that only comes from "knowing you made the effort to do the best of which you're capable"; falling short of your potential can bring its own regrets. Only you can know what is right for you, but it's worth asking yourself what your own expectations might be (see "Do you fear success?" above). It is helpful to distinguish between goals that represent your authentic ambitions and goals that are about staying in your social comfort zone. Changes often mean a world that's new and different, but that can be for the best.

TELLING THE DIFFERENCE

Do you find it hard to distinguish excitement from fear? Drawing a distinction between a stressful memory and an exciting one can be a good way to train yourself to spot the difference if you're getting nervous as you come close to achieving success. Trauma psychologist Susanne Babbel recommends the following exercise:

- Recall a memory of feeling excited and successful from when you were younger. Stay with it for about five minutes, paying attention to the emotions and sensations it stirs up.
- Bring up a more recent memory of excitement and success. Again, stay with it for five minutes and see how it makes you feel.
- Think of an uncomfortable memory. Don't select a real trauma (or at least not without support from a trustworthy professional), but pick something that was, at least, not a nice experience. See how that feels.
- Go back to your recent success story. Does it feel similar to or different from your bad memory?

CHAPTER 4
BASIC SKILLS FOR SUCCESS
AN EVERYDAY GUIDE TO EFFECTIVENESS

A REED IN THE WIND

THE ART OF FLEXIBILITY

The saying goes that it is better to bend than to break. Life means dealing with the unexpected, and, whether the surprises are big or small, your chances of success are greater if you're able to manage them.

We no longer live in a world where it pays to be set in our ways. Technology changes fast, and with it methods of working. The global economy creates ripples in every corner of the earth. Cultures meet and influence each other more than ever before, and the internet means that many of us are seeing and reacting to what other people do and say. Some of us are more comfortable with change than others, but the ability to respond in constructive ways contributes to our growth and success. To feel at ease with this, we need to be confident that we can adapt when changes come along.

Spotting opportunities

The positive way to view change is to see it as an opportunity—you're now facing a challenge to find a new solution. Being open and responsive to new circumstances are attributes well worth cultivating. Researchers at Bradford University in the UK identify a variety of skills relating to flexibility:

1 **Intellectual flexibility.** Keeping an open mind, so that new information is absorbed and made good use of. Being able to balance both the details and the broad overview.

2 **Being receptive.** When change happens, accepting it rather than resisting, and being prepared to learn new ways of meeting goals.

3 **Creativity.** A willingness to try things, improvise, and risk making mistakes in order to achieve your goals.

4 **Adjusting.** Changing methods and working styles when the situation calls for it.

5 **Making it work.** If a solution doesn't work, not dwelling on it; searching for another way that will.

6 **Coming up with new ideas.** Devising new ways to make changes more effective.

The researchers describe these as traits that make their graduates particularly attractive to employers, but whatever your work situation, they're useful skills to practice. They can also be valuable when you're trying to prove your worth to a potential new employer or collaborator; the university recommends the STAR technique (see "Showcasing your skills," opposite) to help show yourself to best advantage.

> A **reed** before the wind **lives on**, while mighty **oaks** do **fall**.
>
> **Proverb**

Seeing the other side

When we work alongside other people, flexibility is essential. A good method for staying flexible in the workplace is to be aware of a common psychological mistake: fundamental attribution error. Put simply, when we make a mistake we believe it is because something happened that was beyond our control, but when someone else makes a mistake we think it is caused by some character flaw or personality "defect" within that person. For example: "I didn't hand in my report because the research took longer than the schedule allowed"; "He didn't hand in his report because he's disorganized and irresponsible." To stay flexible, be aware that we're all prone to this kind of reasoning, and try to put yourself in other people's shoes when you can. It makes you a better collaborator, and it also makes other people's mistakes less stressful for you.

Four ways to flex

A 2015 study at the University of Miami found that cognitive flexibility—the ability to shift your thoughts and adapt to your environment—calls on four traits:

Attention. The ability to detect what's relevant and what's not.

Working memory. Keeping the facts in your mind.

Inhibition. Being able to control your immediate reactions.

Switching. Being able to shift your focus from one task to another.

ADAPT YOUR COPING METHODS

We're sometimes encouraged to follow a one-size-fits-all solution for coping with difficulties, but it pays to be flexible here too. A 2011 study at Stanford University put volunteers through a variety of experiences of differing degrees of intensity. Given the choice between distraction or "reappraisal" (that is, thinking it through and possibly reinterpreting things) as ways of coping with these stresses, they overwhelmingly preferred distraction for more intense moments and reappraisal for milder ones. We have a natural tendency to switch strategies, because when it comes to coping, there is no one "right" way. Be prepared to follow your instincts.

SHOWCASING YOUR SKILLS

Being able to show that you are flexible and adaptable makes you highly attractive to potential employers. Bradford University in the UK recommends the STAR technique, as below. Their advice is to present any setbacks you have faced as part of a story you can tell with confidence:

Step	What to do	Example
S Situation	Define what happened and your position	"I quit my old job to join a start-up, but just as I was about to begin, the funding fell through and the business folded."
T Task	Identify what you needed to do	"I needed to find new work quickly to make ends meet, but I didn't want to take a step backward in my career."
A Action	Describe what you did to fix things	"I had to take a temporary job that wasn't in the right area, so I decided that I'd use my free time to get more training in technical skills, because this is my real interest."
R Result	Show what outcome you achieved	"I was then able to apply for jobs requiring more technical expertise, and now I'm working my way back up the ladder in the right field."

MAKE YOUR OWN LUCK

THE ART OF OPPORTUNITY

Some see luck as the key to success or as a reason for failure. A more balanced view is that good and bad luck will always play a part in our lives; the key is to think positively and spot the opportunities.

When an effort fails to bring about the desired rewards, it is sometimes tempting, or easy, to blame it all on bad luck. Those who do succeed over the long term, however, are unlikely to have been blessed with an uninterrupted run of good fortune; it is more likely that they have accepted that their enterprise will be affected by both ups and downs.

To be able to exploit good luck when it occurs, you need to cultivate a particular mindset. The most important thing is to be open to life's manifold possibilities—the twists and turns of cause and effect. Seeing the potential of an opportunity encourages a positive attitude, which helps to engender success in the long term—even if some of the individual chances turn out to be dead ends.

> **Opportunity knocks often**, but sometimes softly. While blindly **pursuing our goals**, we often **miss** unexpected and wonderful **possibilities**.
>
> **Stephen Shapiro**
> Business author, consultant, and public speaker

Be open and receptive

American psychologist Carol Sansone makes the point simply. "What appears to be luck," she writes, "is really the result of perceptions, personality traits, choices, and actions. And all that is within your control." Those who benefit most from luck have been shown to include a high proportion of extroverts. Such people enjoy a richer weave of fortuitous encounters, simply because they are constantly making new acquaintances; they also tend to keep in touch with a wide range of people.

It helps to be curious about experiences you've never had, as well as curious about other people—especially those who do things beyond your range of experience. Initiating conversations and seeing where they lead can expose you to fresh perspectives and directions.

A willingness to experiment is also key. If you're naturally cautious and worry too much »

10%

Psychologist Richard Wiseman believes that **no more than 10 percent of life** is the result of **pure chance**. Rather, luck is a set of outcomes determined by what you give to life and how you respond to the opportunities that arise.

THE ART OF LUCK

Think of luck as an attribute you have to cultivate and encourage, or as an art you should learn and practice as part of your everyday life. The following techniques will help to improve the chances of new ideas and opportunities opening up for you:

Nurture your network
A good community of friends and acquaintances, made up of people from different walks of life, will help broaden your horizons. Surround yourself with positive people.

Think of yourself as lucky
Be positive and look for the possible upsides in any adverse scenario. This is a much more productive approach than spending time blaming other people or your fate.

Look around
Notice your surroundings. Take breaks and change your routine to open up fresh perspectives. Conscientious people who work hard within narrow parameters are likely to miss good opportunites.

Accept failure
Be willing to deal with ordinary disappointments, even on a regular basis. Recognize that successful people often fail or fall short: it's all part of the process of striving toward a bigger goal.

Break the rules
See a way of doing things differently? Be creative. Of course, listen to your instincts to figure out how much you can push against convention...

Engage with the zeitgeist
Keep abreast of the trends in wider society. This can be a source of inspiration, whatever kind of project you're pursuing.

» about the unknown, you may be blocking opportunities for success before they have a chance to flourish. Relish new experiences: remember that if anxiety overwhelms curiosity, inertia is likely to be the result.

The opportunity mindset

We all suffer setbacks, so how can you survive them best? Part of it is up to "cognitive framing"—that is, what we choose to notice, what we choose to dismiss, and how we understand and explain the broader situation to ourselves. These mental framings affect our decisions and choices: thinking that we are lucky can make us more proactive.

In the early 2000s, British psychologist Richard Wiseman performed a series of experiments with people who viewed themselves as either "lucky" (they were successful and happy, and events in their lives seemed to favor them) or "unlucky" (life just seemed to go wrong for them). What he found was that the "lucky" people were adept at spotting opportunities. In one experiment he told both groups to count the number of pictures in a newspaper. The "unlucky" diligently ground their way through the task; the "lucky" usually noticed that the second page contained an announcement that said: "Stop counting—there are 43 photographs in this newspaper." On a later page the "unlucky" were also too busy counting images to spot a note reading: "Stop counting, tell the experimenter you have seen this, and win $250."

Wiseman's conclusion was that, when faced with a challenge, "unlucky" people were less flexible. They focused on a specific goal, and failed to notice that other options were passing them by. Wiseman identified four basic ways to encourage good fortune:

1 **Create and notice** chance opportunities.

2 **Listen to your intuition**—it's more likely to guide you to a fortuitous decision.

3 **Create self-fulfilling prophecies** by thinking positively.

4 **Be resilient:** tell yourself you can turn bad luck around.

He found that when "unlucky" people adopted these strategies, they experienced an upswing in good fortune: they started being "lucky." By following Wiseman's methods, your odds of turning bad luck to good may be much improved.

STRETCH YOUR BRAIN

Feeling stuck in a rut? Psychologist Clifford N. Lazarus suggests the following exercises to stimulate your thinking and provoke random opportunities:

Try to learn something new every day. It can be small, like a new word or a piece of trivia.

Change your routines. Sit in a different place at the dining table; take a new route to work.

Do new things. Try a new food, watch a film in a genre you don't usually like, or wear a different style of outfit.

Get out of your comfort zone. Regularly do something mildly stressful, such as playing chess against a tough opponent.

THE BANK ROBBER SCENARIO

Picture this: you're in the line at a bank, and an armed robber runs in, firing a gun. The bullet hits you in the arm. Now: were you lucky, or unlucky?

Psychologist Richard Wiseman put this scenario to both "lucky" and "unlucky" people—people whose lives seemed to be better or worse than each others' when compared. Their answers are revealing:

- **"Lucky"** people tended to say they were very fortunate—after all, the bullet could have hit them somewhere fatal.
- **"Unlucky"** people tended to say it was terrible luck—and just *typical* that they were in the bank on that particular day.

The evidence suggests that people who greet misfortunes with an alternative picture of how things might have turned out worse tend to be better at coping and adapting when faced with unexpected challenges.

GOOD OR BAD, WHO KNOWS?

Saeongjima, pronounced "say-ong-jay-mah," is a Chinese-Korean saying that means "the horse of an elderly person living on the border." The phrase comes from a parable in which an old man encounters a series of lucky and unlucky events. But whatever happens, the old man always shrugs off the congratulations or commiserations of his neighbors by saying, "Good or bad, who knows?"

The story goes like this: One day, the old man's horse escapes and runs away across the border. It seems that it has gone forever, but soon enough it makes its way home again, accompanied by a splendid new horse. At the time this appears to be wonderful good fortune.

Months later, the old man's son is badly hurt riding this new horse and ends up disabled, which at the time seems like terribly bad luck.

However, the following year the son is spared from being drafted into a dreadful war because of this injury, and goes on to live a long and peaceful life.

In our own lives, events can have unforeseeable outcomes, so it's always worth remembering "saeongjima": one "unlucky" or missed opportunity might turn into a new and better one later.

CREATING GOOD LUCK

Psychologist Matthew Smith at Buckinghamshire New University in the UK is an expert in the psychology of luck. His research focuses on whether we can take positive action to make ourselves more fortunate, and he suggests five approaches:

1 **Embrace the idea of luck.** Not everything is predictable, and some things happen by chance. We seem to do better if we accept this and make the most of good fortune when it comes along.

2 **Have a "lucky" mindset.** When we think in a positive way, we make ourselves more confident and proactive, and our behavior and expectations make a difference to the events and outcomes we're able to influence.

3 **Be open to opportunity.** By being relaxed, curious, and willing to try new things, we'll be better able to see possibilities, and more comfortable taking risks.

4 **Go with the flow.** If you have specific dreams in mind, it may be uncomfortable stepping off the path you've chosen for yourself, but be prepared to let life surprise you.

5 **Remember that things could be worse.** When you're feeling "unlucky," consider that while things might not be perfect, perhaps they're better than they could have been (see "The bank robber scenario," above left).

TAKING IT IN STRIDE

THE ART OF ACCEPTANCE

If you want to succeed, you will probably want to do so by being yourself, not by being like someone else. It is vital for success that you accept yourself for who you are, and accept circumstances for what they are, too.

Acceptance can create a dynamic and stable person; it is a strong foundation for success. The truth is, however, that many of us aren't happy with every aspect of ourselves or our situation, and even if we are, we don't always stay that way. As Leo Babauta, author of the *Zen Habits* blog, writes, life can be like, "grasping for something solid ... in a river." Life is fluid, and the flow doesn't always go in the directions we'd choose. What, then, if you want to change something about yourself, or you're finding it hard to live with something you can't change?

A question of identity

Entrepreneur and motivational speaker Caroline McHugh poses the question: if you could do anything, what would you do? She points out that we have a tendency to only ask this question when we're feeling unhappy or unfulfiled. Instead, we should ask it when we're feeling strong. We tend to be born confident in our own ideas and can lose that sense of self-belief as we learn to compare ourselves with others, but it's better to forget comparisons and work on being, as McHugh puts it, "good at being yourself." Neither feelings of superiority nor inferiority will help us, she says. Instead, what we need is *interiority*, or a sense of our own inner character. This is "the only place in your life where you have no competition" because your own perspective can't be taken away from you. The first step toward resilience is accepting that it's no good trying to be like someone else—you are who you are, and that's a good thing.

Radical acceptance

It can be hard to like ourselves if we don't like our circumstances (and vice versa). Sometimes, though, things just are what they are. You may be working hard to change your circumstances or compensate for them, but it's harder to do that while you're still struggling to accept them.

In the 1990s, psychologist Marsha Linehan, the founder of Dialectical Behavior Therapy, pioneered a useful concept called "Radical Acceptance." Linehan noticed that people dealing with misfortune tended to react in one of the following ways:

- They tried to change the circumstances.
- They tried to change how they felt about the circumstances.
- They continued to be unhappy.
- They accepted the circumstances.

When the circumstances couldn't be changed, only the fourth group were able to reduce their suffering.

OVERCOMING THE BLOCKS TO ACCEPTANCE

American author and clinician Karyn Hall identifies three main obstacles to Marsha Linehan's theory of "Radical Acceptance," and suggests ways we can overcome them:

Block	Explanation	Reality
Not wanting to let someone off the hook	If you've been wronged, staying angry can feel like justice, and letting go of your resentments can feel like you're excusing the guilty party.	Your anger won't fix an injustice, and the person most affected by it will be you, and possibly your loved ones. You don't have to like the person who hurt you, but you should try to benefit from the experience. Even if you let the anger go, you can still hold on to the lesson.
Acceptance feels like capitulation	You don't agree or approve of what's happened, and accepting it feels like you're saying that you do.	You don't have to agree. You can, however, acknowledge that something is the way it is, and stop trying to live as if it isn't.
Wanting to protect yourself	If you're wearing an armor of anger, sometimes you feel safer.	That armor can be heavy to carry. You may be able to protect yourself better if you lay it down, and instead focus on the knowledge you've gained and how you can use it to protect yourself in the future.

From this insight, psychologists have developed the concept, suggesting that we don't have to accept that reality will always be this way, but we should start by acknowledging that it is this way now. In making this decision, accepting reality isn't a weakness but a strong and active decision that makes us healthier.

Be yourself.
Everyone else is already taken.

Attributed to Oscar Wilde

THE ELEMENTS OF RADICAL ACCEPTANCE

In her theory of "Radical Acceptance," psychologist Marsha Linehan identifies five fundamental elements:

1. Acceptance means acknowledging what is.
2. Acceptance is nonjudgmental. It's not bound up in what's "good" or "bad."
3. To be free from suffering, we have to accept—not resist—reality.
4. It is an act of acceptance if we choose to tolerate distress in the moment.
5. Accepting painful emotions instead of avoiding them actually alleviates suffering in the long term.

WHEN TIMES GET TOUGH

COPING SKILLS

Most of us face hard times at some point during our lives, and we all want to get through adversity and become stronger as a result. What's the secret to dealing with life's difficulties and challenges?

Although there's no single method for making us resilient to difficult times, we can develop a range of attitudes and habits that will help us manage, and which we can adapt to different situations.

GET SOCIAL SUPPORT

There's a large body of research to show that support from friends and loved ones is an important part of dealing with adversity. A well-established model, proposed by psychologist James S. House, divides social support into three categories:

1 **Emotional support:** being reassured that we're liked, trusted, respected, cared about, and loved. This feels good and, when we're in need, it can make an important difference.

2 **Instrumental support:** when someone offers practical help and assistance, such as a lift to an interview, a loan, or a hand decluttering the house.

3 **Information support:** when someone shares their knowledge with us, or points us toward useful resources.

These types of social support are interrelated and, at times, we need all three. In a digital age, there are many ways to seek support. According to a study performed in 2012, however, even regular internet users found face-to-face support (across all three levels) more effective than online advice.

GET YOUR FOCUS RIGHT

In order to feel good about ourselves, it can be more useful to focus on what we want to *do* rather than who we want to *be*. A series of studies focusing on athletes identified two major ways to relate to our goals:

- **Task-involvement:** we focus on gaining knowledge, and improving competence and understanding. We relate to our own skills; other peoples' aren't very relevant.
- **Ego-involvement:** we seek to demonstrate our superior abilities to other people, or to gain their good opinion. Competition and doing better than our peers is important.

Researchers found that task-involved people tended to be less vulnerable to negative emotions and stress, and to have a higher faith in their own effectiveness. Ego-involved people, on the other hand, were more likely to avoid or distract themselves from difficult situations. These avoidant coping strategies tended to impact negatively on their performance and, in turn, their emotions.

More successful ways of coping included reappraising attitudes, restrategizing, and accepting but managing emotions. While you're focused on a goal, it's usually better to think less about your competitors and more about what you need to learn.

KNOW WHEN TO TURN IT OFF

Coping can become a habit, but not a cost-free one. American psychologist Gary Evans points out that our coping strategies can become problematic if we apply them in situations where they're not needed. For example, if you live in crowded conditions, research suggests that you learn to withdraw into yourself to find "space," but that this can lead to having less social support because it's hard to maintain friendships if you can't get out of your shell again afterward.

If you're going through a difficult time, you may need to put up some barriers. For example, if your boss is temperamental, it makes sense to communicate with him or her as little as possible; if you have loud neighbors, it makes sense to train your ears to screen out background noise. For each situation and person you encounter, think about how best to respond in order to optimize the outcome as well as the relationship with the person.

LEARN A NEW STRENGTH

Increasing your confidence in one area can lead to greater confidence in general—this can be especially true if you learn a somewhat risky physical skill. A 2000 US study by Julie C. Weitlauf, Ronald E. Smith, and Daniel P. Cervone found that women who took a self-defense course not only felt less frightened by the thought of being attacked, but six months later they were shown to be both more assertive and less hostile to other people.

Is there anything in your life that you're afraid of, and does that fear make you feel less free? If you can discover a way to make that fear less intimidating, you may find yourself feeling stronger and calmer in other aspects of your life as well.

EXPRESS OR SUPPRESS?

Should you show your feelings or try to hide them? According to a 2004 study for the journal *Psychological Science*, the people who fare best in the long term can do both. Different situations call for different responses, and if you can make adjustments according to what's needed, you'll be more successful as time passes.

TIME MANAGEMENT

PRIMING YOURSELF FOR SUCCESS

Sometimes it can feel like there just aren't enough hours in the day, especially when we're working hard to achieve a goal. Luckily, there are tangible ways in which we can all become more efficient.

Studies show that people who manage their time positively feel more in control, happier, and more relaxed. (Strictly speaking, of course, we can't "manage" time; we can only manage the choices we make about how to use the available time.) Although time management is a much-studied area, some key factors come up again and again. People who handle their time well tend to combine:

- **Time-assessment behaviors.** This involves having a realistic overview of your strengths and weaknesses, and identifying which areas to focus on to optimize your strengths and use your time effectively (instead of wasting time trying to develop areas that might not be worth your investment).
- **Planning behaviors.** Setting goals, making to-do lists, and grouping tasks together are all examples of this. Clarifying your life goals is another example, because it helps you prioritize tasks and keeps you motivated.
- **Monitoring behaviors.** Keeping a time log is a good way to monitor your behavior. Observing how you use your hours and minutes can help you focus on tasks and identify what changes you can make to eliminate activities that sap your time and do not help you to either achieve your goals or to relax and recharge.

TIME FOR A BREAK

In 2014, the Draugiem Group, a Latvian social networking company, tracked their employees' use of time. They found that the most productive didn't work longer hours, but they did take an average of 17 minutes' break time or every 52 minutes of work.

Planning pitfalls

Try not to spend so much time on planning and monitoring that it crowds out the actual tasks you need to do, however. Business experts often recommend limiting planning to 30 minutes at the start of the day. Be wary, too, of "analysis paralysis" (see pp.132–133), whereby you get so caught up in trying to optimize your plans that you don't actually act on them. Time planning needs to be practical, not perfectionistic, to avoid procrastination (see pp.156–159).

THE "EISENHOWER" BOX

If you're struggling to decide which tasks to prioritize, try evaluating each one using this decision matrix. It's based on US President Dwight D. Eisenhower's remark that, "What is important is seldom urgent and what is urgent is seldom important." Crises and deadlines should come first, but usually aren't very common. After that, goals and relationships take precedence over interruptions.

	URGENT	NOT URGENT
IMPORTANT	**Crises and deadlines** For example: a family member in the hospital; an exam to study for; a tax deadline coming up.	**Goals and relationships** For example: improving your skills; developing a healthy lifestyle; maintaining your friendships.
NOT IMPORTANT	**Interruptions** For example: a colleague asks for a minor favor; an email requiring a response arrives; the phone rings.	**Pastimes** For example: watching TV; surfing the internet; window shopping; playing a game.

Should you multitask?

The answer may depend on you. A 1999 US study by psychologists Carol Kaufman-Scarborough and Jay D. Lindquist identified two styles of working: "polychronic" and "monochronic." Polychronic workers prefer to engage in several tasks at once, while monochronics prefer to perform tasks sequentially. Monochronics planned in more detail, but actually found it harder to follow through because it was more difficult for them to manage interruptions. So if you're not comfortable with multitasking, you're likely to need more control over your environment to limit your distractions.

When it comes to managing time, we each have a different personal style. The key is to have a clear understanding of what keeps you productive, and then plan your days to allow for as many of those behaviors as possible.

THE FOUR "Ds"

Bombarded by distracting emails? Occupational psychologist Emma Donaldson-Feilder recommends that you try the following:

1

Delete. About half of your emails can go straight into your trash folder.

2

Do. If it's urgent or won't take long, do it and get it out of the way.

3

Delegate. Could anyone else handle it better? Pass it right along.

4

Defer. If you know you'll need more time, schedule some in and set aside the email for now.

UNTIL WE CAN MANAGE TIME, WE CAN MANAGE NOTHING ELSE.

PETER DRUCKER, ECONOMIST AND AUTHOR

60
15
30
45

DEALING WITH DEADLINES

HOW TO FOCUS ON THE CHALLENGE

Some of us thrive on deadlines, while others can feel daunted by the prospect. For most of us, deadlines focus our attention, so how do you plan effectively to meet your targets while managing your stress levels, too?

Does the thought of a deadline make you feel energized and confident, or create feelings of tension about how you will get everything done on time? Knowing how to manage deadlines is a key part of your success skill set.

Moderation management

Deadlines need to be realistic if you're going to thrive. It's one thing to be busy during a critical period, but an environment in which tight deadlines are the norm is not healthy. A 2012 Danish study found that too many deadlines were associated with worse sleep quality, either because workers had to stay up late to finish their tasks, or because the psychological arousal needed to keep up the pace was difficult to turn off at night. Too little sleep takes a toll on both health and performance, so if you're under that kind of pressure, take extra care of yourself and perhaps start adjusting your plans toward a goal that gives you space to breathe.

In the meantime, however, cognitive reframing is a helpful tool. It's common to think of a deadline as a crisis, but research suggests that people who think of a deadline as a challenge (see "Keeping stress positive," opposite) use the pressure they feel to help them focus on their work, and so avoid distracting thoughts and actions.

Getting started

Some of us jump right in when there's a deadline, but many of us procrastinate and only start to hear the clock ticking when time is running out. This is a question of whether we have what psychologists call an "implemental" mindset—that is, an attitude of getting down to action rather than planning and evaluating. To meet a deadline, we need to put into action whatever plans we have.

Categorizing time

According to psychologists Yanping Tu and Dilip Soman, one obstacle is how we categorize time. We tend to break up time into units, such as weeks, months, and seasons; in a 2014 series of studies among farmers in India and students in North America, they found that if the deadline is on the other side of a "break"—such as in the New Year—we're more likely to see it as remote (see "Getting motivated," opposite), and, as a result, be less ready to jump into action. What you need to do in that situation is find another way to think about the timeframe. For example, if it's November and the deadline is in January, it's better to tell yourself you have to get it done "this winter" rather than "next year."

KEEPING STRESS POSITIVE

Not all stress is bad (see pp.100–101)—there's also a psychological category known as "eustress," meaning positive or beneficial stress (from the Greek prefix "eu-," or "happy"). A 2013 study published in *Organizational Dynamics* identified a positive pattern you can cultivate when the stress of deadlines is getting to you: present the deadline to yourself as a challenge, and you may find yourself taking action instead of stressing out.

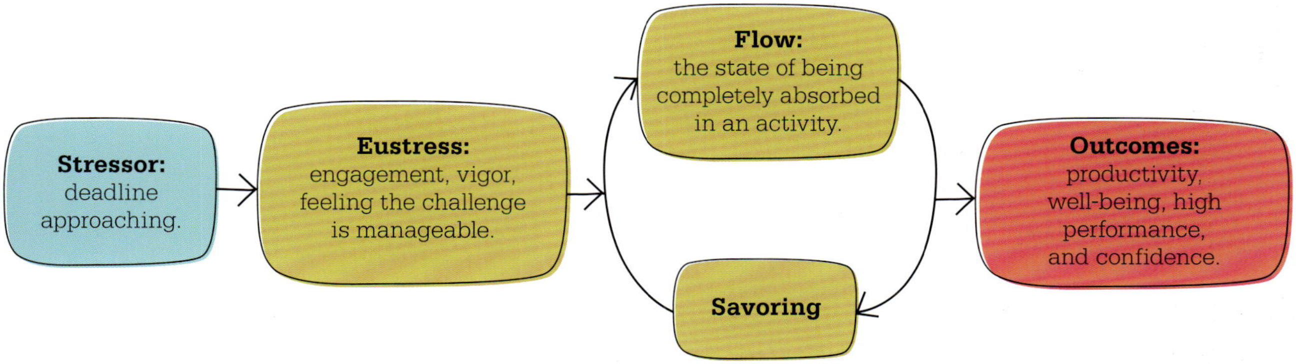

THE DEADLINE BODY CLOCK

Look back over your work during the last 3–5 years and think about whether you tend to meet deadlines on time. Is there a pattern? Some people can hit deadlines right on the mark, some are always a little late, and others are regularly ahead of time. Assuming the deadline is achievable, these patterns are usually consistent: people will almost always take, for example, just the right amount of time, 5 percent shorter, or 10 percent longer than the time allowed. If you're one of the late ones, the solution may be to set yourself a false deadline that's slightly ahead of the real one.

GETTING MOTIVATED

When it's time to plan, a 2014 study in India and North America by psychologists Yanping Tu and Dilip Soman found that it is best to put the deadline inside a timeframe that feels urgent to you. The study found that to get things done, we need to place deadlines in a "like the present" mental space rather than in a "not like the present" category. In the example below, imagine you have a deadline on June 5, and today is May 10. You can take one of two approaches:

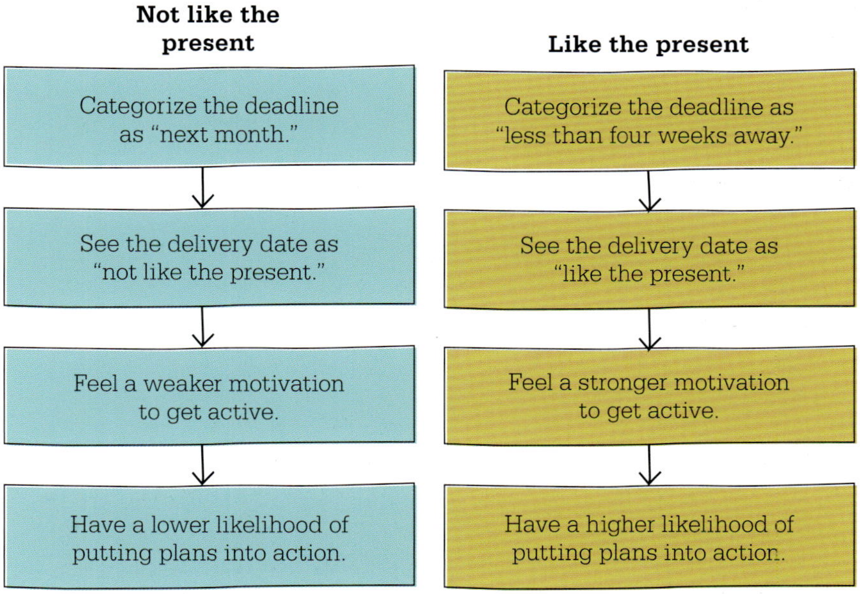

The best approach is to view deadlines as a challenge that you have to meet within a period that's imminent. That way the stress is more manageable, and you have a better chance of starting—and therefore finishing—in good time.

STANDING YOUR GROUND

LEARNING TO SAY "NO"

If you want to be seen as a team player or a "doer," it can be hard to draw boundaries when you really don't have the time or energy for something. Even so, saying "no" is a skill we all need to develop.

Sometimes we have to turn people down. After all, there are only 24 hours in the day and no one has infinite energy. Many of us, however, don't feel comfortable with saying "no" and worry that it will jeopardize our relationship with the person we're turning down. So what's the secret of a good "no" or "not now"?

Saving face

The concept of "face" was developed in 1963 by Canadian sociologist Erving Goffman, and it still applies today. Put simply, we don't like to feel diminished in relation to others. Because saying no to someone can threaten their sense of face, most people feel uncomfortable about being the person turning someone down. Goffman identifies two variants of face:

- **Positive face:** the desire to be seen as a good and respectable person.
- **Negative face:** the desire to remain autonomous.

Psychologists Penelope Brown and Stephen Levinson furthered this idea by categorizing ways of saying "no" into four distinct types (see "Politeness theory," opposite). Each type has a different effect on the listener's sense of face.

If you're saying "no" to someone you don't want to offend, you may need to think about what kind of face they might want to protect. It pays to be particularly aware of this if you are in a position where you are expected to be subordinate to the person you're turning down, such as in a hierarchical organization. Being aware of how your assertion might threaten their sense of face could help you limit the likelihood of a bad reaction.

Once you've made the decision to say "no," there are several other tactics you can use to help make the best of the situation:

- **Find the positive:** Negotiator and presidential adviser William Ury teaches the art of the "positive no." It runs in three steps, yes–no–yes:

> In **saying No positively**, we are giving ourselves a gift ... We are **protecting** what we **value**.
>
> **William Ury**
> Anthropologist and negotiation expert

Affirm: "I'd love to work with you."
Establish a limit: "January isn't a good month for me."
Propose an alternative: "Why don't we compare our schedules for later in the year?"
Ury also adds that we should have a "BATNA"—a Best Alternative To a Negotiated Agreement—so that if the negotiation doesn't go well, we have already prepared a suitable back-up plan.

- **Be specific:** A 2005 study published in the *Journal of Experimental Social Psychology* found that people who talk in abstract terms tend to be perceived as being more biased in their attitudes and motivations than people whose language is more tangible. The person you're saying "no" to will see you in a better light if you're specific about your reasons.
- **Give a reason:** American psychologist Robert Beno Cialdini's research found that providing a reason for saying "no," even if that reason doesn't stand up to scrutiny, is more persuasive than providing no reason at all.
- **Choose your language well:** A 2011 US study found that it's a lot more persuasive to say "I don't" rather than "I can't." Obviously there are situations where this doesn't apply—for example, it's not prudent to tell your boss, "I don't take on more work"—but where the issue is social pressure rather than orders from above, the study found that "don't" sounds less negotiable. So rather than saying, "I can't spend money without checking my budget," try, "I don't spend money without checking my budget," or "I don't make spontaneous decisions about money."

Saying "no" can be an uncomfortable experience for both speaker and listener, but with the right combination of confidence and sensitivity, you can maintain both your boundaries and your alliances.

POLITENESS THEORY

Psychologists Penelope Brown and Stephen C. Levinson suggest that there are four ways of speaking, which might or might not antagonize listeners by undermining their sense of "face." The theory applies in many contexts, including refusals. Different situations call for different kinds of "no":

Ways of speaking	Example phrase	Does it save the listener's face?
Bald on-record	"No, I won't."	Usually not. It can be appropriate in extreme emergencies.
Positive politeness	"It might be a good idea if you asked so-and-so instead."	The aim is to limit the threat to the listener's "positive face"—i.e., it tries to sound friendly.
Negative politeness	"I know you have a lot on your plate right now, but can it wait a while?"	The aim is to show respect for the listener's "negative face"—i.e., it acknowledges that they have their own issues.
Off-record (indirect)	"Wow, I'm looking at a busy week!"	The aim is to save face as much as possible by dropping a hint before it becomes necessary to say "no" openly.

DECISION TIME

BALANCING YOUR CHOICES

To get things done, we have to make decisions. For some of us this is easy, but for others it can be hard not to hesitate. What's the science behind our indecision, and how can we overcome it?

Do you ever panic in the face of too much information, or worry so much about how to make a decision that you never actually make one? This is what psychologists call "analysis paralysis": the state in which your brain becomes so overwhelmed with different possibilities that you can't reach a conclusion. Overthinking and overanalyzing information can undermine us in a number of ways:

- **Productivity and judgment:** too much information, pressure, or anxiety can overload our short-term memory and affect our proficiency and acumen.
- **Creativity:** overthinking makes us less creative. A 2015 study at Stanford University found that participants' most creative work was done when their prefrontal cortex—the center for conscious thought—was less active than their cerebellum, which handles movement and activity.

51%

TIME WELL SPENT?

According to a 2010 study in the US, China, South Africa, the UK, and Australia, white-collar workers spent, on average, **51 percent of their day receiving** and sorting through **information** rather than using it to **do their work**. It's no wonder we can sometimes feel overwhelmed.

- **Happiness:** perfectionism can reduce our chances of happiness. According to economist Herbert Simon, people are either "satisficers" who will settle for something that's "good enough," or "maximizers" who want to make the best possible decision. Maximizers tend to be less happy, have lower self-esteem, and regret their decisions more than satisficers.

Ironically, the more anxious we are about making the perfect decision, the more likely we are to create mental habits that impede our decision-making skills.

Getting to the point

If you find it hard to make up your mind, try the following methods:

- **Imagine you're advising a friend.** Studies show that we find it hard to make decisions when we're too emotionally invested. If you take yourself out of the picture, your choice might become clearer.
- **Limit your information.** Researchers at Princeton and Stanford universities found that information overload is a key cause of indecision. In a digital age, there's always more to review—just don't take on more than you can handle.
- **Realize that "common" doesn't mean "always."** A 2009 study by psychologists Ralph Hertwig and Ido Erev found that we often give too much weight to what's happened recently and too little to events that are rare yet more likely to happen than we think. Don't forget that circumstances can change.
- **Don't waste time on small decisions.** If things will be the same in a year's time no matter what you do, the decision doesn't deserve much of your energy.
- **Set a deadline.** If you haven't made a decision yet, resolve that you must come to a conclusion by a specific date.

Decisions can be challenging, but if you keep your priorities in mind, they become easier to manage.

ARE YOU A "LAY RATIONALIST"?

Do you follow your head or your heart? A 2015 study for the American Marketing Association found that people they described as "lay rationalists"—that is, people who felt more comfortable with facts rather than feelings—were likely to be influenced by what they thought they *should* do, whereas people who were less rational were more likely to be influenced by their emotions and what they *wanted* to do. The two types tend to have quite different concepts of success.

Lay rationalists	Emotion-based decision makers
Are more likely to spend money on material goods.	Are more likely to spend money on experiences.
Like what feels good but choose what they think is sensible.	Choose what feels good.
Have more "useful" friends—that is, people who offer connections.	Have more "fun" friends—that is, people whose company they enjoy.
Are more influenced by objective outcomes.	Are more concerned with fairness and morality.
May cut their losses to salvage something.	May take a loss if the alternative is accepting something unjust.
When donating to charity, pay more attention to the number of people it will help.	When donating to charity, are more influenced by their feelings toward the people it will help.
Are generally more successful professionally.	Are generally happier in their daily lives.

ACTIVE PLANNING

DEVELOPING AND REFINING YOUR STRATEGIES

Planning can be a mixed blessing: a good plan can make you much more efficient, while a bad plan can waste a lot of time. When you have a goal in mind, how do you strike the right balance between strategy and action?

Studies suggest that when we plan well, we perform well, but they also show that we often resist thinking ahead unless someone encourages us to do so. It seems we have a tendency to solve problems opportunistically—as and when they arise—rather than anticipate them beforehand. If we can train ourselves to think ahead, however, we're at a real advantage.

What's stopping us?

Cognitive scientists Wayne Gray and Wai-Tat Fu argue that, when anticipating difficulties, we deal with two kinds of obstacle:

- **Hard constraints:** non-negotiable facts that mean something either is or isn't possible.
- **Soft constraints:** paths of least resistance. We prefer to reach goals with as little cognitive strain as possible. If we can achieve a result one of two ways, and one places more demands on our memory or energy, these "soft constraints" turn us toward the other method.

Sometimes we need to adapt our plans as we work, but it's a good idea to have a strategy laid out. If you know how your mind works, you can anticipate soft constraints and limit their impact. Gray and Fu give the example of assembling a child's toy. Do you like to read all the instructions before you begin, or does that put too much strain on your memory? Do you prefer to read one instruction, follow it, then move on to the next, or is that too much task-switching? Some of us need more time for the early planning stages, while others need wiggle room later in the process. Assess your cognitive approach to simple tasks first, then plan accordingly.

Planning as a group

A good plan needs to accommodate everyone on the team. A useful format to try here is the 1975 "input–process–output" model (see "Group effectiveness," opposite). Some tasks only require that everyone perform to a basic level, but the more difficult the challenge, the more variables you'll have to consider. Here are some important tips:

- The more complex the project, the more you'll need to plan; there will be many tasks and subtasks.
- If your colleagues have limited experience, you should plan in detail, but also be prepared to make changes once the work begins, because they'll be learning as they go. This is known as "in-process planning."

GROUP EFFECTIVENESS

If you're working with others, you'll need to get everyone working together for the best outcome. This "input-process-output" model, devised by psychologists J. Richard Hackman and C. G. Morris, helps predict a group's effectiveness. When drawing up a strategy, try filling out your own version.

INPUT
Variables include: task design; group norms; experience and personalities of all group members; complexity of the challenge.

Examples:
- We need the band ready to perform three new songs.
- We mostly get along, but there's tension between Mike and Jo.
- Jo's a great composer, while Raj and Ben are a bit rusty on their instruments.

PROCESS
Variables include: performance strategies; effort made by everyone; skill and knowledge applied by team members.

Examples:
- How often can we rehearse?
- Will everyone turn up?
- Are we all accomplished musicians?
- Do we all have goodwill?
- Who's leading the group, and can they do it without alienating anyone?

OUTPUT
Effectiveness depends on how the input and process elements combine.

Examples:
- Good basic musicianship and hard work carried us through on the night.
- We were a little ragged for the last two songs.

FEEDBACK
What can you learn for next time?

Examples:
- What did the fans say after we played?
- Does the venue manager have any comments?
- Do any of us have issues we'd like to discuss?

- As well as making a group plan, ask individuals to make their own: research shows that this increases productivity. Other research confirms that people often don't do this unless specifically instructed, so make it clear that everyone on the team should have their own plan.
- Don't oblige people to over-plan if they're doing something they know well: it's not necessary and wastes time.

Groups work at their best when every member has his or her own plan and communicates it clearly to the rest of the team. However, since we don't always plan unless we're told to, be prepared to be the standard-bearer of a good strategy.

KNOW YOUR GOALS

Business leaders suggest that every strong plan includes four stages:

1 **Purpose:** your task, but also your vision and values.

2 **Goals:** what you will do to work toward this purpose.

3 **Strategies:** how you will achieve these goals.

4 **Action plans:** what must be done by when, and by whom.

ASPECTS OF A GREAT PLAN

A 1990 study found that there are five key elements of an effective plan:

1 **Future orientation:** everything should be geared toward the goal and how you'll get there.

2 **Communication:** everyone working together should interact as much as possible.

3 **Know your strengths**, weaknesses, opportunities, and threats (SWOT), and keep reassessing them.

4 **Role definition:** everyone's tasks should be clear.

5 **Action plans:** develop and communicate ideas for what you'll do and how you'll allocate resources.

TAKING THE STAGE

PUBLIC SPEAKING SKILLS

Whether your idea of success is working in perfect isolation or persuading crowds of thousands, it's likely that you'll need to talk in public every now and then. Are you comfortable with being center stage?

According to the *Wall Street Journal*, public speaking is the biggest fear among Americans—even death takes second place! It's highly unlikely that we'll get pelted with rotten tomatoes, even if we do mess up a speech—so what, exactly, are we so afraid of, and what can we do about it?

Fear of speaking

The fundamental fear is that people will reject us en masse—and rejection is literally painful. A 2013 study at the University of Michigan found that the brain releases the same chemicals in the face of social rejection as it does in response to physical pain. When we say rejection "hurts," we're not being metaphorical. Some evolutionary psychologists also argue that the fear of public speaking taps into the ancient part of our brain that believes if we lose social support, we'll be left alone, not just to sulk, but to starve. It's not surprising that so many

IN GOOD COMPANY

According to leadership consultant Beverly D. Flaxington, writing in *Psychology Today*, **three out of four people fear public speaking**. Despite this, most of them speak perfectly well when it comes to it.

ALL HAIL

In 2013, UK sound consultant Julian Treasure devised a useful acronym to help you inspire your audience, and ensure that they will want to hear what you have to say.

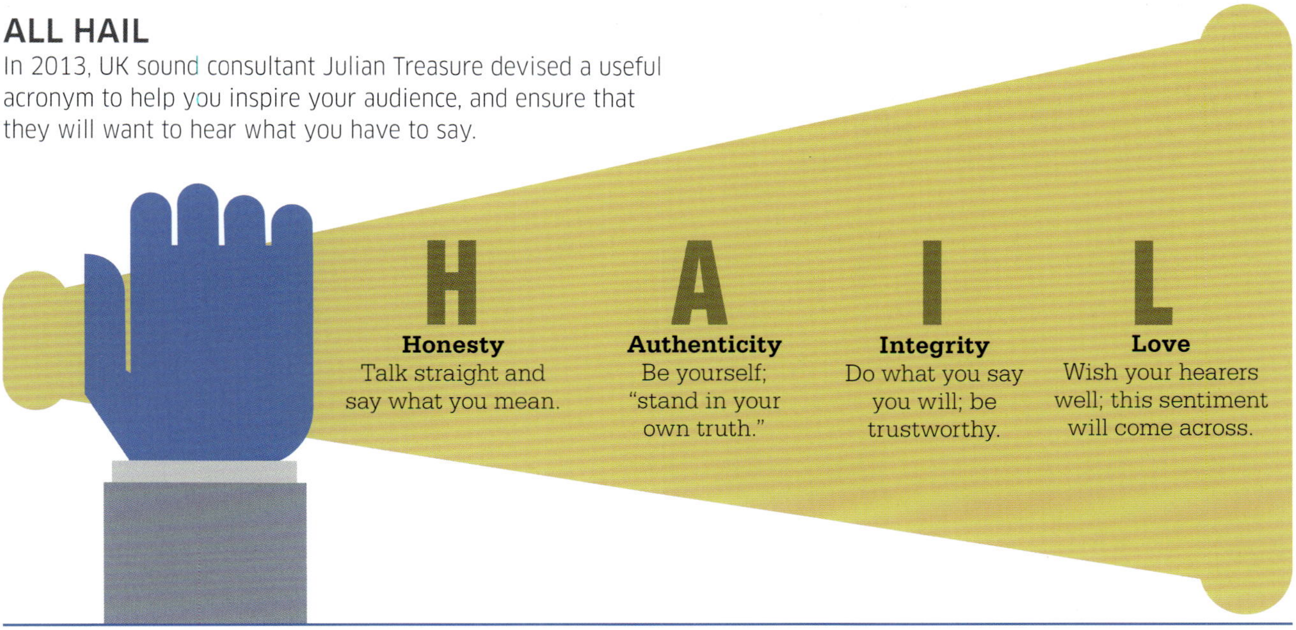

of us fear public speaking, but it's probably time to become more proactive about it.

Get in the right mood

Some researchers argue that our brains contain cells called "mirror neurons" that not only notice what somebody else is feeling but produce an image of that feeling in us, too. If you've ever flinched when someone else got hurt, or caught the giggles from a friend, that's your mirror neurons at work. You can use this in public speaking. If you are excited by your subject, the audience will mirror your enthusiasm.

Be generous to the audience

The popular educational TED lectures advise speakers to give the audience something to take home with them—an insight they can apply to their own lives—and to think about benefiting them rather than selling to them. We can all spot a mechanical pitch, and we usually feel pressured rather than engaged. Instead, see yourself and your audience as members of the same common humanity, and think about how to speak so that they'll feel all the better for knowing what you have to share.

See it as a skill

Public speaking isn't a measure of your inherent worth: some of the finest people in the world might mumble and drone if you put them in the spotlight. Instead, adopt a growth mindset (see p.26): you're a lifelong learner, and public speaking is just one thing you may need to improve with practice.

Don't just read it out

Finally, a note on notes. Use them if you want to, but don't write a script that you'll deliver verbatim. It takes an experienced performer to deliver blocks of text with an air of freshness, and if you're reading aloud, you have the added problem of staring at the page instead of looking at your listeners. Keep your notes to brief points you can grasp at a glance, and use them as jumping-off points to remind you of your key ideas. From that structure, you can speak directly to the audience; it'll sound much more engaging.

HARNESSING YOUR FEAR

A little tension can actually be good for your performance (see pp.100–101). Anxiety gets adrenaline flowing, and adrenaline gives us energy. You can use that energy to power yourself forward. Put on a confident face, which can feed back into your mood, and remind yourself that feeling nervous doesn't prove you're going to fail, it just means your body is gearing up for a challenge.

MAKING A PITCH

THE ART OF SELLING

It's one thing to know you have a great idea—it's another to convince other people. Whether you're raising funds, looking for a job, or sharing a passion, you'll do better if you can present your plans persuasively.

Pitching is the art of presenting your own value—or at least the value of your work—to others. This doesn't always come naturally to many of us, so here are some useful tips based on a number of psychological studies.

BE PREPARED

- **Research your market.** What are the demographics of the people you're appealing to? How would they benefit from what you have to offer? Bear in mind that people buy things for their own reasons, not because they want to please a stranger.
- **Think price.** If you're selling something expensive, address people with a good level of disposable income.
- **Know your competition.** If there are a lot of people doing what you're doing, compete by adding a twist, beating them on quality, or offering better value. If your idea is unique, what need does it fulfill and what else is currently fulfilling that need? Sell the idea that you can satisfy it better.
- **Think flexibility.** If you're appealing to a range of people, modify what you're offering to meet individual needs.
- **Practice speaking.** Hone your public speaking skills (see pp.136–137)—a bad speaker makes their idea look poor, too.

HAVE THE RIGHT APPROACH

- **Know your value.** If you have a track record of past successes, or something unique to offer, make it a central part of your pitch.
- **Embrace salesmanship.** We all recognize the stereotype of the slick, pushy hustler, but don't let negative associations interfere with your pitch. Remember, you're presenting something meaningful and honest, so try to see the art of selling in a positive light.
- **Keep your body language calm and confident.** Gesticulating or fidgeting will distract from your message.
- **Look people in the eye.** You're trying to connect with them, and eye contact makes a big difference.
- **Be willing to learn.** Encourage discussion, ask questions, and take feedback on board. It can take courage, but a responsive seller is a good seller.
- **Become comfortable with negotiation.** Even a strong salesperson doesn't always get everything they ask for, so role-play with friends until you feel at ease with the back-and-forth of negotiations.
- **Be passionate.** This is your idea, and you believe in it. Let everyone see this.

STRUCTURE YOUR PITCH WELL

- **Open with your conclusion.** According to executive coach Patricia Fripp, you should let people know from the start why you're there. Everything else you say will support that.
- **Keep it simple but memorable.** Lead with something that's easy for people to grasp and repeat to others.
- **Describe the benefits and the costs.** Don't be shy about either of these elements—your audience wants to hear both.
- **Be specific about what you need.** The crisper and more accurate you are, the more professional you'll sound.

CHOOSE YOUR STYLE

In 2015, sales training provider TACK International reported that 50 percent of the listeners they polled preferred discussion-based pitches and presentations:

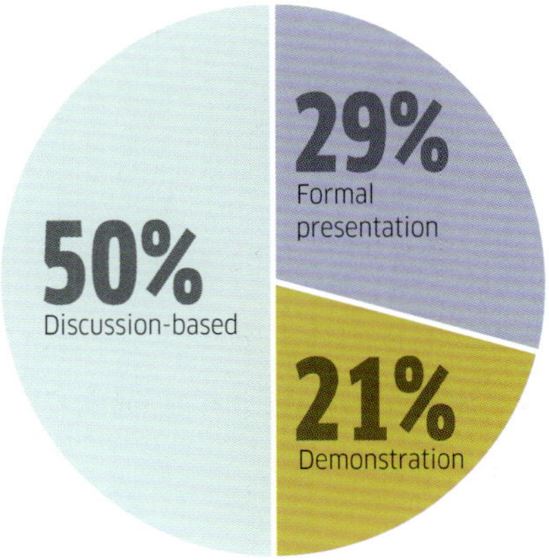

MAKE OR BREAK?

Kimberly D. Elsbach, Professor of Organizational Behavior at the University of California, identifies four common speaking styles that can ruin your pitch:

1 **The pushover.** It's good to adapt to your listeners' needs, but if you offer to make changes at every turn, you look like you're not sure about your own idea—and if you're not sure, no one else will be, either. Take feedback on board, but explain and defend yourself when necessary.

2 **The robot.** Don't just read from a script or answer questions with pre-prepared speeches. Interact and respond to the people you are talking to so they feel "heard" and understood.

3 **The used-car salesman.** Wheedling, outlandish claims, and a hard sell will put people off you, never mind your idea. Take yourself seriously and be credible.

4 **The charity case.** Don't sound too needy, and if people say no, don't beg. Generally people are interested in what you can offer them, not what they can do for you.

KEEP IT SHORT

52%

of clients want initial proposal documents to be **fewer than 3 pages** in length.

SAFEGUARDING YOUR TEAM

HOW TO PROTECT YOUR PROJECT

Tackling a project as a team brings many different factors into play, and sometimes things can go wrong. What's the best way to maintain productivity and enhance group harmony?

Any group can experience conflict, low morale, and a lack of cohesion. How do you avoid these issues and give your team the best chance of success?

A good plan

It may be common sense that a well-planned project has the best chance of success, but science backs it up too: a 2013 Australian and Fijian study, for example, found that it was particularly helpful to anticipate potential risks (see "Types of risks," opposite). Carefully planned projects enjoyed a double benefit:

- When there was a high level of risk, well-planned projects were more efficient—that is, more likely to finish on time and budget.
- When there was a low level of risk, well-planned projects were more effective—that is, more likely to achieve good results.

For everyone to stick to a plan, they need to stay motivated and work collaboratively, which is why good management skills are important.

The key question

Multiple studies confirm that the most important part of keeping a team together is being able to answer one simple question: "Why are we doing this?" It's discouraging and confusing not to be clear on this point, and teams that aren't tend to lose focus and be more prone to conflict.

There are many reasons why we might not ask this question. A Massachusetts Institute of Technology (MIT) study in 2013 gave several possibilities, including a bias

THE QUALITIES OF A GREAT TEAM

Management professors Dov Dvir and Aaron J. Shenhar have studied more than 400 projects in various industries worldwide since the 1950s, and found that the outstanding teams had several traits in common:

1 They worked on offering something unique or of exceptional value.

2 They began with a long period of project definition, after which everyone was clear about the overriding vision and purpose.

3 They could create a revolutionary project culture. If old habits didn't work, they set them aside for whatever would best serve the real goal.

4 Their leaders had good personal and communication skills, and constantly stayed in touch with the next tier down in the chain of command.

5 They didn't try to reinvent the wheel. If relevant knowledge already existed, they used it.

6 Their teams were diverse enough to be adaptable if the market changed.

7 They had a strong ethos of team spirit and pride in their work. Team members had a sense of joint ownership, and the leaders respected this.

toward action (the team jumps to work before they've considered the big picture) and reaching for a familiar solution (you've faced similar situations before and fail to consider whether this situation is unique in some way). Instead, the MIT team suggests that you ask yourselves:

- What is our most important problem?
- Will this course of action address the real issue?
- How many potential causes can we find? Are we looking at a big enough picture?
- Are we agreed on the reason that drives the need for the project?
- Have we had frank and open discussions to bring any unspoken questions to light?
- Are we keeping to our goal, or are we straying?

That way, personal conflicts take second place, and new information can be handled in the light of your bigger, shared purpose.

TYPES OF RISKS

While making your plans, try to anticipate potential future risks. Different theorists suggest different areas of consideration, so decide what feels right for you.

Project management expert Max Wideman suggest these five areas of consideration:

- **External, unpredictable, and uncontrollable risks:** e.g., weather damage to your building adds a sudden extra cost.
- **External, predictable, and uncontrollable risks:** e.g., your main supplier seems to be heading for bankruptcy.
- **Internal, non-technical, and controllable risks:** e.g., staff tensions are lowering productivity.
- **Internal, technical, and controllable risks:** e.g., your computer security is weak.
- **Legal and controllable risks:** e.g., there are copyright concerns to be investigated.

Management expert Avraham Shtub and his team suggest these three areas of consideration:

- **Technical performance risks:** e.g., can you ship your fragile product safely?
- **Budget risks:** e.g., will you have enough money to pay everyone next year?
- **Schedule risks:** e.g., can you meet an upcoming deadline?

TAKING CHARGE

MANAGEMENT AND LEADERSHIP

Whether you're heading up a department or speaking out as part of the team, there are times when you have to step up and use your influence. What's the best way to get your message across?

It's common to assume that management and leadership are one and the same. However, it's probably more accurate to say that leadership is one of the many skills that a manager needs.

It's possible to act as a leader even if you're not in charge. For example, a person who tries to persuade their group to change for the better is showing leadership—whether or not they're the boss. Management, on the other hand, involves a balance of authority and organizational skills that can be challenging. Managing well may be your aspiration, but you can be a leader based on the actions you take, not your job title or position.

Getting your style right

Successful people often like to say they know the "secret" of leadership, but different situations often call for different approaches. An idea proposed by contingency theorists Robert Tannenbaum and Warren Schmidt (see "The leadership continuum," opposite) divides leadership styles into four groups, depending on how much authority is used:

1 **"Tell."** As the leader you are autocratic, although not necessarily harsh. The rules are already in place and it's your job to monitor how people follow them.

2 **"Sell."** The decision has already been made, but it's your job to present it to the team. Key skills here are being persuasive and encouraging.

3 **"Consult."** You know what you want to achieve, but the team has a lot of say in how to go about it. Your job is to motivate and delegate as well as to direct.

4 **"Participate."** You define what is needed and what the task's parameters are, but rely on the skills and motivation of your team to find productive ways of working. You allow them as much responsibility as possible.

Depending on the task and the people you're working with, you may need to adjust your leadership style. A good leader doesn't rely on not being questioned, but can shift their approach to meet the needs of each situation.

> **Leadership** is not about titles, positions, or flow charts. It is about **one life influencing another**.
>
> **John C. Maxwell**
> Leadership author and speaker

Inspiring people

Think back to favorite bosses, teachers, or people of influence within your community. What was it about them that impressed you? What can you learn from them?

Different cultures value different personality traits, but studies suggest that the following qualities almost always inspire confidence:

- **Be clear about what you mean.** In a changing world, leaders may have to switch strategies, which can confuse their teams. Let your overarching goal be seen so that your integrity is clear even if you have to adjust your tactics.
- **Don't pretend that listening and agreeing are the same.** A leader who doesn't listen is discouraging, and a leader who won't own their authority is frustrating. Be receptive to feedback, but when decisions have to be made, make them.
- **Hold yourself accountable.** Everybody makes mistakes, and it creates needless tension if you fail to acknowledge yours and make amends.
- **Be confident, but not arrogant.** The antidote to overconfidence is openness. Others may always have something more to teach you.
- **Monitor outcomes** and follow up on what you've learned.

A good leader can improve things for everyone around them. If you can embrace your responsibilities and find a style that works for everyone, your whole group will be the better for your commitment.

THE LEADERSHIP CONTINUUM

This important leadership model was developed in the US in 1958 by contingency theorists Robert Tannenbaum and Warren Schmidt. Different groups and tasks, they found, will do best under different kinds of leaders:

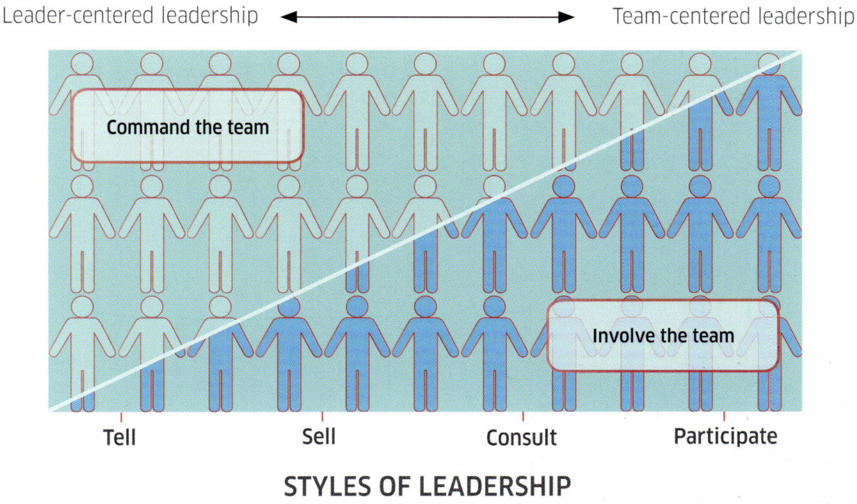

EVERYONE IN AGREEMENT?

Psychologist Anna Lebedeva identifies three different responses among stakeholders (such as team members, customers, or sponsors) when change is brought in:

1. **Active supporters:** people who like and endorse the new idea. A good leader recognizes and publicly thanks such people.
2. **Fence-sitters:** people who want to wait and see how things turn out. The best way to persuade them is to surround them with active supporters.
3. **Active blockers:** people who oppose or criticize. These people need more direct persuasion.

A LEADER'S OVERVIEW

Management expert John Adair argues that group performance is dependent on how leaders balance the competing needs of the "total" situation. When you're in charge, you need to be aware of all these aspects:

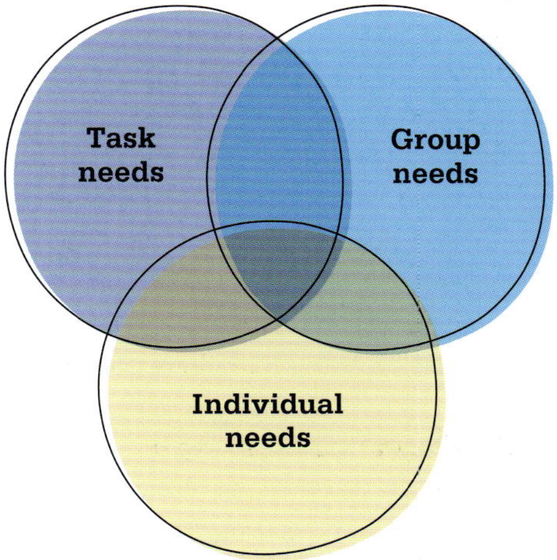

MAKING MEMORIES

MAXIMIZING YOUR MENTAL RESOURCES

Memory is part of our ancient survival kit—but how do we make a Stone Age brain work for us today? Whether we're trying to retain information or maintain our optimism, it helps to know how memory functions.

Why do we have the capacity to make and access memories? The most likely explanation is that this function evolved not so much to allow us to recall the past, but to inform us how to react in the present and attempt to predict the future. Knowing this can be useful to us as we look for ways to retain information, and it can also help us to manage our expectations.

Think about the context

Need to remember something? Studies show that our memory is adaptive—that is, it is hardwired to help us fit into our environment the best we can. A 2007 study (see "Survival instinct," opposite) found that we're far more likely to remember ideas that we associate with survival, so if there is a piece of information that you have to remember, try picturing it in that context. Not to the extent that you panic yourself, of course—the scenario could be imaginary, or related to positive "survival" traits such as making allies or attracting potential partners.

Don't discount the positive

Memory may help us survive, but it can also undermine us. Studies find that we're highly prone to a fallacy known as "duration neglect," and that this can lead to negative thinking.

Psychologists Daniel Kahneman and Jason Riis give the following example: a music lover listens with delight to a long symphony, only to be shocked in the final bars by the

SURVIVAL INSTINCT

A 2007 international experiment asked three groups of volunteers to read lists of randomly selected words, such as "stone" and "chair." Each group was then asked a different question:

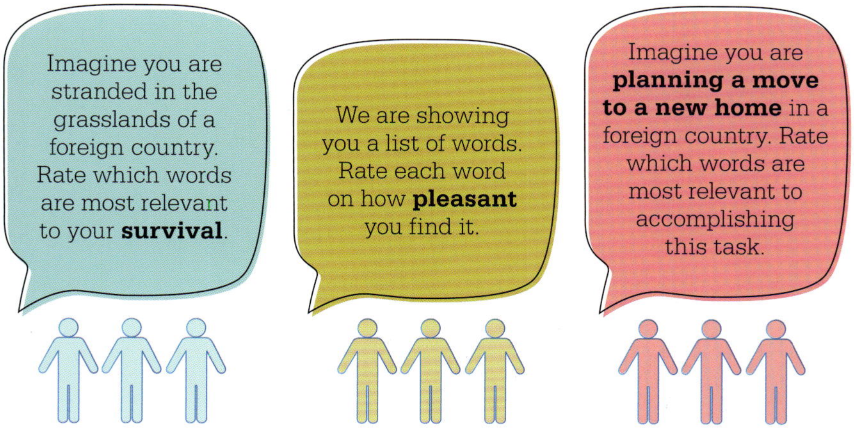

Even though the word list was the same for each group, the volunteers who were asked to think in terms of survival had the best recall. This is "adaptive" memory: we remember best what helps us adapt to—and survive in—our environment.

Percentage of words remembered correctly:

scratch of a damaged recording. The listener is likely to say that the experience was ruined, but in fact, only the memory has been spoiled—for more than an hour, the experience was very pleasant.

We tend to evaluate remembered experiences based on either their most dramatic moment or their ending—a phenomenon known as the "peak/end" rule. When motivating yourself, be aware that you may be liable to putting too much emphasis on bad moments purely because they were intense. Don't let that intensity discourage you. A "failure" may have had months or years of success preceding it. Remember all the facts, not just the dramatic ones, and you're likely to feel more confident.

THE MEMORY PALACE

The ancient Greeks and Romans were master speechmakers, and they worked without notes. Their trick was to create a "memory palace," in which they placed outlandish reminders in a familiar setting. You can try it yourself. Suppose you want to make a speech about growing the market for a product, an advertising campaign you developed in Canada, and your desire to test it out on social media. Picture this:

- You are outside your home. There is a huge plant on the doorstep, shooting up at great speed. (This reminds you of the word "grow.")
- You enter your house. There is a dancing clown in the hallway with a maple leaf for a nose. (This looks like the leaf on the Canadian flag, which reminds you of the ad campaign.)
- You walk into your kitchen, but it's full of tiny computers gossiping about your toaster. (That's your reminder for "social media.")

Classical rhetoricians remembered their speeches not word for word, but topic by topic. Contemporary science proves they were right to do so, because our visual-spatial memory is more powerful than our ability to retain verbal and numerical information. If you need to remember something, try creating your own memory palace, populated with outlandish cues.

CRITICAL THINKING

THE POWER OF SKEPTICISM

When we want to succeed, it's tempting to follow any advice that sounds hopeful. The key, however, is to use your judgment, ask questions, and be a little cautious when listening to "success stories."

Critical thinking doesn't always come to us naturally—in fact, studies suggest that most of us are rather poor at it unless we have been explicitly taught how to do it. When it comes to making important choices, however, some skill with logic can be indispensable.

Information literacy

If you are about to embark on a new project, the first step is to gather relevant information. To do this effectively, try applying the set of skills below. They are defined by the Association of College and Research Libraries as key to an "information-literate individual":

- Define the nature and extent of the information you need.
- Acquire that information as efficiently as possible.
- Critically evaluate that information, including how reliable or biased the source might be.
- Use the information effectively, ethically, and legally to achieve a specific goal.
- Remember that information literacy is an ongoing part of lifelong learning.

The first part of critical thinking is to make sure you have all the facts at your disposal. From that solid base, you can make your decisions.

Listen to the right people

Whatever your aspirations, you'll probably have role models and people you admire. If so, it's natural to follow their advice about how to succeed—after all, if their path worked for them, doesn't it follow that it ought to work for you, too?

In fact, it's wise to be wary of that assumption. Critical thinking reveals the reason—successful people are, in effect, an incomplete data set. For example, a person who risked everything they owned on a business venture and became

> We think we **make decisions** because we **have good reasons** ... [but] we believe in the reasons because we've **already made the decision**.
>
> **Daniel Kahneman**
> Israeli-born psychologist and Nobel laureate

a billionaire is likely to recommend bold strategies and total commitment. However, there may be other people who took the same course of action and went bankrupt; they would advise caution and securing your assets instead. If you only hear the success stories, you are listening to a self-selecting group who can't give you the full picture.

Survivorship bias

"Survivorship bias" is a common logical fallacy. We're prone to listen to the success stories—the survivors—because the others aren't around to tell the tale. A dramatic example from history is the case of statistician Abraham Wald who, during World War II, was hired by the U.S. Air Force to determine how to make their bomber planes safer. The planes that returned tended to have bullet holes along the wings, body, and tail, and commanders wanted to reinforce those areas because they seemed to get hit most often. Wald, however, saw that the problem was that these bullet holes had not destroyed the planes, and what needed more protection were the areas that *weren't* hit. Those were the areas where, if a plane was struck by a bullet, it would never be seen again. His calculations based on that logic are still in use today, and they have saved many pilots.

When taking advice on how to succeed, make sure you have all the facts. Gather your information as fully as possible, and be aware that life's "winners" may not have all the answers. It's your decision how to proceed, so ask questions and come to your own conclusions.

THE CLASSICAL SYLLOGISM

The ancient Greek philosopher Aristotle taught a form of reasoning that became central to Western thought: the three-part syllogism, or pattern of deductive reasoning. This remains a useful way to see if our evidence makes sense. Consider these two syllogisms below, and try to spot the false one.

Both conclusions are technically correct, but the syllogism on the right is based on bad reasoning—in this case, it overlooks the possibility that Socrates might be some other mortal creature. Arguments can reach a conclusion that sounds right, but always be alert to their actual logic.

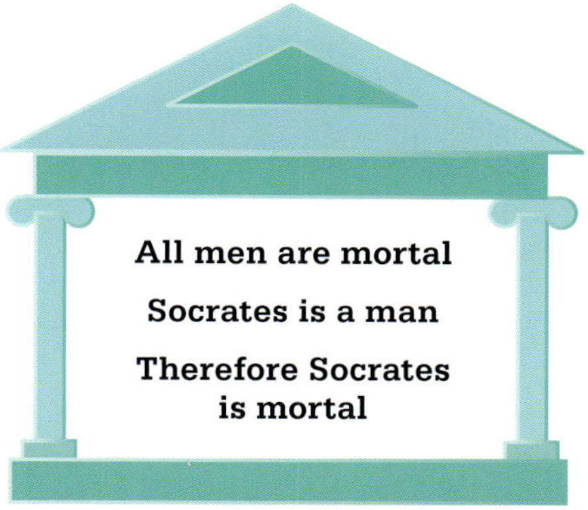

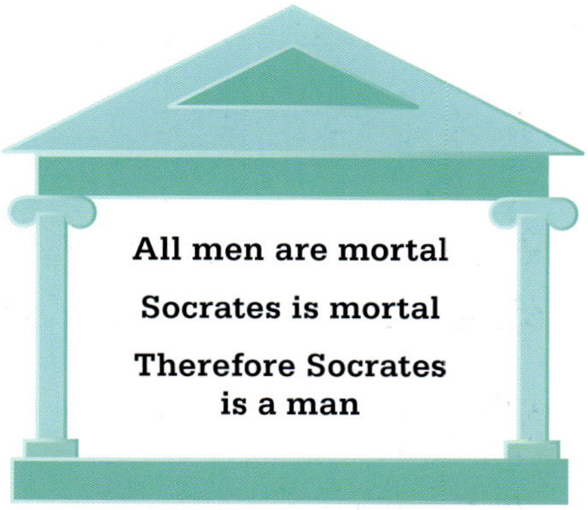

HOW DO WE MANAGE INFORMATION?

The psychological theory of "dual processing" argues that when we assess information, there are two kinds of thought processes at work: decision-making and reflective thinking. When facing a choice, ask yourself which process seems to be dominating, and whether you might benefit from balancing it with the other.

Thought process	How it works	Pros	Cons
Decision-making	Quick, automatic, and based on past experience.	In everyday situations, it's efficient and saves needless agonizing.	It's unreflective, prone to biased thinking, and vulnerable to misinformation.
Reflective thinking	Consciously rational and focused.	When facing new or complex situations, it's much more likely to reach a correct conclusion.	It places demand on the working memory and requires more time and concentration.

KNOWING YOUR BLIND SPOTS

HOW TO KEEP A RATIONAL PERSPECTIVE

When it comes to taking a gamble, whether in a casino or on the stock market, many of us believe we'll win. Knowing the psychological reasons behind this false assumption can help us on the road to success.

We don't always act in a rational way when we make decisions about what's in our best interests. In fact, if we're in a bad situation, we can often make it worse by pursuing an unpredictable course of action rather than simply accepting our losses and trying to prevent further damage.

The sunk cost fallacy

If we've invested in something that hasn't repaid us—be it money in a failing venture, time in an unhappy relationship, or chips at the roulette wheel—we find it very difficult to walk away. This is the sunk cost fallacy. Our instinct is to continue investing money or time as we hope that our investment will prove to be worthwhile in the end. Giving up would mean acknowledging that we've wasted something we can't get back, and that thought is so painful that we prefer to avoid it if we can.

PROSPECT THEORY

If a choice or product offers an uncertain reward, we are liable to evaluate it on its prospect rather than on its utility. This is to say that we tend to assess something's value based on what it *might* be worth later rather than what it's *actually* worth right now—and if that "might" is temptingly high, we're more likely to make irrational decisions and invest too much in something whose utility isn't worth what we give for it. It pays to be aware of possible future outcomes, but don't let them rule you: a prospect is not a certainty.

The problem, of course, is that if something really is a bad bet, then staying with it simply increases the amount we lose. Rather than walk away from a bad five-year relationship, for example, we turn it into a bad 10-year relationship; rather than accept that we've lost a thousand dollars, we lay down another thousand and lose that too. In the end, by delaying the pain of admitting our problem, we only add to it. Sometimes we just have to cut our losses.

The power of the near miss

A 2016 experiment for the *Journal of Gambling Studies* found that subjects who narrowly missed out on a win showed elevated heart rates and a greater desire to gamble again than if they lost by a large margin. Always remember that a narrow loss is still a loss, and take a deep breath before you act on it.

QUANTITY VERSUS ODDS

In 1994, psychologists Veronika Denes-Raj and Seymour Epstein offered US volunteers a chance to win a dollar if they could pick out a red jelly bean from a mixture of red and white jelly beans. Offered either a large, covered bowl with more red beans but worse odds, or a small, covered bowl with fewer red beans but better odds, most of the subjects—even though they knew the odds beforehand—chose the big bowl with the worse odds. The sizes of the bowls outweighed their rational judgment about which was the better bet. When making decisions, don't let quantity blind you to the actual odds.

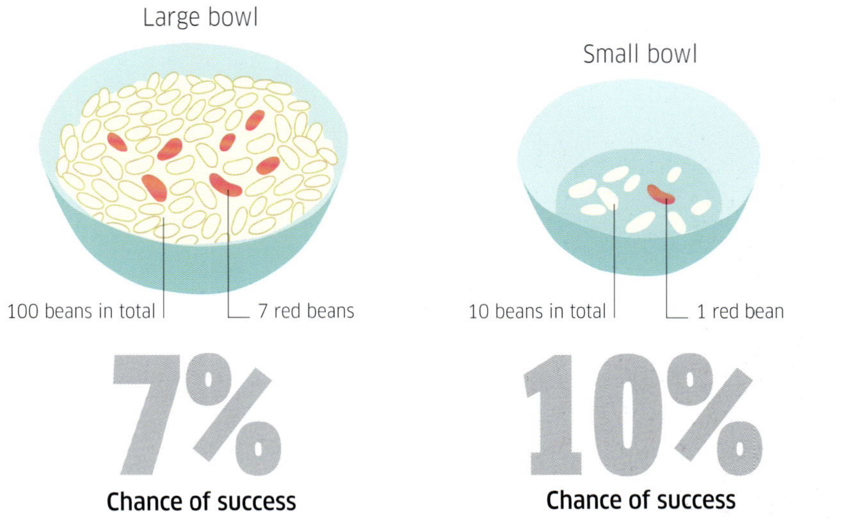

THE GAMBLER'S FALLACY

Do several losses in a row mean a win must be around the corner? Sadly not: this is the gambler's fallacy, which assumes that the odds of an event happening next time are lowered by it having already just happened. For example, if you flip a coin six times and it lands on heads, what are the odds of it coming up tails? If you guess anything higher than 50–50, that's the gambler's fallacy. Evaluate each chance on its own probabilities.

THE FALLACY OF COMPOSITION

We can sometimes assume that the whole will be as good as each of its parts. Suppose, for example, you're in charge of a startup, and you know that everyone you've brought on board is productive and efficient. It might seem logical to assume that, as a result, the startup will be productive and efficient, too—but this isn't necessarily true. The fallacy of composition fails to allow for how the different "parts" interact with each other—if, for example, your efficient administrator and your highly skilled head of IT each assumes the other is in charge of collating prototype test results, then you have a problem. Equally, a unit composed of good people can still be working on a doomed project, and a project composed of good ideas may lack a stable center. When assembling a team with a common goal, always check the overall view as well as the individuals involved.

CHAPTER 5

IN YOUR SIGHTS

GOAL SETTING AND GOAL GETTING

MASTER OF YOUR FATE

KEEPING YOURSELF MOTIVATED

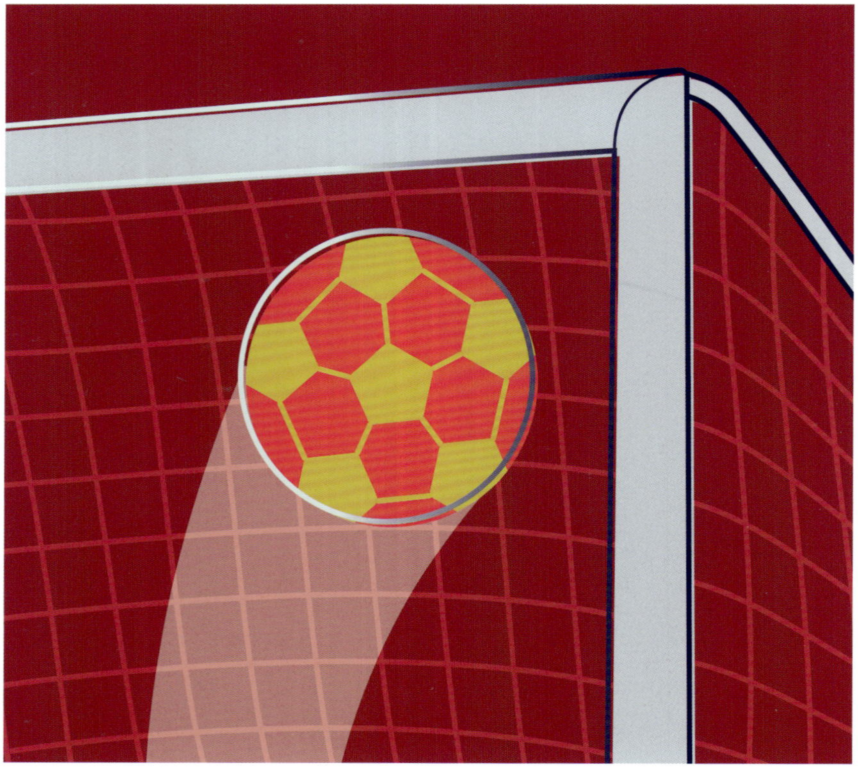

Do you see yourself as a dynamic self-starter, or is it hard for you to get going on a project without somebody else pushing you? How you view yourself can have a surprising impact on your success.

Do you think you have the power to change your own world? How much of your life would you say was the result of luck? Your response to questions such as these can affect your ability to achieve your goals.

The locus of control

In 1954, American psychologist Julian Rotter originated a now-famous theory known as the "locus of control." In Rotter's own words, this is the degree to which people expect that "an outcome of their behavior is contingent on their own behavior or personal characteristics." Put simply, it concerns where you think the control over your circumstances resides: either within you, or in external factors.

Many studies have found that people with a high *internal* locus of control tend to be more successful, perform better, enjoy their work more, are better able to delay gratification, and are more willing to challenge themselves. Believing that you can make a difference leads to higher self-esteem and stronger motivation. (Though it can also make you more judgmental,

MOTIVATION FOLLOWS ACTION

Starting something new? Take a tip from Cognitive Behavioral Therapy (CBT) expert David D. Burns: "Motivation does *not* come first, *action* does!" Sometimes the best way to get started is simply to start, and wait for the motivation to catch up with you.

INTERNAL OR EXTERNAL?

Do you have a high or low internal locus of control? See which of these statements you agree with—the more red statements you pick, the higher your internal locus of control:

- You reap what you sow.
- No matter what you do, some people just won't like you.
- I'm usually confident in my plans.
- If you're properly prepared for an interview, you stand a better chance of success.
- I often feel I don't have much control over what happens to me.
- Life is a game of chance.
- You can usually get along with everyone if you make the effort.
- You can never know how things will turn out.
- There's no point preparing, because so much depends on the interviewer's whim.
- I don't believe luck plays a big part in my life.

and likely to take failures more personally.) If, on the other hand, you find it difficult to act without someone else's encouragement or authority, you might have a relatively high *external* locus of control, and could benefit from seeking out areas where you can exert more control.

Does it help?

We can't control everything in our environment. However, a 1980 study by American psychologist S. M. Miller found that even an incorrect perception of control tends to improve well-being. When it comes to motivating yourself, developing an attitude that you are in control, even if you have private doubts, can be the best way of spurring yourself into action. To sustain motivation over time, focus on what you can control and enlist the help of others when you need to. You may find that you have more control over your world than you believed possible.

WHEN YOU CAN'T GET INTERESTED

According to Self Determination Theory (SDT), workers suffer less stress when they find their work intrinsically motivating (see pp.72–73)—that is, they enjoy it for its own sake. If, however, there's nothing intrinsically rewarding about a task, these motivating factors may help you instead:

- **External motivators.** You do it to get paid, or because it meets somebody's expectations.
- **Self-worth motivators.** There is pride in doing it well, or guilt and anxiety in doing it badly.
- **Internalizing motivators.** You try to identify with the external reasons. You might say: "I believe in what my company does, so even the small details count."

TROUBLE DECIDING?

A 2015 study of US, Israeli, and Chinese people facing career decisions investigated what factors made it easier or harder for them to make up their minds. Across all these cultures, the most successful decision-makers showed:

- An internal locus of control.
- Less procrastination.
- Greater speed when it came to making decisions.
- Less dependence on others.

They also found that most people benefited from more comprehensive information gathering (with the exception of the US volunteers) and from being less worried about pleasing others (with the exception of the Chinese volunteers).

THINKING LIKE A WINNER

TEN BELIEFS TO MOTIVATE YOU

What goes on in the minds of highly successful people? If you want to stay focused and persistent in the face of challenges, try adopting some of these helpful, positive mindsets.

Success comes in many different forms, and we all have our own ideas about what achievement looks like. Studies show, however, that the world's high achievers have a similar outlook on life. If you find yourself struggling to get motivated, try out these ways of thinking and see if they get you moving again.

1 **Achievement matters more than power.** People can rise to management positions if their main goal is authority, but people who really carve out their own place in the world tend to be those who feel best about themselves when they are achieving something important. Some authority may be necessary to attain your goals and to make things happen, but it's a means, not an end in itself. The goal is to feel you've done something that is, by your own values, meaningful.

2 **It's my responsibility.** Successful people tend to have a high internal locus of control (see pp.152–153), and believe that their own efforts are what will make the difference. The focus is on doing what needs to be done and not waiting for others to encourage you or give you direction. Taking responsibility also means knowing when to ask for help.

3 **It's an opportunity, not a threat.** When a challenge comes along, top performers are more excited about the chance it offers than worried about what may happen if it goes wrong. They know that nothing worth having is easy, so difficulty is just a sign that the project is worthwhile.

4 **I'll enjoy this.** Perseverance brings its own satisfactions, and go-getters can get hooked on that feeling. Staying focused over the long term can be approached like a game, with every day that you stick to your goals feeling like a win. If you can feel playful about your efforts, you're likely to be less stressed: the sense of threat goes down, and the fun increases.

> You don't learn to walk by following rules. You **learn by doing**, and by **falling over**.
>
> **Sir Richard Branson**
> Founder, Virgin Group

43%

MORE PRODUCTIVE

The global consulting firm Hay Group found that companies with **motivated employees** were 43 percent **more productive** than workplaces with unmotivated staff.

ENGAGED WORKERS

A 2014 Gallup poll found that, while less than one third of American employees were motivated and absorbed by their work, levels of engagement were at their highest since 2000—when only 26 percent were engaged. Make it your business to identify and seek out such people—their motivation will feed into your own.

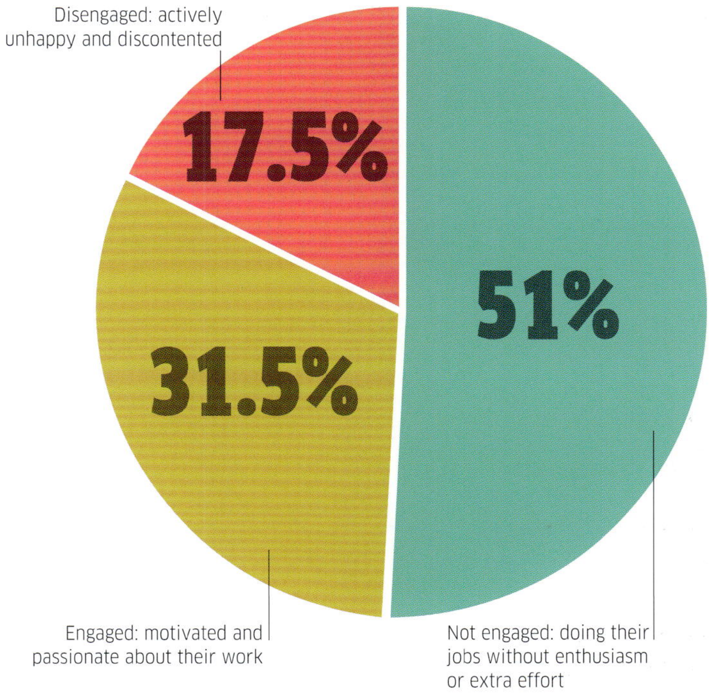

5 Talent isn't worth worrying about. The ability you're born with can set the baseline for potential success but, without practice, natural talent won't develop, just like a muscle that's not used. While there's very little we can do about the attributes we were born with, there's a great deal we can choose to do with these attributes. Even gifted people have to work on continuing to develop their skills, so it's more productive to focus on what you intend to do and learn than it is to worry about whether you're naturally "good" at it.

6 Hard work is impressive. People who excel at what they do see hard work as admirable, and dedicated people as interesting. They feel good about themselves for living their values and are willing to work hard over time.

7 Failure doesn't mean much. If something doesn't work the first few times, successful people tend to brush this off as a learning process and carry on. It takes many more setbacks before they start to consider something to be impossible.

8 Don't burn bridges. You may not like someone, but you might still have to work with them in the future. Even if you don't, having adversaries is not good for your reputation. It's a lot easier and less stressful to remain at least reasonably civil and be known as someone easy to collaborate with. You never know who might get to hear of your behavior, so it always pays to be professional.

9 No staying in a rut. Practice doesn't improve us if we practice the same things over and over again. What works is "deliberate practice"—that is, constantly practicing at a slightly higher level than our comfort zone.

10 What's my next step? We continually develop as we go, so your goals are likely to change as you progress. High achievers build regular feedback into their schedules and identify what to do next based on new information. Assess and update your goals as you keep learning.

BEATING PROCRASTINATION

USING YOUR TIME AND RESOURCES WELL

If you've ever thought, "I know I have to do it, but I'll just do one more thing first …," then you're familiar with procrastination. It's time to stop delaying and get down to business. Here's how to do it.

Most of us realize it's a bad idea to put things off. Indeed, studies confirm that procrastination can lead to worse academic performance; less self-care; poorer health; worse employment records; higher levels of stress, anxiety, and depression; and even increased loneliness. Given these negative effects, you might think we would be motivated to avoid procrastination at all costs. However, feeling bad about yourself is likely to make you procrastinate *more*, not less. A better strategy is to tackle the practical causes of procrastination.

Why do we do it?

Psychology defines procrastination as a "self-regulatory failure," which means that we find ourselves unable to manage our own behavior, even when we know we should. The true nature of this behavior is clear from the word's Latin origins: "pro," meaning "put forward," and "crastinus," meaning tomorrow. Its causes are complex and still being studied, but various factors contributing to procrastination are known, and are as follows:

> Time is what we **want most**, but what, alas! we **use worst**.
>
> **William Penn**
> English Quaker and founder of the colony of Pennsylvania

DOUBTS GETTING YOU DOWN?

If you're delaying getting started on something because you don't feel up to the task, try a technique discovered in a 2010 study published in the *Journal of Experimental Social Psychology*. The researchers found that uncertain people found themselves feeling more confident if, when they expressed their doubts, they shook their heads at the same time, as if disagreeing with their own words. If you make your gestures "doubt your doubts," your mood may follow.

THE PROCRASTINATION CYCLE

When we tell ourselves we'll do something later, we're hoping that we'll feel more motivated when the time comes. The trouble is, the stress of leaving tasks undone tends to create a negative cycle. If you think you'll feel more like doing something tomorrow, you're probably wrong, so you might as well start now.

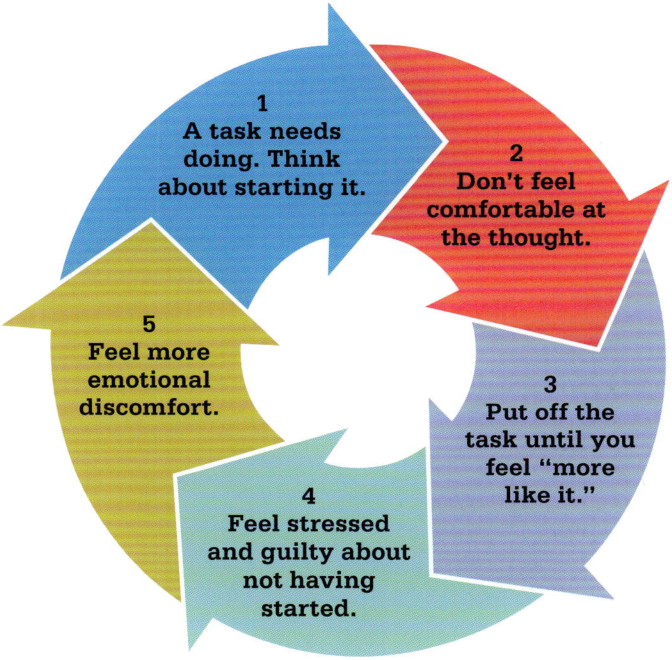

- Some of it is innate. A 2003 twin study, for example, found that about 22 percent of the cause was likely to be genetic.
- The appeal of a task plays a big factor. This is known as "task aversion": the more aversive or unpleasant something is, the more likely we are to put it off.
- On the Big Five personality test (see pp.18–19), people who rate high for neuroticism and/or low for conscientiousness tend to procrastinate more.
- Perfectionism, fear of failure, and anxiety about being judged all correlate with procrastination. This suggests that some of us delay because the stress of a task not done is less frightening than the stress of doing it and being found inadequate.
- Impulsiveness goes hand in hand with procrastination. If we struggle to control our passing desires, the desire to do something more fun than the task at hand is overwhelming.
- We can "self-handicap." People who believe their actions don't have much power to change things are likely to focus on trying to manage their feelings about a situation instead of acting to try and change it.
- Just as procrastination can lead to depression, so people prone to depression procrastinate more—largely because depression saps our energy.

What can you do about it?

If you tend to put things off, what's the solution? The first thing to realize is that false logic has a role to play in procrastination. According to American psychologist Joseph Ferrari, we are subject to two false assumptions:

1 **We delay taking action** because we feel we're in the "wrong mood."

2 **We assume that (somehow) our mood** will spontaneously improve in the near future.

In fact, our mood for doing the task is only likely to grow less favorable the more we put it off (see "The procrastination cycle," above), as guilt makes us less productive. More effective methods include:

»

- **Get someone else to set you a deadline.** A study by Israeli-American psychologist Dan Ariely found that, given three passages of text to proofread, students with external deadlines consistently outperformed those who were allowed to manage their own time—especially when they were given a single end date for all three passages, as this added a further level of constraint to the deadline. Set a deadline and share it with someone to hold yourself accountable.
- **Trick yourself.** A study by Ferrari (see p157) found that students who put off a "cognitive evaluation" puzzle did this exact same puzzle just as readily as everyone else when they were told it was a game. You can do this particularly well if you use the technique of "impulse pairing" or "fusing." This means you blend a necessary task with the kind of fun task that you might otherwise be tempted to do instead—for instance, if you avoid studying to socialize, create a study group so you can do both at once.
- **Limit your distractions.** If you just can't do your tax return when you could browse the internet instead, put a temporary blocker on your computer or phone. If you know you always end up doing housework instead of studying for that examination, go somewhere else, such as a library, to focus your attention.
- **Find the challenge.** A 1995 US study observed that difficulty isn't as much of a deterrent as we might think. In fact, tasks that are too easy are boring, and boredom is off-putting. We find it more satisfying to do something that feels like an achievement, so if something is simple but necessary, try to add a level of challenge to it so that it feels more meaningful.
- **Find your role models.** A 1997 study by American psychologist Albert Bandura found there were two particularly effective ways of making a task more achievable. The first is "modeling," or learning by example, because it helps to observe other people completing tasks. The second method, "performance accomplishments," involves knowing your own track record of success and reminding yourself that you've finished things in the past. Even if they're small things, make a note of them so you can see yourself as a finisher, not a delayer.
- **Remember you're a learner.** Psychologists talk of "learned industriousness," meaning that you can teach yourself good habits. The way to do this is to give yourself rewards, which don't have to be substantial—a 2000 study published in the *Journal of Applied Behavior Analysis* found that pennies

CONCRETE THINKING

A 2008 study published in *Psychological Science* found that people are more efficient when they think in practical terms. Participants were split into two groups:

1
Abstract construal
The first group was shown an image of Impressionist painter Georges Seurat's *La Parade*, and told it was a good example of color evoking emotion and harmony.

2
Concrete construal
The second group was shown a close-up detail from the same painting, and told it showed Seurat's use of pointillism (painting with dots) to build an image with constrasting colors.

They were then asked to complete a survey and return it within three weeks. The "abstract construal" group took an average of 20.5 days to complete it–right up to the deadline–while the "concrete construal" group averaged 12.5 days. Just being encouraged to think in specific terms shortened the response time.

GROWING OUT OF IT?

Who procrastinates the most? According to a 2015 German study, people who are 14–29 years old score highest, but the numbers don't fall substantially with increased maturity. If you're young now, you'd be well advised to start improving your habits right away, as good timekeeping doesn't develop automatically.

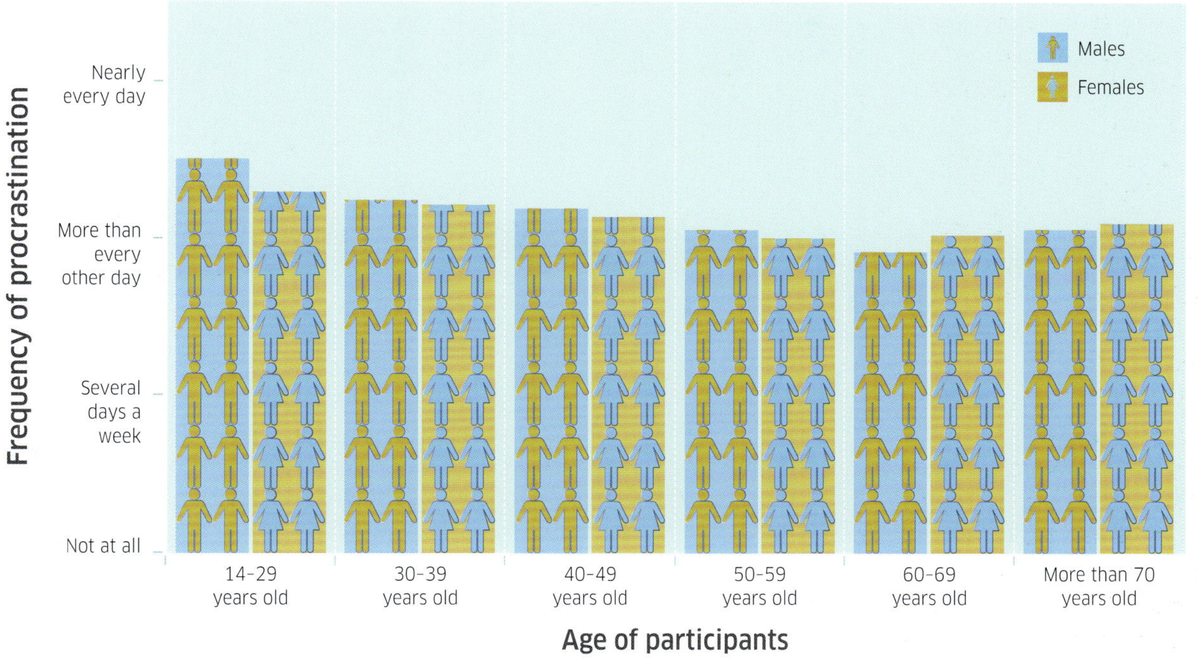

and praise did the job. The important point about the rewards is that they must meet two criteria. First, they must be reliable, so don't skip rewarding yourself. Second, they have to come immediately after you have completed the task—after all, your brain is primarily focused on the short term.

All of us are guilty of the occasional delay, but for some of us it's a more serious problem. The best solution is not to feel ashamed, as this will only increase your stress levels, and research shows that the more stressed we feel about a task, the less likely we are to get started. Instead, try to see each task as a challenge that will make you feel good when you finish it. Even a moderately efficient working pattern can lead to substantial success.

15–20%

FOREVER DELAYED

A 1996 US study found that 15–20 percent of adults describe themselves as **chronic procrastinators**.

1/3

LOST IN TIME

In a 2007 study, American students estimated that procrastination consumed as much as **one third of their day**.

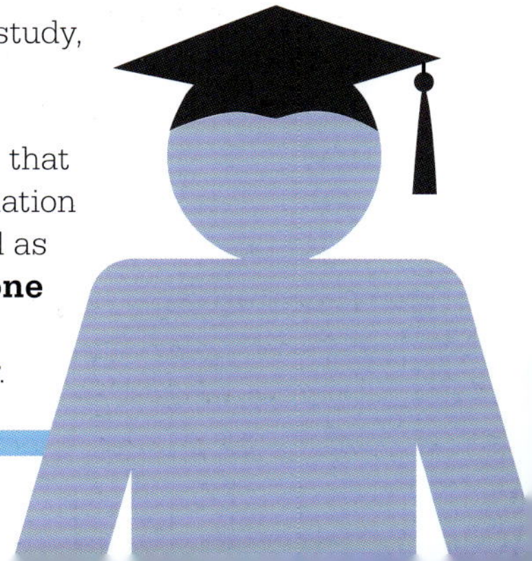

THE PERILS OF PERFECTIONISM

WHEN IT'S WRONG TO BE RIGHT

If you're set on success, you're likely to have high standards. This can be a good thing, but if you're afraid to be anything less than perfect, those standards may end up being more of a hindrance than a help.

Does everything have to be exactly right before it's acceptable to you? Do you struggle to forgive yourself for small mistakes and flaws? While we might think that success means being the best we can be, being set on perfection can actually undermine our performance.

The origins of perfectionism

Why are some of us so worried about getting everything right? A series of studies in the early 2000s found that one factor was our upbringing. People raised by authoritative parents—who set and enforced reasonable rules, but were open to their children's feelings—tend to be comfortable with things being "good enough." People raised by authoritarian parents, on the other hand—who enforced rules rigidly, and emphasized and rewarded obedience—experience a more anxious childhood and are more likely to become adults afraid of making mistakes. There are two types of perfectionism: "adaptive," which works for the situation, and "maladaptive," which undermines us. Children of authoritarian parents are affected by both types.

Our childhoods are not the whole story, of course: some of us are born more worried than others, and life experiences influence us, too.

> The **perfect** is the enemy of the **good**.
>
> **Voltaire**
> Writer, historian, and philosopher

Whatever the cause, studies show that perfectionism doesn't help us with our strategies for success.

Undermining yourself

When faced with a problem, we need a solution. The trouble with perfectionism is that it can make us worse at finding it. Numerous studies have found that perfectionists are less proactive when faced with stress. People whose standards are high but realistic tend to engage in "active coping"—they try to deal with the problem or reduce its impact. Perfectionists who are ruled by a fear of mistakes, on the other hand, tend to resort to "avoidant coping"—trying to ignore the problem or deny its impact. As a result, their problems are more likely to persist.

What can I do about it?

If you are feeling under pressure to be perfect, try to find the root cause (see "Where does the pressure come from?," opposite). Also, keep in mind the following pieces of advice:

AVOIDING PERFECTIONIST PITFALLS

Maladaptive perfectionism, which means being unable to tolerate even minor flaws, can lead to a host of problems. Developing a more forgiving approach creates several advantages:

- More realistic standards (both for yourself and for others)
- Reducing procrastination
- Lower stress levels
- Greater decisiveness
- Higher self-confidence
- More comfort with ambiguity
- Less vulnerability to obsessiveness
- Finding it easier to make career choices

- Avoid black-and-white thinking: between "perfect" and "terrible" there's a lot of middle ground.
- Decisions aren't irreversible. You can leave a job you don't like, or change a project or plan that isn't working.
- Change your point of comparison. If you compare an adequate solution to the idea of a "perfect" one, you may find yourself unable to act. Instead, compare your adequate solution to having no solution at all.

The adage "nobody's perfect" is true. Instead of being a failure, it turns out that being "good enough" can in fact be the most efficient way to get ahead.

WHERE DOES THE PRESSURE COME FROM?

According to a 2014 Canadian study, we can define perfectionism as a combination of two basic factors–stress from social pressure, and stress from the pressure we place on ourselves. If you tend to be hard on yourself, it can be helpful to ask where the pressure is coming from: that way, you have a clearer picture of what areas in your life might benefit from a more tolerant attitude.

	Low social pressure	High social pressure
Low self-imposed perfectionism	"People are not expecting me to be perfect and I do not strive to attain perfection."	"People are putting pressure on me to be perfect but I don't personally decide to aim for perfection."
High self-imposed perfectionism	"I am the one who personally decides to aim for perfection."	"People are putting pressure on me to be perfect and I personally decide to aim for perfection."

SEEING YOUR WAY
VISUALIZATION TECHNIQUES

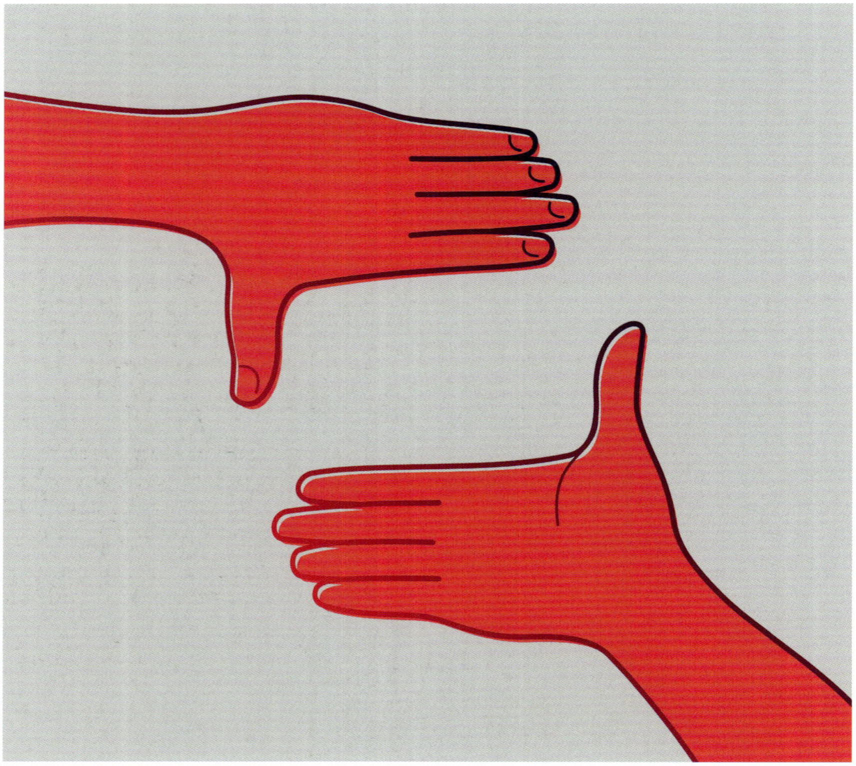

You may be familiar with the idea that visualizing what you want can make it more likely that you'll get it. What does the science say about this idea, and how can you apply it to achieving your goals?

The idea that we can think our way to success is an appealing one. Studies show that visualization can help—but we need to be cautious and precise about how we do it. Picturing success isn't a magic charm; the most it can do is help motivate us to act. Some kinds of visualization can even make us *less* motivated.

A word to the wise

There's an important difference between action-oriented visualization and fantasizing. Studies have found that people who fantasize a lot about their dream job—which you could call "visualizing" it—tend to submit fewer applications, get fewer job offers, and have a lower income than those who don't. The reason is that these dreams can drain our motivation. A 2011 US study by psychologists Heather Kappes and Gabriele Oettingen found that participants who were encouraged to "mentally indulge in a desired future" were far less proactive than those who were told to consider the potential tasks and challenges they might meet along the way.

When we imagine that we have something we want, we trick our brains into feeling as though we already have it. This may be pleasant, but it doesn't motivate us.

The right picture

If we want to use our thoughts to propel us toward a brighter future, we need to focus on the *process*, not the outcome. Mental images are, as British psychologists Martin Conway, Kevin Meares, and Sally Standart put it, a "language of goals," and we need to send ourselves the right message. This means using our imaginations as a kind of simulator for our actions, focusing not on where we want to be, but on how we'll get there.

A 2010 New Zealand study published in the *Journal of Behavioral Medicine* defined two types of mental imaging. The first type—"outcome simulation," or picturing the end result—was found to increase desire, but didn't translate into action. The second type—"process simulation," or picturing working toward the outcome—was more likely to produce "goal-directed behaviors."

When we picture what we need to do to achieve a goal, we are mentally anticipating the potential challenges, which means we'll be less daunted by them when they come along. If you can keep your focus on the right things, it may help you to take the right actions.

THE PLANNING FALLACY

When we plan a project, we often underestimate the resources we will need to complete it–such as time and money. Picturing the work we'll need to do along the way (known as "process simulation"), instead of imagining the end result, can help us be more realistic. In a 1998 study at the University of California, students performed better in exams when they had included process simulation in their preparations.

FANTASY VERSUS SIMULATION

When visualizing success, we need to see ourselves as problem-solvers rather than dreamers. Suppose, for example, you want to run a marathon to raise money for charity. The different thought processes shown below can have a very different impact on your motivation:

Fantasy: picturing the end result

Mental picture: "I'm a successful athlete and a charitable person."

You enjoy the positive feelings that go with that self-image.

You feel like you've accomplished something.

Real-life event: "It's raining. Shall I train today?"

Outcome: "Maybe I'll put it off. It's not like I'm a bad person, after all."

Simulation: picturing how you'll get there

Mental picture: "I'm going to jog every morning, come rain or shine."

You rehearse the challenges you'll face.

You prepare yourself for moments when you'll need to push yourself.

Real-life event: "It's raining. Shall I train today?"

Outcome: "OK, I planned for days like this. Where's my waterproof jacket?"

CATCHING A MOOD

THE POWER OF EMOTIONAL CONTAGION

Feeling happy isn't just pleasant; it can also influence how other people react to you. How can you tap into the energy of your positive emotions to achieve what's important to you?

Human beings are social creatures and, as such, we tend to notice each other's moods. This goes further than simply being able to tell whether someone is happy or sad: we actually experience an unconscious echo of our companions' emotions.

Mood on the job

This echoing is known as "emotional contagion," and it can affect how people respond to us. In a 2011 study conducted in China, actors were hired to serve in a restaurant and were asked to follow either "positive" or "negative" scripts. Positive scripts included things like, "I just received a bonus, so I'm feeling happy," while negative scripts included, "I'm frustrated with my manager." Customers were more forgiving about poor service if they believed that their waitress was in a good mood. Happy people feel like better company, and so we're more likely to excuse their mistakes.

The halo effect

A psychological concept known as the "halo effect" states that we tend to make inferences about other people's actions and behavior based on limited information. If we have a positive impression of them, we see them with a kind of halo that casts everything else in a more positive light. A 1994 US study confirmed that being in a happier mood at work could translate into better appraisals and higher pay. Happy and warm people were seen as competent and trustworthy. When it comes to success, we benefit from being seen as a cheerful person.

SETTING THE LEVEL

Is emotional contagion (see “Mood on the job,” opposite) just about acting happy or sad? Psychologists R. J. Larsen and E. E. Diener developed a chart (below) that captures the relationships among our moods and our levels of “activation.” We can be influenced by each other’s positive or negative moods, but also by each other’s apparent levels of activation. Put simply, activation is how geared up for action your nervous system is, whether that action is “fight or flight” or joyous engagement. Research has found that it’s easier to catch an “activated” mood (whether pleasant or unpleasant) than a “deactivated” one, probably because activated people are more demonstrative. If you want to be emotionally influential, it’s a good idea to make sure you’re rested and healthy enough to keep your energy levels up. Use the chart below to identify your own mood and activation levels as well as those of the person you’d like to influence. This will help you to model the mood you want them to “catch.”

MOOD AND ACTIVATION LEVELS

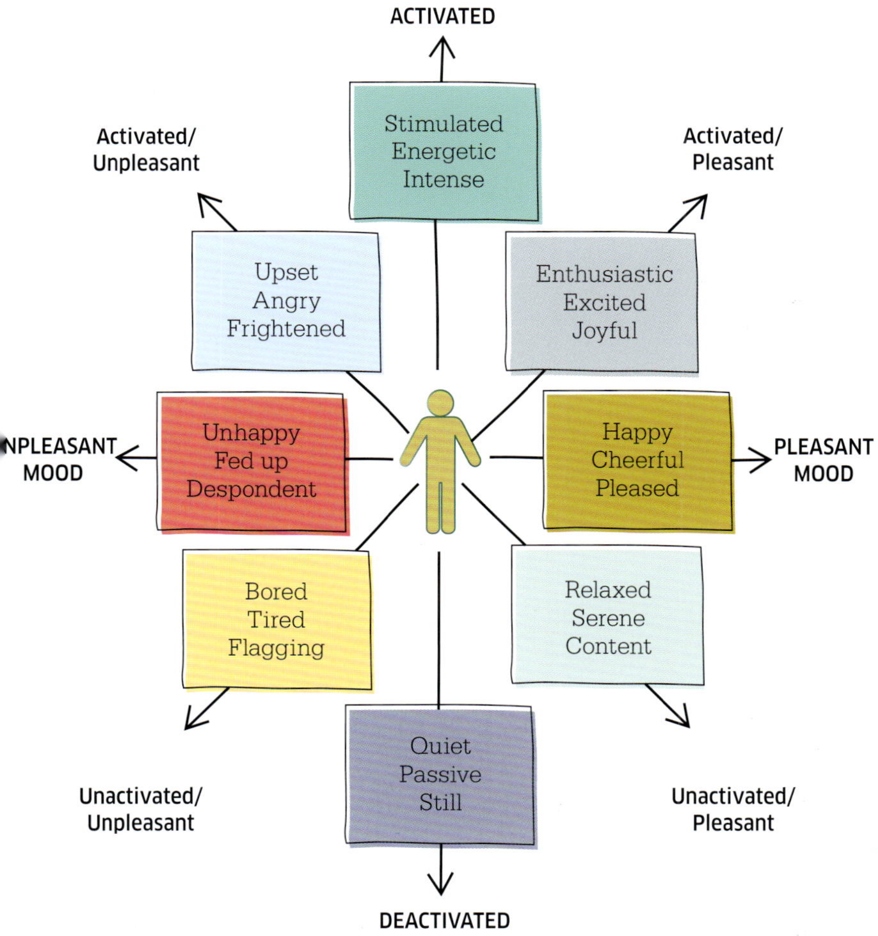

CONSCIOUS AND SUBCONSCIOUS

Emotional contagion (see “Mood on the job,” opposite) happens on two levels, the “conscious” and the “subconscious.” You have more control over your conscious reactions, but when trying to influence other people—or resist their influence on you—try to be aware of the subconscious signals being sent. If you can assume a physical posture that reflects the mood you want to project, it may help you set the right emotional tone. To make emotional contagion work for you, follow these steps for conscious emotional contagion, and also be aware of the stages of subconscious emotional contagion.

Conscious emotional contagion:

1 Try to figure out what the other person is feeling.

2 Use this as information about which emotional tone would suit the situation.

3 Assume the mood that seems most appropriate.

Subconscious emotional contagion:

1 See another person’s expression and body language.

2 Automatically mimic them.

3 Start to feel the emotions you’re displaying.

FINDING FLOW

A STATE OF ENGAGED FOCUS

For a task to be truly satisfying, we need to be able to enjoy the work for its own sake, instead of just taking pleasure in the end results. For that to happen, we need to become fully absorbed in what we do.

Flow is an important part of any kind of success. It's a word that's often used in positive psychology (see pp.48–51) and it describes a state of complete engagement with a task, to the point that you lose track of time and want to continue working on the task as long as possible. If you've ever forgotten to eat lunch because you were so absorbed in finishing an essay, or hit a sweet spot on the running track where you were aware of nothing but the rhythm of your feet, you've experienced a "flow" state.

These experiences are intrinsically rewarding: we enjoy them whether or not they bring us any other benefits. A task that allows us to be in a state of flow brings us clarity and feelings of accomplishment, whether it's great or small.

How do we find flow?

A key to creating flow states is to find tasks that let us feel what Robert J. Vallerand, Professor of Psychology at the Université du Québec à Montréal, calls "harmonious passion." This comes when we engage with tasks that we feel are a part of us, as opposed to what Vallerand terms "obsessive passion," which happens when we fear we will suffer or be punished if we don't complete a task that we don't really identify with.

Suppose you teach mathematics, and you not only find your work interesting but consider it central to who you are. In this situation, you're not just someone who teaches. In your self-concept (who you believe yourself to be), a very important part of your personal definition is that you are "a teacher." Under the right circumstances (see "Harmonious passion," opposite), tasks that you enjoy and that fully engage your attention when teaching, will usually lead to a state of flow. The same is true no matter what our vocation: flow comes from tasks that we are passionate about and that align with our values and identity.

Conscious control

Of course, sometimes we need to do everyday tasks that aren't central to our identity. In these situations, we're required to use "attention" as opposed to "absorption" (see "Quality or quantity?," opposite). A 2011 international study for the *Journal of Management Studies* found that, perhaps predictably, workers who felt a harmonious passion for their jobs were more likely to become absorbed in them, and also found it easier to pay attention. The unexpected news, however, was that people who didn't feel this harmonious passion were nevertheless capable of both absorption and attention—they just needed to approach their jobs in a flexible way so that they could still create a flow state for themselves. This might involve taking ownership of a task, or fostering an interest in it.

When it comes to managing your focus—whether it's a project that you're passionate about or just a mundane task—it's useful to have some self-knowledge. What's at the core of your identity? What are your values and real interests? The more you can approach a task in this spirit, the better chance you'll have of becoming absorbed in it—and the more rewarding the experience will ultimately become.

QUALITY OR QUANTITY?

Psychologist N. P. Rothbard identifies two factors that are crucial to cognitive engagement.

1—Attention: the *quantity* of our focus. It is concerned with the amount of effort we put into keeping our minds on a task. It:

- Is under our conscious control.
- Is finite, and wanes when we grow tired.

2—Absorption: the *quality* of our focus. It is concerned with how intensely immersed we are in a task. It:

- Arises spontaneously from the right mix of circumstances.
- Is self-rewarding; we may get tired, but can still stay focused and may not notice time passing.

AN ENGAGING CHALLENGE

The concept of flow was first proposed by Hungarian psychologist Mihaly Csikszentmihalyi. According to Csikszentmihalyi, we achieve this state of contented immersion when we meet a task that's reasonably difficult–not beyond our capability, but something that stretches us and demands our full concentration. In the graph below, flow is shown as one of a number of mental states that can result from attempting a task, depending on how challenging the task is and how skilled we are.

FLOW AND OTHER MENTAL STATES

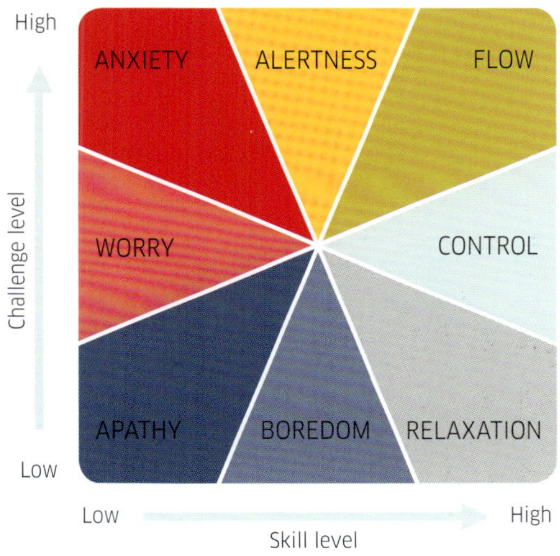

HARMONIOUS PASSION

Psychologist Robert J. Vallerand observes that feeling a harmonious passion for a task–that is, our interest in it is deep enough to be part of our identity–can greatly improve our performance. If we feel we're doing something that reflects our feelings and values, it adds another layer of engagement, because it involves us on a deeper level.

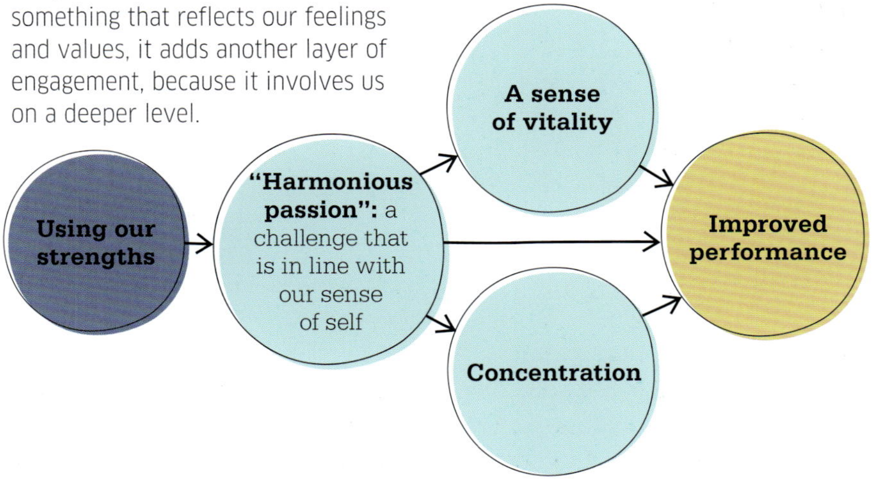

ENJOYMENT APPEARS AT THE BOUNDARY BETWEEN BOREDOM AND ANXIETY, WHEN THE CHALLENGES ARE JUST BALANCED WITH THE PERSON'S CAPACITY TO ACT.

MIHALY CSIKSZENTMIHALYI, PSYCHOLOGIST AND PIONEER OF THE CONCEPT OF "FLOW"

PERSONAL COST CONTROL

WHEN TO HOLD ON, WHEN TO LET GO

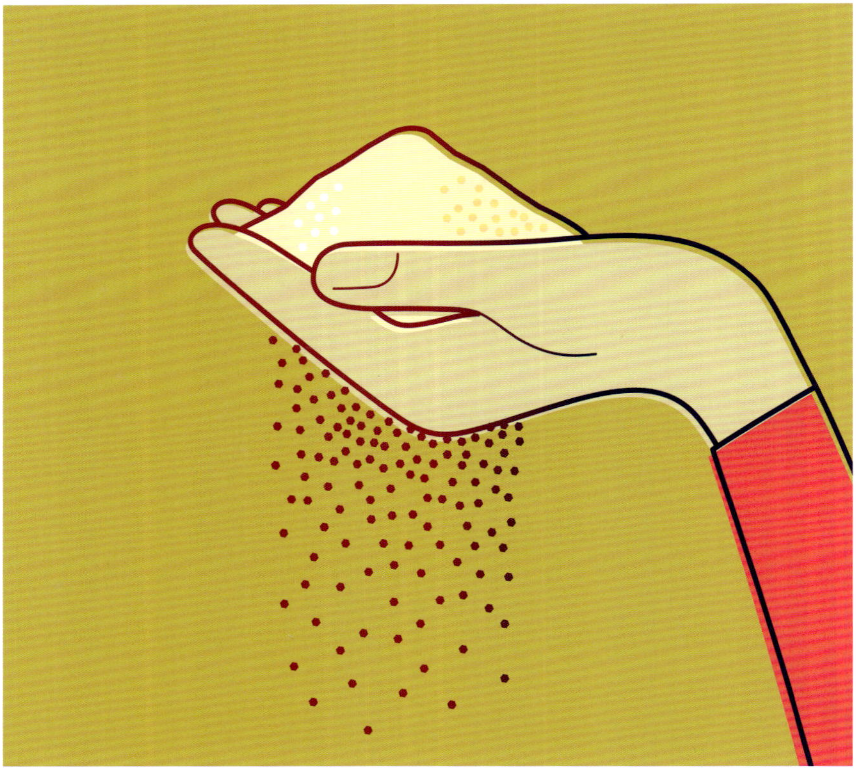

Achieving our goals often involves choosing between competing priorities. When we decide to give something up, how do we deal with the feelings of discomfort this can cause?

Have you ever held onto an item of clothing that no longer fits, or a bond that's fallen in value? You know you'd like to have more space in your wardrobe or a better investment, but somehow the pain of losing what you have, even if it's not useful, seems to outweigh the clear benefits. This is what psychologists call loss aversion.

The endowment effect

In 1990, economist Richard Thaler joined psychologist Daniel Kahneman and behavioral economist Jack L. Knetsch in an experiment. Half of the study's participants were given coffee cups, and the other half only shown them. The two groups were then asked how much they would be prepared to either sell or buy the cups for respectively. The "owners" wanted about twice as much for their cups as the viewers were willing to pay. This is the endowment effect: simply owning something, even briefly, makes us put a higher value on it. It seems we dislike giving things up simply because it's a sacrifice, even if we wouldn't otherwise value the thing we're giving up very highly.

Ownership and self-image

Why do we sometimes act in an irrational way? In a 2013 study by American psychologists Sara Loughran Dommer and Vanitha Swaminathan, one group of volunteers was asked to describe a "social self-threat" situation, such as a romantic rejection, while a second group was asked to describe an average day. Both groups were then given a relatively worthless item—a ballpoint pen—before being asked to part with it. The study found that people were less willing to give up the pen after they experienced social self-threat situations. When we own something, we start to incorporate it into our sense of who we are—and the more threatened we feel, the less willing we are to forfeit even unimportant things.

If you need to give something up, try to bolster your sense of identity first. Remind yourself that self-worth doesn't depend on particular possessions or relationships—it's inherent, and the more confidence you have in yourself, the easier it can be to let things go.

LOSS AVERSION

A knowledge of loss aversion can be useful when you are seeking to influence others. When making pitches, marketing psychologists propose the following approaches:

- Suggest your audience already possesses something desirable, and that your product will stop them from losing it. (For example, "You could lose hundreds of clients if you don't...")
- Encourage them to imagine themselves owning or using your product. ("Picture yourself sitting behind the wheel...")
- Let them "own" your product for a limited time, such as a free sample or a trial period. That way, not buying it once the trial ends would mean giving it up.

WEIGHING THE CHOICES

When you have to decide what to give up, it can be useful to think in terms of different types of goals. A 1997 study published in the *Journal of Personality and Social Psychology* suggests weighing four different types of goals when trying to make a decision. Suppose you're trying to decide whether to cancel date night with your partner in order to get some extra work done. Assessing the situation in the context of the following types of goals may help you settle whether, in this instance, your partner or your work should take priority.

Type of goal	Should I go out for dinner...	...or should I work late?
Task-specific goal: meeting a specific short-term goal.	I have planned a romantic evening, which I know would please my partner.	I have a deadline to meet; that's my specific task. Staying late would help.
Situation-specific goal: the overall purpose of a particular activity.	I want to be a good partner. Canceling dinner could be seen as me not caring about our relationship.	I want to impress my boss so I stand a better chance of promotion next year.
Personal goal: an individual aspiration that transcends particular situations.	I want a loving relationship. I know that means acting in a thoughtful and caring way.	I want to do well at work. Can I do that without putting in the work tonight?
Personal values and images of your ideal future self: ideas of who, in the long term, you want to be.	Some day I'd like to get married and have a family. I need to demonstrate that I'm a reliable partner.	I'd like to be seen as the best candidate for the next promotion opportunity. I need to sustain a good professional reputation for that to happen.

YOUR EVOLVING NETWORK

MAINTAINING A VARIETY OF RELATIONSHIPS

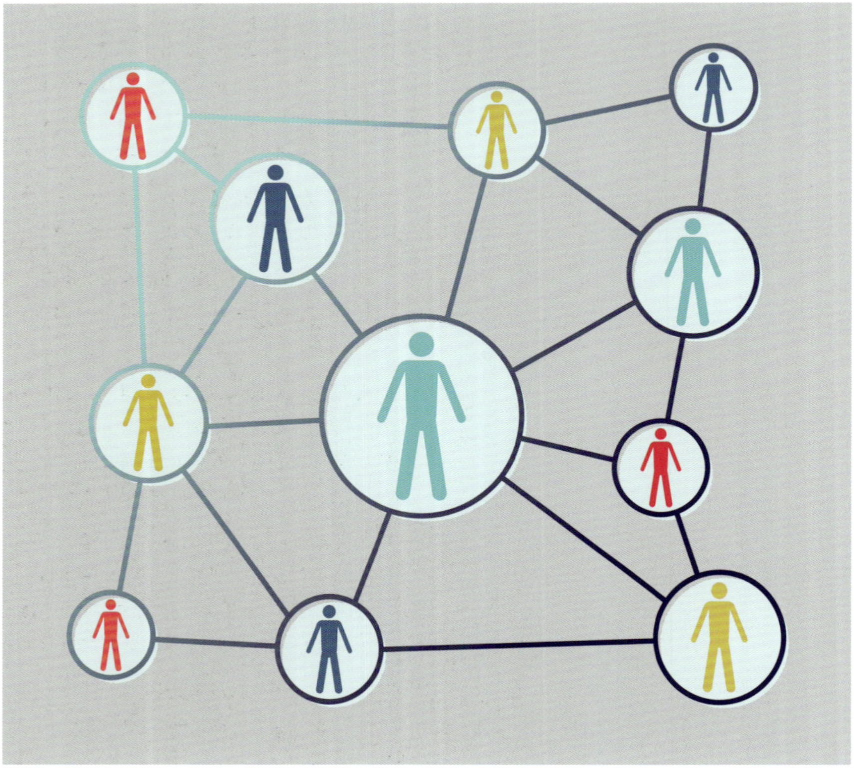

The effort you put into networking will pay dividends. Think of it as building a community of people you can rely on, learn from, and share ideas with over time. The key is to foster relationships with a wide range of people.

The ties within our communities can be a strong support to us. But when it comes to networking, do you prefer to align yourself with people based on your feelings toward them, or an assessment of what they can do for you? A 2008 American study found that some people are "affect-based"—that is, they're led by their feelings and are bonded to others by empathy, rapport, and self-disclosure. On the other hand, "cognition-led" thinkers are guided by rational calculation and prefer people who offer them tangible benefits, such as career guidance and task-specific advice. The researchers concluded that some people value friendliness more than practical help, while for others it is the reverse. When getting along with your colleagues and friends, it's useful to know which is which.

The strength of weak ties

"Weak ties" refers to the connections we have with people with whom we are on good terms but don't see often—such as friends of friends, people we meet at conferences, and old colleagues. Such contacts are still worth cultivating: sociologist Mark Granovetter, researching randomly selected professionals, discovered that the majority had found their job through people they saw only rarely. Granovetter deduced that such connections don't overlap our social circles much, and so they can introduce us to new people and opportunities: those who may not seem to have much influence on your prospects now may make the most difference in the future.

CLOSE-KNIT OR DISTANT

A 2004 Italian and American study analyzed group dynamics in the Italian television industry—a field that calls for both creative and technical expertise—to examine which sorts of teams were the most effective. They found that when it came to completing tasks, groups with a moderate level of closeness were the least productive, as they were interconnected enough to be insular, but not close enough for the members to have a profound mutual understanding.

Low level of closeness

- Variety
- Innovation
- Entrepreneurship
- Freedom to differ

Moderate level of closeness

- Lack of fresh ideas
- Creative stagnation
- "Groupthink"
- Lower productivity

High level of closeness

- Trust
- Mutual support
- Efficient habits are self-reinforcing

CONNECTING OTHERS

Silicon Valley entrepreneur Adam Rifkin argues that most of us think of our network as a series of spokes, like a bicycle wheel, with ourselves in the center. Instead, we should conceive of ourselves as part of a community: connecting people to each other still places us in the center of that community, even if we aren't particularly connected to each individual. This broadens the depth and size of our network, and by empowering others, we benefit in the long run too.

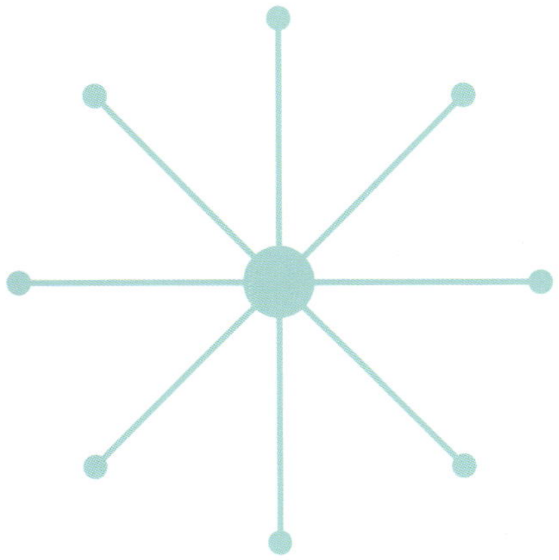

Hub and spoke network

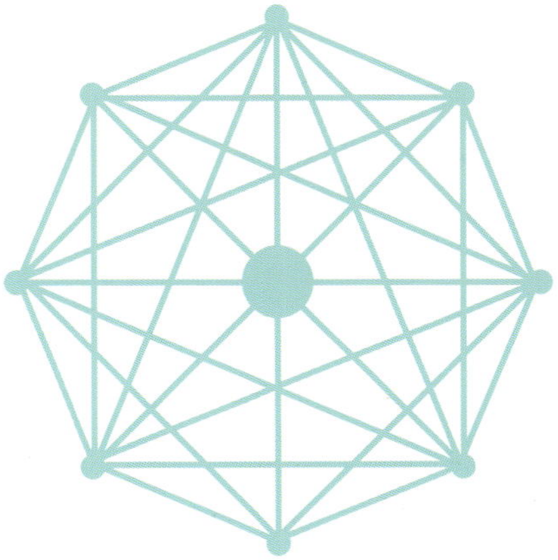

Community network

HOW TO NETWORK

American management consultant and entrepreneur Ken Morse offers these eight tips for successful networking at an event:

1 **Do your research.** If information is available about who will be present, read it, and see if you know anyone in your network who could help you make a connection to these people.

2 **Perfect a short speech.** This is your "elevator pitch": be able to say what you can offer people in one or two sentences.

3 **Show up early.** This is an opportunity to meet the host.

4 **Act with confidence.** Take the initiative by introducing yourself to others.

5 **Hang around by the food.** Blocking the bar will irritate people, but food boosts people's mood and makes them friendlier.

6 **Approach speakers before their talk.** Afterwards people will be clustering around them and it will be hard to get their attention.

7 **Ask for introductions.** If you know someone with credibility (see pp.200–201), being presented by them makes you look credible too.

8 **Focus on other people.** Ask questions. People enjoy sharing their opinions and perspectives, so listen closely, and make space for conversations to flourish.

BUILDING YOUR SOCIAL CAPITAL

GIVE YOURSELF AN EDGE

Positive relationships are good for our emotional health, but there's more to it than that. A dynamic network is also one of the center points of a productive community. This is social capital, and you can help create it.

The concept of "social capital" was first coined by author Lyda Judson Hanifan in 1916. The term refers to the fact that connections within the broader community enrich life both for the individual member and for the group as a whole. The idea enjoyed a revival in the popular consciousness when American academic Robert D. Putnam published his 2000 book *Bowling Alone: The Collapse and Revival of American Community*, and has since been taken up by promoters as influential as Bill Clinton, George W. Bush, and the World Bank.

Working together

World Bank social scientist Michael Woolcock describes three kinds of social capital:

1 **Bonding.** This means ties between people in similar situations, such as family, close friends, and neighbors.

2 **Bridging.** This is similar to the concept of "weak ties" (see pp.172–173): connections between people who are fairly alike but not especially intimate, such as casual friends and ex-colleagues.

3 **Linking.** This is based on connecting people who are in different situations and do not know each other: reaching out to, and sharing resources with, other communities.

The most productive scenario is a healthy mix of all three. Bonding social capital is supportive and reciprocal, and studies find that it is often the source of the most reliable support. On its own, however, it can lend itself to insularity and "us-versus-them" thinking. Bridging social capital allows us to fill gaps in our resources,

BENEFICIAL CONTACT

A 1998 American study found that the most successful managers spent:

10% **more time communicating and liasing** than their counterparts; and

70% **more time** engaged in **networking activities**.

as long as we make good use of them—that is, we seek and exchange information and resources instead of simply "schmoozing" for schmoozing's sake. Linking social capital keeps us vital by bringing us into contact with new ideas and encouraging us to be generous and see the bigger picture. Combining all three allows us to have both solid support and a sense of ourselves as part of the wider human family. Building success means establishing a foundation of social capital that is both solid and diverse.

Beyond networking

Staying active in your social circles is a good way to develop social capital, but the best way to sustain it is to develop a reputation as being trustworthy (see pp.200–201). A community depends on the good faith of its members, so the more you can show yourself a dependable participant, the greater the rewards for everyone, including you.

> **Social capital**... is not simply the sum of the institutions which **underpin society**—it is also the **glue** that **holds them together**.
>
> **The World Bank, 1998**

CREATING VALUE TOGETHER

A 1988 study published in the *Academy of Management Journal* suggests we view the creation of social capital as the result of several factors. To establish good ties with people you need an established arrangement that supports this, such as regular meetings, activities, or communication (the "structural dimension"). You also need to appeal to what you share beyond these circumstances, by finding the values you have in common: even if you're very different, there will be underlying principles you all hold (the "cognitive dimension"). By spending time together and working over shared ideals, you each have an opportunity to establish yourselves as someone to be trusted (the "relational dimension"). From there, you've built the social capital to create outcomes that are greater than the sum of their parts. Use this diagram to help you foster social capital.

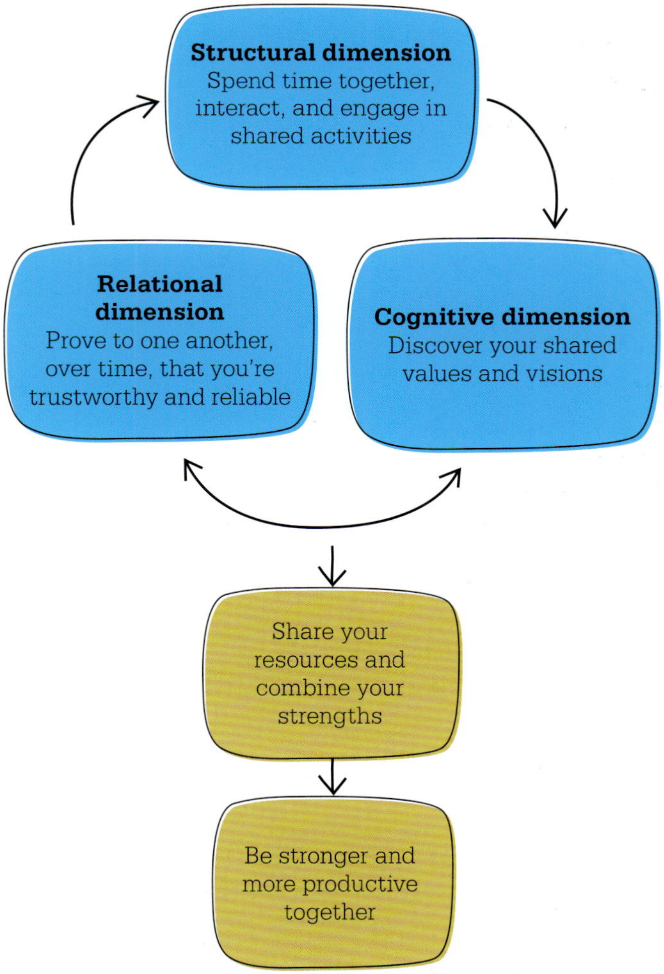

CREATIVE RESPONSES

FINDING INVENTIVE ALTERNATIVES

Creativity can be defined as the ability to reimagine existing elements in a new way. If you are inventive, you can solve problems in a unique way and find new channels to achieve your goals.

Are you an artist, a scientist, or a combination of the two? According to research, it doesn't make much difference: creativity is creativity, whatever end it serves. A 2001 American study even found that the works of Albert Einstein and Pablo Picasso were based on similar elements, such as a strong sense of aesthetics and an interest in how spaces are experienced by different observers.

You may not think of yourself as a naturally creative person, but evidence suggests that how you think about the situation makes all the difference. Using this framework, think of creativity as a mental state that everyone can access. Use the seven methods below to stimulate your imagination and curiosity.

1 IDENTIFY THE PROBLEM

When you're faced with a new challenge or problem, start by spending time in mindful observation, identifying, defining, and redefining the issue. Keep your mind as open as possible: it's easy to get used to the status quo, especially with modern life being so fast-paced and full of distractions. Instead, try to be alert to how things are and how they might be improved—and be prepared to see the big picture and consider *why* they are the way they are. Resist simple or familiar explanations and probe as deeply as you can to develop your understanding.

2 ABSORB YOURSELF

Groundwork and immersion are crucial. Don't become fixated on the idea of a sudden epiphany. There's nothing uncreative about preparation: many of the best "inspirations" are actually the result of long and serious involvement in a field of work. The more you know, the better your ideas will be, so do your research and familiarize yourself with your subject.

3 PRACTICE GENERATING IDEAS

Your neural networks are designed to run along familiar paths—your brain saves energy that way. We tend to have established categories and rules in our head, but these can be a barrier to innovation. We also have an awkward tendency to play it safe the more stress we're under: research shows that volunteers pressured to be creative and given an example will, on 9 out of 10 occasions, "create" something that's a close copy of the example. The best protection against this is practice: think of new ideas regularly in low-pressure situations where it really doesn't matter if they're useless. That way, you can strengthen your creative muscles in a comfortable environment, and build your confidence in the fact that you can create new options and alternatives. We're creatures of habit, so make a habit of thinking outside the box.

4 CROSS-POLLINATE IDEAS

Combining ideas and opinions is something that comes naturally to us: you may have heard someone say that a situation or concept is like, "such-and-such meets such-and-such." When seeking new solutions, put different concepts and solutions together and see whether they generate any chemistry. If they do, pursue this path and see where it takes you.

5 LET IT INCUBATE

When you have an idea, you don't have to leap into action and develop it right away. You might wish to seize the moment, of course, but the creative process also runs on rest periods (see p.178), so letting an idea ferment for a while can often improve it. Allow your subconscious some time to enrich things.

6 EVALUATE AND SELECT

Being creative involves vetting your ideas. Which ideas have a good benefit-to-risk ratio? Which ones feel worth the energy it will take to carry them out? Which best reflect your values and aspirations? Good support and a chance to discuss your plans in a safe environment can be particularly useful at this point.

7 TEST AND IMPLEMENT

There's no point testing the plot of an unwritten novel or the rough sketch of a new kind of engine, because your idea has to be at least at the first draft or prototype stage before anyone can have an informed opinion about it. However, once you have something tangible to show for your work, test it as soon as you can. Every creative endeavor involves uncertainty and the chance of failure, and discovering and correcting mistakes early on is much better for your confidence than detecting a flaw when you're a long way down the line. Try it out while it's still not polished—it's a good way to get around performance anxiety because at this point, no one expects perfection.

> The most **exciting phrase to hear** in science, the one that **heralds new discoveries**, is not "Eureka" but "That's funny [curious]..."
>
> **Isaac Asimov**
> Author and biochemist

Balance your mental space
Brain scans show that there are two major neurological states associated with creativity:

1 **A relaxed, quiescent state**, similar to dreaming. This is when you are feeling inspired and ideas are starting to form.

2 **An energetic, active state** in which you elaborate on the idea you've "dreamed up" and put it into practice.

Studies show that highly creative people are good at switching between these two states. Forcing yourself to create is likely to deny you the calm moments when the inspiration can incubate. Don't strain yourself: rest periods are part of the creative process.

Forget the "lone genius"
There may be times when you need periods of peace and quiet to work on your ideas, but getting others' ideas and perspectives can accelerate the creative process in ways you never imagined. The idea of the solitary intellectual pioneer is something of a myth. Numerous studies confirm that creativity is influenced by our social and cultural context, and even some of the greatest minds in history, including Albert Einstein and Charles Darwin, were working with collaborative teams when they made their breakthroughs. History may credit the lead scientist or artist, but this isn't to say that they weren't part of a professional community. Contact with other minds keeps us challenged and supported, and that's good for creativity.

THINKING CAPS

In the 1990s, psychologist Edward de Bono developed a game to encourage creative problem-solving. If you and your team are struggling, you might try putting on his different-colored thinking caps, with each of you taking on a prescribed role as you discuss the challenge or opportunity you're facing. Don't just pretend: research shows it works best if you actually wear party hats!

Stay curious
Happiness researcher Todd Kashdan defines curiosity as a willingness to seek out new experiences and to be at ease with the ambiguous and the unpredictable. Keeping an open mind means we're always able to learn from new experiences as they come along, and tolerating uncertainty means we're more persistent when it's not clear how things will turn out. The Romantic poet John Keats described "what quality went to form a Man of Achievement" as "Negative Capability, that is when a man is capable of being in uncertainties, mysteries, doubts, without any irritable reaching after fact and reason." Don't be afraid of uncertainty: it can be the root of great work.

Be confident and persistent
The price of creativity is that sometimes things fail. According to research from the Howard Hughes Medical Institute, scientists given full creative freedom published twice

as frequently in the top journals, but also twice as frequently in less well respected journals—in other words, they had as many unsuccessful ideas as successful ones. The nature of creativity is that we move away from reliable certainties and take a chance on a possible dead end. The higher your belief in your own efficacy (see pp.102–103) and the more willing you are to accept that not everything has to be perfect (see pp.160–161), the more likely you are to free your mind and make a great imaginative leap.

SUPERHEROES

In 1985, consultants Steve Grossman and Katherine Catlin developed a game to stimulate creativity, called "Superheroes." Everyone pretends to be—and might even dress up as—superheroes such as Superman and Wonder Woman. They then describe their special powers and characters, and approach the problem in those roles. The sense of empowerment and silliness can result in surprising solutions.

> **Genius** means little more than the faculty of **perceiving** in an **unhabitual way**.
>
> **William James**
> Psychologist and philosopher

IN EVERY FIELD...

According to a 1981 study published in the *Annual Review of Psychology* journal, creative people in every domain share the following personality traits, which you may wish to cultivate in yourself:

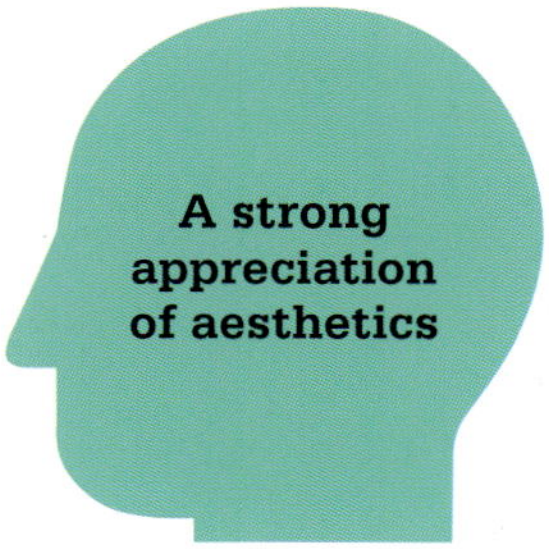

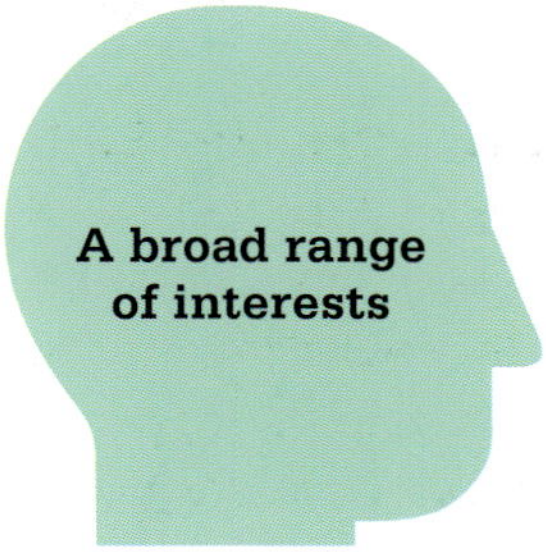

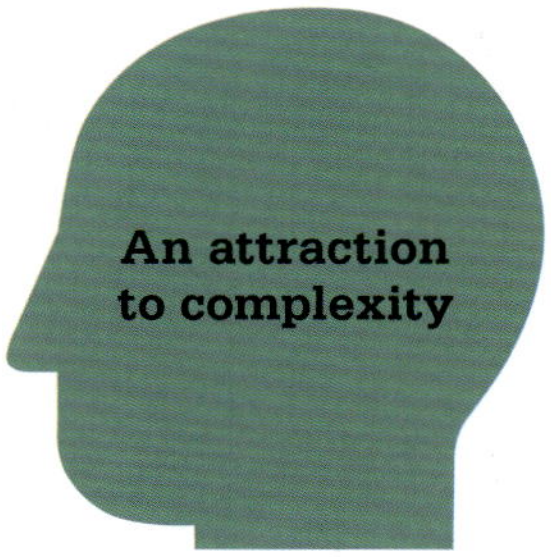

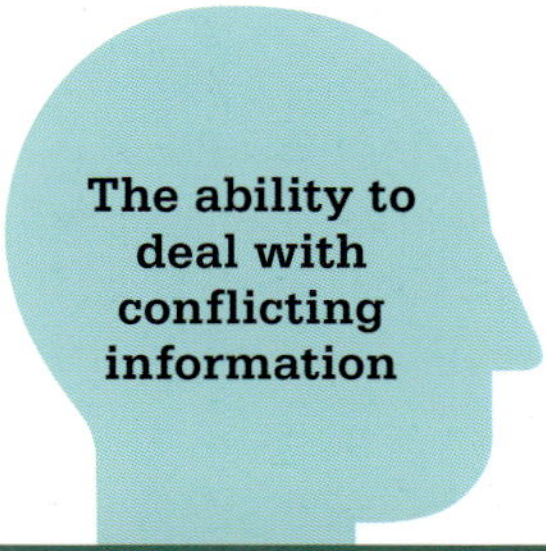

LEARNING FROM FAILURES

HOW TO KEEP AN OPEN MIND

Nobody likes the idea of falling short, but in order to keep moving forward, we need to be able to learn from our mistakes. This means being able to accept failure instead of fleeing from the discomfort it causes.

Learning from our mistakes can be critical for our success. A 2015 US study, for example, found that serial entrepreneurs were not only more likely to change industries if a venture failed, but were more likely to fail in the new industry too, not least because they were new to it, lacked expertise, and assumed that what *did* work in the old field *should* work in the new. It's easy to get stuck in a pattern of doing things automatically, but what really helps us develop is being able to step back and identify what we can do differently in the future based on the mistakes we made in the past.

Seeing straight

Humans are prone to a particularly awkward cognitive error: we see what we expect to see rather than what's actually there. "Schema theory" argues that this can even include what's right in front of us, from minor mistakes such as putting the cereal box in the fridge because we were thinking about the cupboard, to fatal mistakes such as a nurse attaching a patient to the wrong drip because of nerves or the pressure of the job. The less reflective we are, the more we fail—and we need to be able to learn the right lessons from our failures.

Defensive thinking

If we're intelligent, surely we should be good at learning from mistakes? In fact, according to business specialist Chris Argyris, smart people often lack this skill. The problem is one of mental habits. High achievers usually succeed at

LEARNING LOOPS

Business theorist Chris Argyris points to two different ways of learning from mistakes, the single and double loop. A single loop can be efficient if you're pursuing a specific goal, but if you want to broaden your mental scope, it's better to add another loop to your thinking that looks at the bigger picture as well—not just whether you did a particular task "by the book," but also examining the nature of the task itself. Argyris uses the example of seeing yourself as a thermostat set to 68°F (20°C), and imagines that it could be programmed to add in another level of calculation.

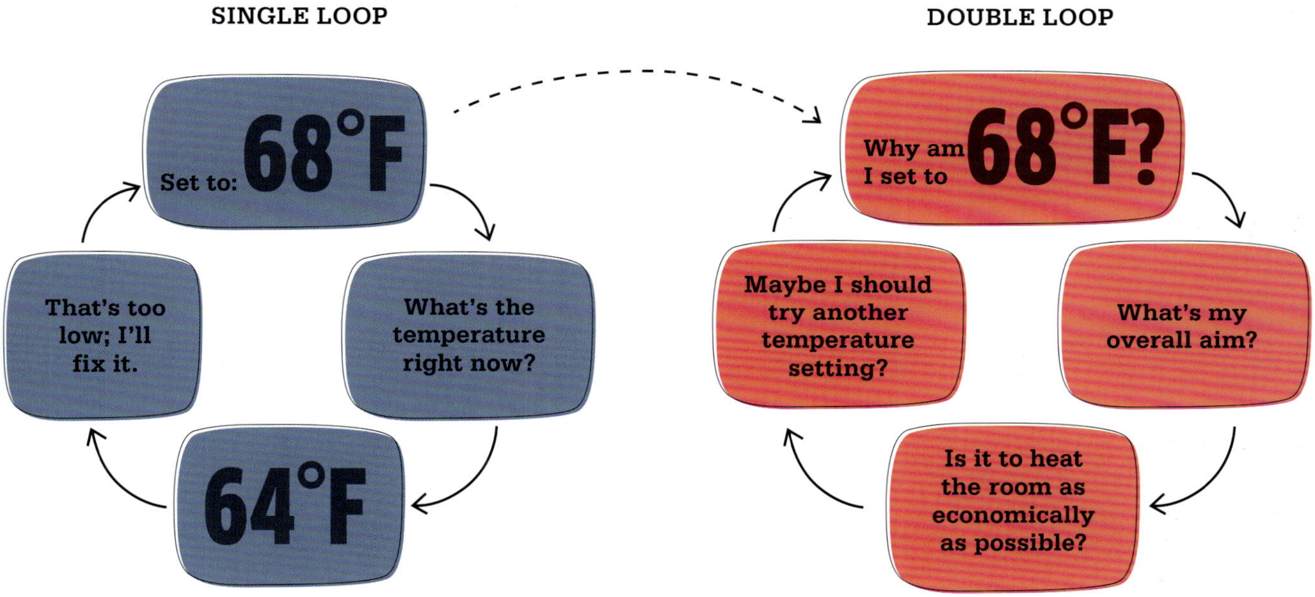

what they attempt. As a result, they don't experience failure on a regular basis and so don't have much practice at learning from it. Many of us are problem-oriented: if something is wrong, our instinct is to fix it as quickly as possible and move on. This may feel efficient, but it doesn't help us examine the causes, which could include the need to revise our own approach (see "Learning loops," above).

When we fail to get the result we want, we tend to go into defensive reasoning. We tried, it didn't work, and we don't want it to be our fault, so we redirect our energy into proving that it wasn't. This is a sure way to shut down our problem-solving abilities.

Changing habits

While we like to think of ourselves as consistent, Argyris argues that our principles tend to be undermined by a pattern of thinking that aims to:

- Keep us in control
- Maximize "winning" and minimize "losing"
- Suppress negative feelings
- Be "rational," which, in practice, means evaluating our behavior on our own terms.

At their core, all of these elements are about avoiding anxiety and shame, and they don't help us to improve. To learn from setbacks, we need to embrace vulnerability (see p.109) and cross-check our actions and assumptions to make sure we're not denying ourselves an important learning opportunity. We all make mistakes: the key to success is to accept them when they happen, understand what caused them and, if necessary, modify our approach. If we can do this, the mistakes themselves may matter much less.

AVOIDING BURNOUT

SUSTAINING YOUR PROGRESS OVER TIME

Burnout doesn't happen overnight, but if you've been pushing yourself for too long you may not realize you're heading for trouble until it's too late. Learn to recognize the signs and take steps to look after yourself.

We all have days when we're tired, but burnout is more serious. Burnout occurs when chronic stress (see pp.96–97) overwhelms you to the point where everything in your life starts to suffer. Your efforts need to be sustainable over the long term, and protecting yourself is much more effective than waiting until you are spent to take action.

The telltale signs

To know when it's time to give yourself a change or a rest, watch out for these problems:

- **Lots of minor health complaints.** Your immune system weakens when you're exhausted, and this means you're more susceptible to bugs and illnesses. You may also develop stress-related symptoms such as headaches, palpitations, dizziness, chest pains, and stomach problems—in which case, see a doctor.
- **Chronic tiredness.** If you're tired after a big effort, that's one thing, but if you're tired all the time—especially if you feel too tired to get simple, everyday things done—you may be suffering from burnout.
- **Trouble sleeping.** If you're chronically stressed, you're in a state of constant arousal, which means it can be hard to shut off and relax at the end of the day.
- **Impaired memory and concentration.** Too much pressure pushes your body into a state of "fight or flight." In the short term this can help by diverting all our cognitive resources to a single problem, but we're not designed to live like this over an extended period. If you're developing tunnel vision or feeling confused, you may need a proper rest.
- **Diminished job performance.** Compare your current performance to how you were doing a year or two ago. Burnout tends to reveal itself in a slow but steady decline.
- **Interpersonal problems.** Are you having more disagreements and quarrels than usual? Or are you feeling detached from others?
- **Poor self-care.** Are you forgetting to eat, or living on junk food? Are you going without exercise or sleep?
- **Dark emotions.** Anger, depression, anxiety, cynicism, and numbness indicate that you may be reaching your limit.

Preemptive measures

If you notice any of the warning signs, follow these steps to get yourself back on an even keel:

- **Say "no" where you can.** Some things may be non-negotiable, but don't take on any more than you absolutely have to (see pp.130–131).
- **Forget perfectionism.** Your aim is to be "good enough," not perfect (see pp.160–161).
- **Don't ruminate.** Rumination is when we lapse into a spiral of brooding (see "The ruminative cycle," right): remind yourself of the positives or distract yourself with something else to break the pattern.
- **Know when to get out.** Potential causes of burnout are situations of unfairness, insufficient reward, unsupportive communities, and lack of control. Sometimes the solution is to change your environment.
- **Take care of yourself.** You have to eat, drink, sleep, and get some exercise: neglecting your physical well-being is a false economy.
- **Have a place to be vulnerable**, preferably with other people who are going through the same problems as you.
- **Live your values.** A big cause of burnout is a disconnect between what you believe in and what you're working toward. Find ways to do things that align with your principles.

Put your own well-being first: it helps no one if you run yourself into the ground. It's more efficient to function at a level you can comfortably sustain over the long term—this is a key component of achieving and maintaining enduring success.

THE RUMINATIVE CYCLE

Reflecting and planning can be helpful, but beware of the "ruminative cycle," shown below, in which dwelling on negative thoughts can become self-reinforcing. If you find yourself getting mired in worries, resentments, or bad memories, remember that the solution involves breaking a habit. When the problem is overthinking bad feelings, you can't *think* your way to a solution—it's better to go and do something completely different. Listen to music, read a book, cook a meal—whatever it takes to get your mind running along pleasanter lines. It may take some effort at first, but persevere, and you may find your mood lifts.

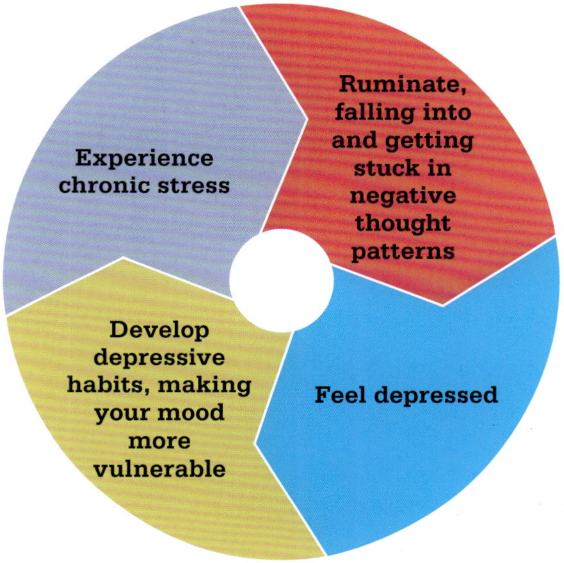

OPTIMUM WORKLOADS

The type of control we have over our work can have an impact on our health. A 2010 Australian-Canadian study found that people who are self-motivated and have a high level of control become *less* prone to illness as their workload increases. Try to identify your own optimum workload: it may seem counterintuitive, but an increased workload may improve your health.

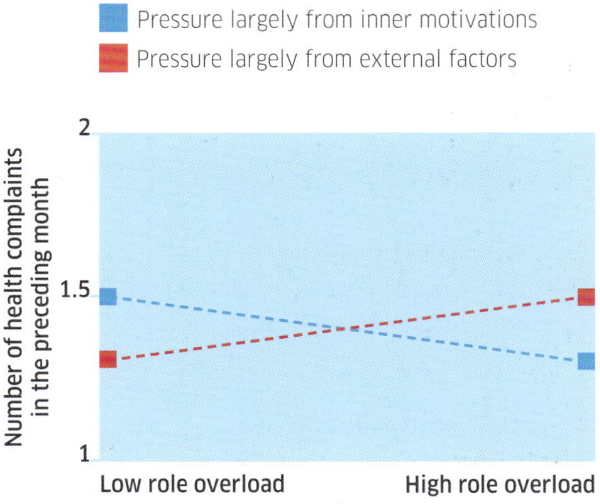

THE RELATIONSHIP BETWEEN WORKLOAD AND HEALTH

FREE TIME

OPTIMIZING YOUR LEISURE TIME TO NURTURE SUCCESS

When your life is focused on planning for success, it can be easy to treat leisure time as a low priority. In fact, though, you may find it easier to attain your goals if you plan your free time equally well.

Our time is valuable. Yet when it comes to enjoying our recreation time, we can find it slipping away. It's understandable that we may feel reluctant to plan our downtime—with all the pressures of life, we don't want to turn fun into yet more work—but a bit of forethought can mean the difference between time lost and time relished.

The universal goal

The desire to enjoy our leisure time spans nations and generations. Research conducted by the World Health Organization in 2008 found that an enjoyment of leisure time, especially when it produces "flow" experiences (see pp.166–167), improves people's quality of life in a range of countries around the world. Meanwhile, a 2006 Brazilian study found that a structured outdoor adventure program markedly improved the quality of life of citizens aged between 60 and 80. Whatever our age or place of origin, we need free time—but it's more "freeing" when it's at least moderately planned.

Making it worthwhile

When we're tired and overwhelmed, we often long for more time to relax. Sometimes, though, quality is better than quantity.

A 2010 study published in the *Journal of Happiness Studies* documented the lives of 403 students over the course of a month. It found that simply having more free time didn't necessarily lead to an improvement in the students' well-being. What mattered was how well they *used* their free time.

WHAT FILLS YOUR TIME?

Psychotherapist and business coach Lynn Grodzki states that our time can be divided into three basic categories:

- **Work time.** Activities that bring us either joy or money.
- **Spirit time.** Meaningful activities that rejuvenate our souls.
- **Buffer time.** Time spent on practical and psychological "inessentials" that can eat into the two other, more important categories.

How much of your time is being spent on buffer activities? Could you fill it with something more effective?

Those who did benefit from their free time had a proactive approach to it. They tended to:

- Engage in physical activities
- Engage in social activities, with both friends and family
- Engage in specific leisure activities, such as excursions and hobbies

TYPES OF LEISURE ACTIVITY

What do we get out of leisure? Working from Maslow's "hierarchy of needs" (see "Our deepest needs," right), psychologists Mounir Ragheb and Jacob Beard identified six types of activity that give us satisfaction:

1 **Psychological.** Look for activities that reward you on an emotional or cognitive level.

2 **Educational.** Find activities that improve your knowledge and understanding.

3 **Social.** Involve your friends and family in your leisure activities.

4 **Relaxation.** Seek out peaceful and unchallenging activities.

5 **Physiological.** Enjoy pleasant physical activities.

6 **Aesthetic.** Engage in activities in which you can enjoy beautiful places and things.

- Set specific goals, such as, "I want to improve my fitness"
- Schedule activities in advance.

If we assume that our leisure time will take care of itself, we are more likely to end up feeling bored and unsatisfied. This can raise our stress levels, as the sense that time is slipping away is more likely to make us feel anxious than rested. Research suggests we thrive most when we see "time off" as a period for doing things that matter to us, rather than just a spell when we're not working.

OUR DEEPEST NEEDS

In 1943, American psychologist Abraham Maslow first advanced his theory of the "hierarchy of needs"—the idea that we meet our most basic needs first, and then seek to meet "higher" needs, which help us achieve our full potential. Maslow based his theory on his study of outstanding individuals, such as physicist Albert Einstein and abolitionist hero Frederick Douglass, believing that such people represented the healthiest in human psychology. Leisure activities tend to represent the upper tiers of the hierarchy. Which of the following needs do your leisure activities satisfy?

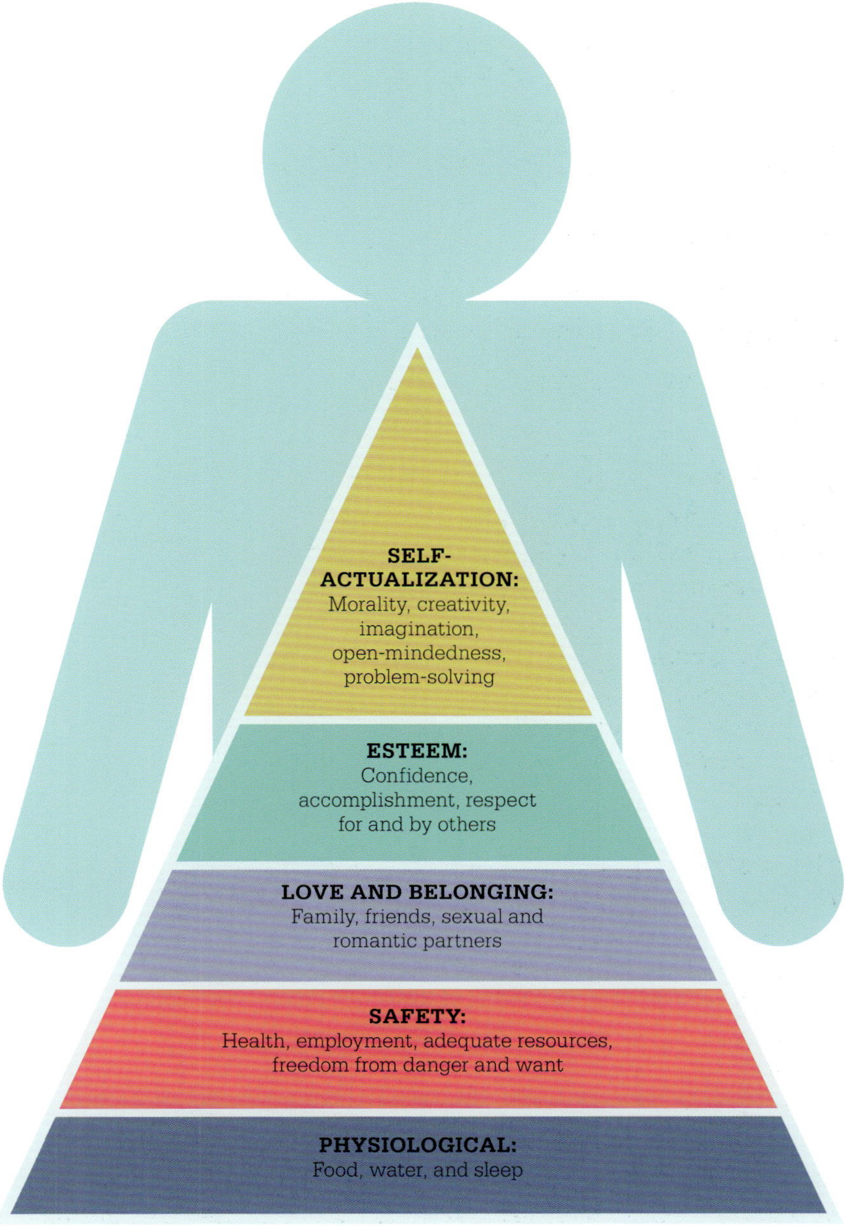

CHAPTER 6
SUCCESS
A WHOLE-LIFE PROCESS

BUILDING RESILIENCE

FORTIFYING YOUR INNER RESERVES

Success involves coping well with challenges and crises, but also relishing good things when you find them. That way, when life does get difficult, you can benefit from a well-rounded outlook based on positivity and optimism.

A positive mindset is a long-term investment that prepares you for life's challenges. Research has found that when we experience good moods, this tends to broaden our outlook and allow us to respond to situations—including bad ones—more flexibly than usual. If we can cultivate this positive mindset, it's likely to help us build maturity of character. If you want to get through life with a robust attitude, don't push yourself to be "tougher," but instead open yourself to the full range of life's experiences (good, bad, and challenging). Here are some approaches you may find useful in your journey.

SAVOR THE GOOD MOMENTS

In the *Journal of Happiness Studies*, psychologists Michele Tugade and Barbara Fredrickson point out that if we have something good to report, we commonly call friends and family, wanting to tell as many people as possible. This is partly about maintaining social connections, but it's also about prolonging the happy mood: sharing the good news keeps the pleasure fresh in our minds. We can prolong the mood at any time, by looking forward to a positive experience, enjoying it while it lasts, and then relishing the memory afterward. All are ways of "capitalizing" on something pleasant—which is to say, getting as much value out of it as we can.

ENJOY ALL YOU CAN

Psychology distinguishes between two kinds of well-being:

- **Hedonic well-being.** From the Greek *hēdonē*, meaning "pleasure." This describes subjective, in-the-moment experiences that we find enjoyable.
- **Eudaimonic well-being.** From the Greek *eu*, meaning "good" and *daimōn*, meaning "spirit." This describes long-term activities that allow us to grow, have positive relationships with other people, and feel good about ourselves.

It's not only life's challenges that foster our resilience; it's also our experiences of life at its best. So make enough room for enjoyment in your life.

KEEP A BALANCED PERSPECTIVE

While a positive attitude is undoubtedly good for success, in some circumstances this needs qualification. As psychologists Robert Cummins and Mark Wooden remark in the *Journal of Happiness Studies,* "the extremes of optimism are [...] maladaptive"—which means too much can be as unhelpful as too little. Too little optimism makes us discouraged and fearful, but an excess can make us impulsive in situations where caution would serve us better. Balance is the key to success: being optimistic but also realistic.

FIND THE SILVER LINING

We can't prevent the bad moments, but we can learn to experience at least some positive emotions within them. According to a 2000 US study, useful approaches for turning negative to positive are:

Reappraising the situation, trying to find a positive aspect.

Problem-solving as a boost to self-esteem: searching for solutions is satisfying.

Finding positive meaning within daily events, such as appreciating a compliment.

Finding the funny side even of difficulties—as if seeing things through someone's else's eyes.

Don't wait for a big problem to arise before you put these coping methods into effect. Instead, see them as faculties you can exercise at any time so that you'll be strong and ready for whatever life brings you.

CHOOSE YOUR AFFIRMATIONS WISELY

If you wish to boost your self-esteem, it can be productive to give yourself positive messages or "affirmations." However, a 2009 Canadian study published in *Psychological Science* adds a caveat to this. If your self-esteem is robust to begin with, repeating positive statements like, "I'm a lovable person" can help—but if your self-esteem is low, this can backfire. The researchers found that the people whose confidence most needed reinforcement tended to feel worse after repeating generalized, nonspecific positive affirmations. It seems they didn't feel that these statements were true, and having to articulate them only served as a reminder that these were painful subjects. If you decide to use affirmations to lift your spirits, choose statements that you feel describe positive attributes about your talents and what is important to you, such as, "I am excellent at attending to details and planning."

LIFELONG LEARNING

THE PATH OF DEVELOPMENT

As we progress through our lives, we can learn from experiences in work, at home, and in our communities. Development is continuous and keeps us motivated and focused on, "what's next?"

The most reliable path to success is to assume that learning is not a process that you finish, but a way to approach every situation you encounter. There are always opportunities to seek out new situations in which to learn and develop. With the help of a "growth mindset" (see p.26), you can always stay vitally and rewardingly engaged.

Seeking out knowledge

Do we ever reach a point where we "know enough"? Certainly we can acquire enough skills to meet a particular challenge, but there are far-ranging benefits to continuing our learning:

- **Learning makes us more confident and resilient.** The experience of meeting challenges and using our intelligence to overcome them boosts our sense that we can cope with difficult situations.
- **Learners are better able to cope with change.** Mastering new concepts accustoms us to encountering unfamiliar and perhaps challenging beliefs. The more we come to terms with unknown ways of thinking, the less daunting the unknown becomes.
- **Learning enriches our experiences.** Life becomes more interesting as we learn and develop. The more we can approach the world as students, the more we are likely to thrive in it.
- **Learning makes us more well rounded.** A 2015 study published in *Adult Education Quarterly* found that the best measure of lifelong learning was "human capital"—the understanding we can gain by educating ourselves. "Social capital," or the extent to which we build on connections with others to help us develop, was also helpful, especially for those with less formal education. But the greater their "human capital," the better the subjects of the research were able to make effective use of their skills in a variety of situations.
- **Learning preserves our well-being as we age.** Studies confirm that older people who embark on education enjoy higher levels of health and happiness, and the connections and insight they foster enrich the community as a whole.

Learning to learn

It may sound like a narrow topic, but learning itself can be a skill to develop. In 2006, the European Parliament and Council listed this

THE LEARNER IN SOCIETY

How should we understand our learning in the widest context? Danish Professor of Lifelong Learning Knud Illeris argues that we learn in three dimensions: through our thoughts (cognition), our feelings (emotion), and our place in the world (environment). This creates balance:

- ✔ **COGNITION:** our personal abilities and understanding
- ✔ **EMOTION:** how we achieve psychological balance
- ✔ **ENVIRONMENT:** how we positively integrate into the world and culture around us.

as one of several "key competences" we can improve throughout our lives. Here is the complete list:

- Communication in our mother tongue
- Communication in foreign languages
- Mathematical, scientific, and technical competence
- Digital and computer competence
- Learning to learn
- Social and civic competence
- A sense of initiative and entrepreneurship
- Cultural awareness and expression.

If you need a general recipe for success, one of the best things you could do is follow this curriculum.

REACHING FOR MEANING

According to Portuguese psychologist and education expert Roberto Carneiro, learning is a process that grows more complex—and more fulfilling—as we develop. We begin with approaching basic information, and progress from there to knowledge, which gives us a grasp of the facts. Then, we approach genuine "learning," in which we refine our understanding of the knowledge we've gained. Finally, we reach a sense of meaning, in which the application, value, and worth of all we've learned starts to become clear.

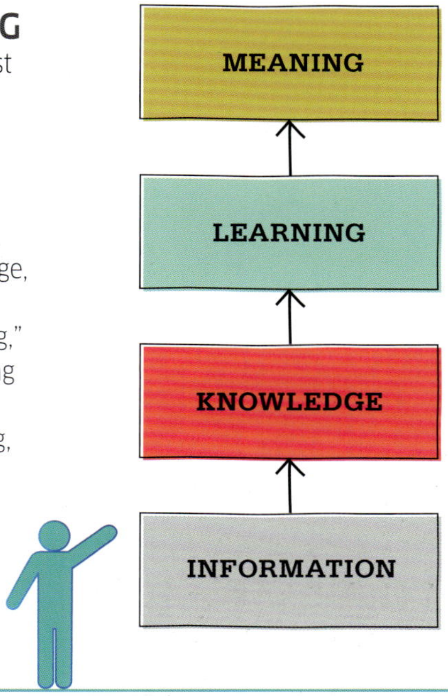

TO ADAPT OR GENERATE?

Thinking of learning as a way of gaining information is useful but limited. Professor Roberto Carneiro proposes a distinction between "adaptive" and "generative" learning. Adaptive learning helps us to manage within our environment; generative learning helps us to change our environment. To be successful, we need to cultivate both types of learning.

Adaptive learning helps us to ...	Generative learning helps us to ...
■ "Fit" our environment	■ "Stretch" our environment
■ Adjust to change	■ Expand our capacity
■ Cope with threats	■ Develop creativity
■ React to symptoms	■ Identify causes
■ Identify signs	■ Anticipate the future
■ Gain conventional knowledge	■ See things in a new way

DESIRE IS THE KEY TO MOTIVATION, BUT IT'S THE DETERMINATION AND COMMITMENT TO AN UNRELENTING PURSUIT OF YOUR GOAL—A COMMITMENT TO EXCELLENCE—THAT WILL ENABLE YOU TO ATTAIN THE SUCCESS YOU SEEK.

MARIO ANDRETTI, RACE CAR DRIVER

FEEDBACK

SHARING IDEAS AND HEARING OPINIONS

Cooperating well with others means being comfortable with feedback—both giving it and receiving it. Opening channels of response, in both directions, is often the key to a successful endeavor.

No matter how much confidence we have in our own opinions, we can all benefit from views expressed by others. Both in and out of the workplace, knowing how to gather feedback is often a significant factor in attaining success. However, you must be prepared to have your own ideas criticized—even, at times, demolished.

Taking it well

Neurological evidence suggests that we're wired to fear criticism. There's even some research to suggest that negative comments are processed by different, more sensitive neural circuits than those that handle positive input. Fundamentally, fear of criticism is fear of rejection. No matter how tactfully a negative comment is phrased, a part of our brain hears the threat of, "You're fired" or, "No one will love you." Faced with anxiety-inducing feedback—for example, a negative appraisal from your manager—try the following:

- **Listen for the facts.** It's helpful to separate fact from opinion. Even if you don't agree with the conclusions, you can often pick up good information and store it for later use.
- **Consider the motivation.** Is the speaker trying to help you, even if they're being blunt? Or are they trying to reinforce their own authority or score points? These different motivations require different responses.
- **Make it impersonal.** If you did make a mistake, present yourself

85%

PEER TO PEER

According to a 1994 Australian study, 85 percent of students felt they **learned more** from **peer assessments** than reviews from authority figures.

as an ally with your criticizer: "Yes, I notice I sometimes do that. What can you suggest?"

- **Ask for time.** If you don't think you can respond constructively at once, say you appreciate the feedback and you'd like time to give the matter serious thought.

Giving as well as taking

Numerous studies confirm that giving feedback to people who share your goals can be at least as helpful as receiving it. Having to assess somebody else's efforts forces our brains to think objectively about:

- The purpose of what everyone is trying to achieve
- What criteria this can be judged by
- What a good example might look like
- Possible remedies when things aren't quite as they should be.

Such an approach will develop your critical-thinking skills in ways that can benefit all areas of your life.

BET AND BEAR

American psychologists Patricia L. Harms and Deborah Britt Roebuck describe two different models for giving positive and negative feedback—"BET" and "BEAR," respectively. If you have to tell someone what you think of them, follow one of these approaches:

Step	Action	Example
B Behavior	Describe what someone is doing that benefits everyone	"You are really making everyone feel that they are appreciated."
E Effect	Outline the result of this positive behavior	"This has led to a greater sense of well-being within the group and a better outcome for all."
T Thank you	Show appreciation	"The people involved are really happy to be working with you. Thanks!
B Behavior	Describe the action that caused a problem	"You said you could handle the contract, but you didn't start on it until last week."
E Effect	What effect is this having?	"There was so much to do I had to stop and help you, which caused problems with my other projects."
A Alternative	Suggest how someone could do things differently in the future	"Please let me know as soon as you anticipate there being a problem."
R Result	Describe what positive effects making that change would create	"That way, it will be much easier to find the right person to help you out."

LISTENING SKILLS

HOW TO TUNE INTO WHAT YOU HEAR

We all know the importance of learning from others, but it can be surprisingly difficult to really "hear" what someone else is saying. How can we become better listeners and absorb the best of what we are told?

A good listener is someone able to absorb more information. If you want to improve your listening skills, what are the best strategies?

Mirror, mirror

If you see two people "mirroring" each other's body language in conversation, you may think this shows the pressure of social conformity. But in fact it may be part of an attempt to understand each other. One scientific theory calls this "embodied simulation" (See "Picture the listening process," opposite). We can't see into people's minds, but we believe that private thoughts and feelings will be reflected in overt motor behavior such as facial expressions and body posture—and if we mimic these things, the feedback into our brains can help us fully understand. We tend to do this subconsciously, but if you're having trouble grasping someone's motivations, try making a deliberate effort to discreetly copy their body language to increase your intuitive understanding.

Active listening

Psychologists are increasingly recommending the process of "active listening" for effective learning. Whereas "passive listening" involves simply staying quiet and hearing what's being said, active listening is the practice of engaging so that the conversation really connects. Try the following techniques:

- **Listen with your body.** Mirror, smile, make eye contact, lean in slightly. Don't fidget, as that distracts the speaker: make your whole posture about paying attention.
- **Share the viewpoint.** Show from what you say in response to the other person that you're trying to see how things look from their perspective.
- **Be composed and pleasant.** The speaker will pick up on your manner just as you pick up on theirs, so maintain a calm and approachable presence.
- **Show "altercentrism"** (focus on the other person). Ask open questions; don't interrupt; reflect back or paraphrase some of what they say; if you're not sure what they mean, ask them to clarify.
- **Defer judgment.** Don't anticipate what they'll say or jump in with counter-arguments. Let them finish before you form your opinion.
- **Validate.** If someone is distressed, always focus on showing that you support their right to feel what they feel. This may make them more coherent.

PICTURE THE LISTENING PROCESS

American psychologists Graham Bodie, Debra Worthington, and Lynn Cooper, along with German psychologist Margarete Imhof, propose a "unified field theory" of how we manage conversations. This graphic shows how a conversation operates. The more care and skill we can deploy at the process stage, when we make our contribution, the more valuable the outcomes of any discussion will be.

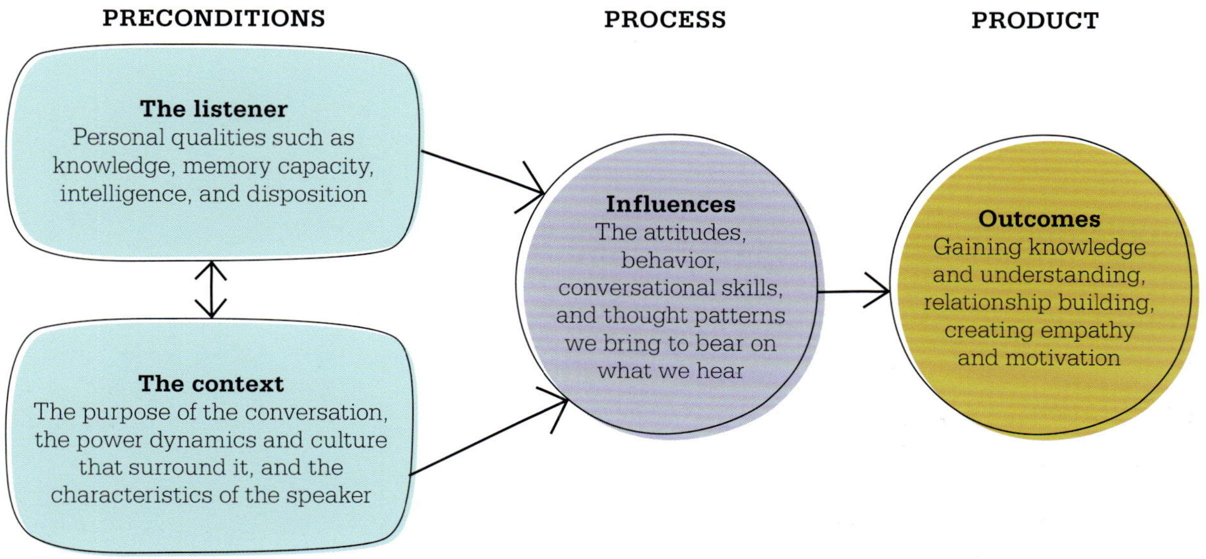

- **Reflect.** Say something like: "So if I understand you, what you're saying is..." This gives them space to correct any false impressions and shows you're striving to understand.
- **Summarize.** Recap what they say at regular intervals. This proves your interest, and gives them the chance to stress anything you've missed.

Any social situation gives you the opportunity to practice listening, so begin as soon as you can and see where your new skills can take you. Test your own memory, and resolve to listen better. Bear in mind that a good listener is a facilitator, who empowers others to communicate.

ACTIVE LISTENING DOS AND DON'TS

Active listening means creating an open verbal space. Here are some suggestions and taboos:

Avoid: Questions that risk sounding accusatory, such as: "Why did you do that?"
Do say: "Can you tell me more about what happened?"

Avoid: Pushing too hard for sensitive information.
Do say: "If you're willing to talk about that, I'm happy to listen."

Avoid: Presumptions, such as "I know just how you feel."
Do say: "How are you feeling about that?"

Avoid: Unwanted advice, such as: "You should just quit."
Do say: "Do you want to brainstorm some strategies?"

Avoid: Patronizing expressions of pity—such as "You poor thing!"—which is different from empathy.
Do say: "That does sound difficult. How are you coping?"

Avoid: Bluntness, lack of courtesy.
Do say: "Might I suggest...?" "Please excuse me...?"

MENTORS AND GUIDES

THE VALUE OF MUTUAL SUPPORT

A good mentor can be a precious asset. To build a strong mentoring relationship, work creatively to optimize your learning and growth, and be clear about how both sides can benefit from the process.

When a person with greater knowledge or experience takes you under their wing, it can make a positive difference to your life in a variety of areas. Mentoring is a key way for skills to be passed on, both inside and outside the professional sphere. A mentor can benefit you when you're embarking on a new kind of activity, seeking help with life's challenges, or trying to grow yourself creatively, intellectually, or professionally.

Finding a mentor

Good mentors don't come along every day, so what's the best way to recruit one? When seeking someone to be your guide, bear in mind the following factors:

- **Decide at the outset why you want a mentor.** For example: do you need introductions in a particular field, a reliable critic of your performance, or someone to watch in action? Having a clear idea of your expectations can prevent disappointment.

90%

VALUE FEEDBACK

A 2009 US study found that more than **90 percent of mentors** thought it was important to encourage **candid feedback** from their protégés.

- **Identify, and make use of, networking opportunities.** Many industries offer mentoring programs: you might wish to find out where your colleagues found their mentors; look into places where the people you admire spend time and are open to socializing. Remember, no one mentor will "have it all"—to optimize your success, you will need multiple mentors.
- **When meeting people, be sensitive to their responses.** If somebody doesn't seem willing to help you, there's no point in pushing—this will only alienate them. But don't expect them to read your mind. Say clearly that you'd value any advice they can offer you. If they're polite but vague, that's probably a "no."
- **Be open to unexpected connections.** The right mentor for you might work in a field you hadn't thought of, or have a very different personality from you. They don't have to be the person you aspire to be yourself: all that matters is good rapport.

Maintaining the relationship

Once you've established a good connection with someone, put careful thought into how you can continue to get the best out of the mentor–mentee dynamic. Try out these methods:

- **Be reciprocal**. Offer them any connections or introductions you can. Support and promote their work. Be prepared to assist them. A mentee with staying power knows to give something back.
- **Show initiative.** It's not very rewarding to mentor someone who seems too dependent. What a mentor values is a protégé with energy and enthusiasm, who is worth helping because they'll make the best of what you give.
- **Accept what's offered.** Some mentors may not wish to provide emotional support, for example, but can still give good practical help. If you need something your mentor doesn't want to give, look elsewhere to fill that need.
- **Finish the mentor–mentee dynamic when it feels right.** If you're no longer finding your mentor helpful, maybe it's the natural time to move forward.

MENTORING CONSTELLATION

Support from those with more experience can obviously be valuable, but don't overlook "sideways" and even "upward" mentoring. A 2013 US paper for the Center for Creative Leadership describes a "constellation" of relationships in which mutual support and guidance between equals, as well as backing from those below you in a hierarchy, can be just as fruitful as a top-down pattern.

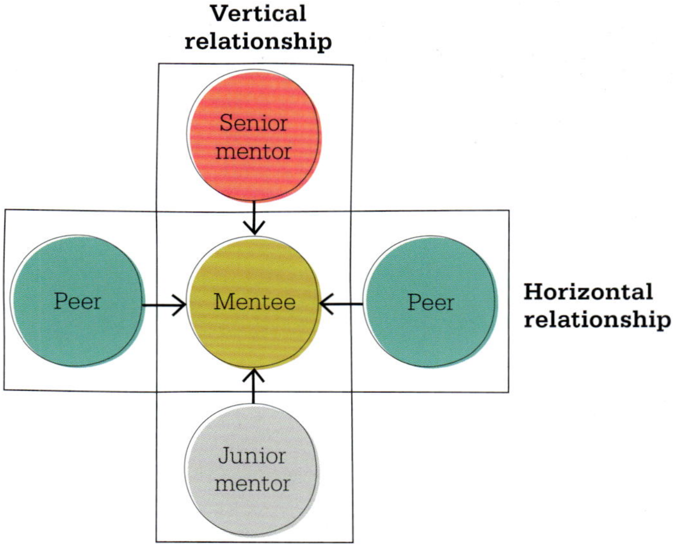

25–33%

KEEP IT IN THE FAMILY

A 2013 study asked managers **which relationships** most helped them **develop professionally.** Family members accounted for **25–33 percent** of the people cited.

The key to any relationship with a mentor is to appreciate the value of what is given, and to show courtesy, consideration, and support as well. Whether this results in a lifelong friendship or a temporary but helpful interaction, look for the benefits and enjoy them for what they are.

CREDIBILITY

TALKING THE TALK AND WALKING THE WALK

A reputation for being trustworthy is an essential asset. A person with low credibility misses opportunities, while a good track record wins loyalty. Each action and decision we make has an impact on our credibility.

Credible people are those whom others believe in. Without credibility, you'll find that your judgments or even the "facts" you present are mistrusted, and that you fail to inspire confidence. The essential thing is to make sure that what you say and what you do line up. It's easier to lose credibility than to restore it, so be mindful of how authentic you're being, and how you appear to others. And if things do go wrong, be prepared to do the serious work necessary to address the situation directly.

Align what you say and do

Numerous studies confirm that credibility comes down to a very simple fact: if somebody's statements don't align with their behavior, if they profess ideals they don't uphold, or if they make promises they don't keep, then we don't trust them.

A 1994 US study funded by the National Institute of Mental Health and the Stern School of Business found that volunteers presented with ambiguous messages were much more likely to trust sources seen as credible—and that on relatively low-stakes decisions, credibility was the *only* factor people considered, no matter how strong or weak the arguments they heard. When it comes to day-to-day living, credibility may be the only currency that counts.

Amending mistakes

Hopefully your aim is to live with integrity, but everybody makes mistakes. Sometimes it's impossible

THE TIMELINE OF TRUST

How do we decide whether we can trust someone? American psychologist Tony Simons argues that the question involves first making a judgment of someone's "behavioral integrity," based on their past actions. From there, we decide on their "credibility" and anticipate their future behavior—as shown in the example below. To strengthen your own credibility and inspire confidence, try to make sure that your deeds align with your words: do what you say you will. That way, you will be perceived as an honest and credible person.

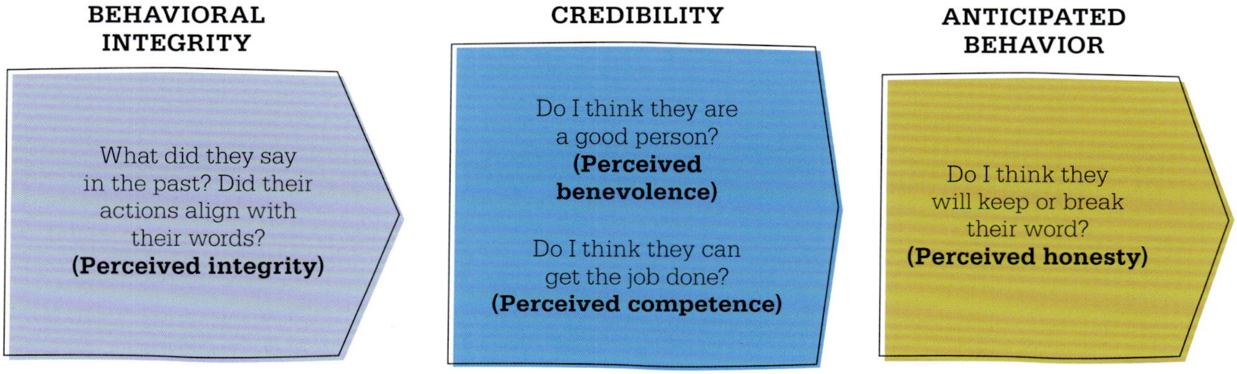

to keep a promise, or our self-control weakens and we bend our own rules. If others observe you doing this, you have a problem.

If you go wrong, what can you do? Studies suggest that if you're seen as untruthful, that extends to your "excuses," so apologies and promises need to be carefully formulated. A 2002 study published in *Organization Science* found that the question, "What will it take for you to cooperate again?" proved much less effective than, "What *can I do* to get you to cooperate again?"—shifting the burden of action onto the wrongdoer. The same study found that offers of making amends tended to obtain forgiveness, but they didn't need to be large: small ones worked equally well in showing goodwill, as long as they made a real attempt at reparation.

THE RATCHET EFFECT

We know from experience, and multiple studies confirm, that it's far easier to lose trust than it is to gain it. Psychologist Tony Simons calls this the "ratchet effect." In the same way that the angled teeth of a ratchet allow it to turn in only one direction, so each time we are perceived as unreliable, our credibility is damaged in a way that's hard to reverse—even if most of our actions are perfectly honest.

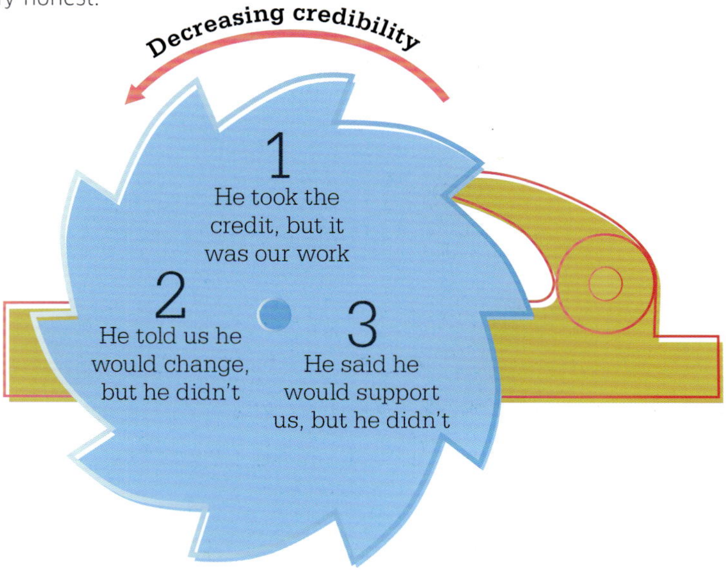

RESPECT

HOW TO GET OTHERS TO RECOGNIZE YOUR WORTH

We often hope other people will approve of our character, actions, and opinions. However, this can leave us with a dilemma: to what extent should we try to win respect by doing as others wish?

Feeling respected in our community gives us peace of mind: it is one of the best boosts for our confidence and our relationships with ourselves and others. But how do we present our most admirable self while being true to who we really are?

Presenting a respectable self

Social disapproval is a powerful deterrent, and all of us, to some extent, will want to maintain a public face that people accept. Psychologists refer to the process as "impression management" (IM). This can sound rather manipulative; and indeed studies confirm that individuals with a high IM score are more willing to be economical with the truth when their reputation is on the line. Recent research, though, has argued that such people are not truly confident—instead, they are defensive, and anxious about losing face. Israeli psychologist Liad Uziel argued in 2010 that a more accurate term would be "interpersonally oriented self-control," a useful phrase that flags the difference between negative covering up and positive self-presentation. Showing yourself worthy of respect can be a skilled performance, but it needn't be a cynical one. At times it may even increase your creativity (see "Not so shallow," opposite).

> Respect for ourselves **guides our morals**; respect for others **guides our manners**.
>
> **Laurence Sterne**
> Irish novelist and clergyman

Respect and giving

While it's good to be generous, it's also common knowledge that people don't usually respect a pushover. When considering this aspect of your standing with others, ask yourself a few questions:

- Do I have a hard time refusing unreasonable requests?
- Do I often feel taken for granted?
- Do I often put my own needs last?
- Do I do more favors for others than they do for me?
- Do I get the low-grade work no one else wants?
- Do I worry people will reject me if I say no?

As anthropologist David Graeber observes in *Debt: The First 5,000 Years*, nonreciprocal giving is a mark of hierarchy rather than

STEPPING OFF THE GUILT TRACK

If you feel under pressure to accept every responsibility pushed your way, you're probably a decent person–but you may gain more respect if you can draw some reasonable boundaries. This may mean letting go of guilt. Here is one example, showing a possible set of negative thoughts about a situation, alongside alternative, more positive responses.

Situation

A friend asks for a favor when you're too busy

"I can see they need help, but I've got all this work to do."

Negative responses

- "If I say no, that'll make things worse for them"
- "That's selfish of me"
- "People don't like selfish people"
- "Maybe I'll lose my friendship"

You feel guilt and anxiety

- "OK, I guess I'll make time"

You do, and your work suffers

- "Why am I so inadequate? Maybe people are right not to respect me."

Positive responses

- "This favor is something I just can't manage right now"
- "I don't have to sabotage myself to be a good person"
- "If I take care of myself, I can be more help to them another time"
- "If they're my friend, they'll understand this"

You feel regret combined with confidence

- "I'll make it up to them later."

You say no, and your own life stays under control

- "If I ask for respect, I can expect to get it."

equality—think of giving candy to a child or bringing a tribute to a king. In such imbalanced relationships, giving once creates the expectation that you'll give again.

If you give too much, you may actually be indicating that you consider yourself lower-status. If so, finding ways to say no (see p.131) might actually raise your standing.

Respect begins with respecting yourself, so work on showing your value and following your principles.

Maintaining respect

Respect, lost in a moment, may take great effort to restore—though at times a single great effort can win over others and recover your position. Don't skimp on what's needed to rebuild your standing: respect is worth striving for.

NOT SO SHALLOW

There's a tendency to think of people who pay a lot of attention to their "impression management" (IM) as more superficial than those who don't. A 2010 study by Israeli psychologist Liad Uziel, however, found that a desire for respect may increase creativity in front of an audience. Asked to create stories in a test setting, people rated as having low IM performed better when alone. However, given an audience, it was people with high IM who carried the day.

THE EFFECT OF "IM" ON CREATIVITY

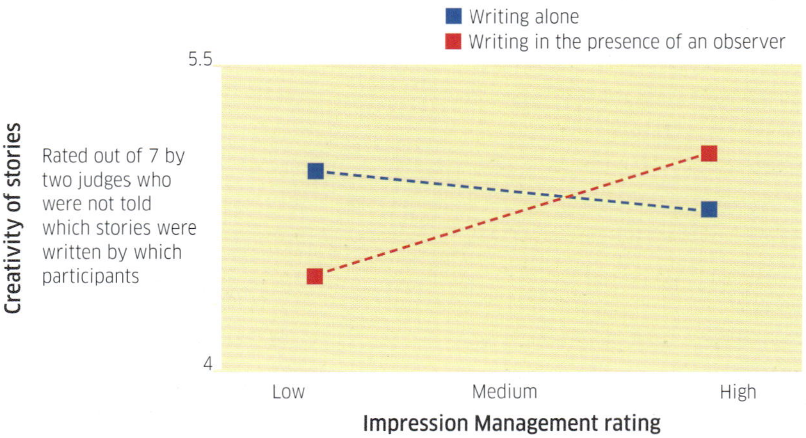

THE PSYCHOLOGY OF WEALTH

HOW DO YOU RELATE TO MONEY?

Success doesn't necessarily mean acquiring great wealth, but lack of financial resources may make you feel like an underachiever. Money can be an emotional subject, so how do you cultivate a healthy attitude?

Ever since psychologist Sigmund Freud defined the need to hoard wealth as a sign of an "anal-retentive" personality, psychologists have been studying our relationship with money. How can you get a balanced view of this difficult subject?

What does it mean?

Is money a source of stress, a moral pitfall, or a valid symbol for one of life's winners? In the 1990s, psychologist Thomas Li-Ping Tang developed what he called the "Money Ethic Scale" (MES), which is a good way to judge how we value money. Tang found that people who ranked money highly as a sign of achievement tended to experience less life satisfaction, and also that people working to a modest budget tended to be more content. Hence, the evidence suggests that treating money as a practicality rather than as a measure of your worth may make you happier. He also found that people who value money highly aren't necessarily richer than those who don't, so giving money low priority probably won't end up impoverishing you!

What can it buy you?

What do you see as the main purpose of money? A useful three-point scale was devised by American psychologists Kent Yamauchi and Donald Templer, alongside a questionnaire you can use for self-testing (see "Test your money focus," opposite). These writers posit that our relationship with money can be measured by the following three factors:

1 **Power and prestige.** Using money to obtain influence over and/or impress other people.

2 **Security.** Using money to protect ourselves against various types of fear or want.

3 **Retention.** Saving for the sake of saving itself, sometimes to the point of parsimony or even obsessiveness.

They note that security and retention can overlap. Both, for example, can be apparent in a desire for "time retention," which is when we're motivated to be prepared for a rainy day. And both

> He is rich or poor according to **what he is**, not according to **what he has**.
>
> **Henry Ward Beecher**
> American social reformer

can be a sign of distrust, such as when we worry about someone cheating or overcharging us.

Money as opportunity

The sense of our being poised to embark on some new project or other experience can be very satisfying—especially when we're conscious of having enough money to pursue a chosen plan.

Issues, however, may arise when we aren't yet ready to commit to—and spend money on—a particular course of action. Perhaps we haven't made up our minds between alternatives. Having to spend cash may heighten the importance of certainty. Or even if we *have* decided, our sense of cutting off an alternative future for ourselves, for which the money could equally well have been used, can result in paralysis: unable to commit, we do nothing. In such situations, it's good to reassess your relationship with money. If you believe it should be a tool, what's the point of a tool you don't use?

Money magnifies

All this illustrates how money can magnify our psychological issues. It can make relationship problems much harder to deal with—just think of money's role in many celebrity divorces. And having no spare cash can further lower an already low sense of self-esteem.

The message from all this is: don't allow money to have symbolic force unless you want it to. And by extension, don't mistake a wealthy lifestyle for happiness. True wealth lies elsewhere.

TEST YOUR MONEY FOCUS

Research on attitudes about money by American psychologists Kent Yamauchi and Donald Templer was based on asking participants to answer a revealing questionnaire. Use the same questions for your own self-assessment. Which of the three statements in each bubble resonates most with you? Use the concluding summary for self-assessment, and work on the action points given.

A When I want people to do things for me, I use money to influence them.
B I like to plan for my financial future.
C I haggle or complain about the price of things.

A If I'm honest, I buy things to impress people.
B I save regularly.
C I tend to say I "can't afford" something, even if I can.

A It's very tempting to boast about how much I earn.
B I'm being careful to prepare for my old age.
C I don't like spending, even on necessities.

A I know money isn't everything, but I do find wealthy people impressive.
B It bothers me if I've bought something I could have gotten cheaper elsewhere.
C I like to keep track of my money.

A I often try to find out if other people make more than me.
B I keep a cushion of money in case of bad times.
C I'd describe myself as a prudent person.

A I'll spend more to get the best products or brands.
B I worry that I won't be financially secure.
C I follow a very careful budget.

Mostly A: Power and prestige are motivators for you.
Action: Avoid obsessive ambition. Be sure not to neglect love and friendship.
Mostly B: You're motivated by security.
Action: Check that you're not neglecting opportunities. Challenge yourself.
Mostly C: You have a tendency toward "retention," or hoarding.
Action: Make sure your behavior doesn't turn to meanness. Give generously.

GOOD FRIENDS

THE VALUE OF SUPPORTIVE RELATIONSHIPS

While working to make a success of your life, consciously attend to building and nurturing relationships and friendships. Human connection is the core of well-being, and good relationships can make us more productive.

Studies confirm that friendships aren't just for mutual support and shared leisure: people with a good social circle tend to enjoy better mental and physical health and greater life satisfaction, and are even longer-lived. If friendships are the key to well-being, productivity, and success, is there a key to friendship?

Are we all alike?

It is commonly believed that female friendships are more intimate than male ones—or that closeness between men tends to be through bonding over shared activities rather than shared revelations. This way of looking at things distinguishes between "side-by-side" and "face-to-face" closeness. However, this distinction does not hold; men value and need the same dynamic in their friendships. Studies confirm that men, too, rate "self-disclosure" as an important part of friendships, and feel less satisfied when their friends are not confiding. Research suggests that when it comes to platonic

> **Good relationships** keep us **happier** and **healthier**. Period.
>
> **Robert Waldinger**
> Psychiatrist, psychoanalyst, and director of a 75-year study of adult development at Harvard Medical School

relationships, men and women's needs are more similar than we might think.

What seems clearer is that the number of our friendships shrinks as we move through adulthood. According to the studies, though, this doesn't necessarily mean older adults are lonelier. Instead, we go through what longevity psychologist Laura Carstensen calls a "pruning effect": in our thirties and forties, as family and work responsibilities limit our free time, we drift away from people who can't support our "new normal" and become closer to those who do. Older social circles tend to be smaller, but also more robust: in our maturer years we replace quantity with quality.

The essence of friendship

What are the essential qualities of a friendship? Canadian psychologist Beverley Fehr, in a series of surveys in 2004 with both men and women, found that certain ideas of what a friend should provide were rated more "prototypical"—that is, closer to the core concept of friendship—than others (see "Dimensions of friendship", right). Both men and women were more likely to be upset by violations of prototypical friendship rules than of more peripheral rules—but at the same time, more likely to forgive transgressions by friends whose prototypical support could be relied upon. Friendship seems to be a mix of support, acceptance, loyalty, and trustworthiness: if someone can give us those, other things matter less.

SELF-ASSESSMENT

75% of **women** and

72% of **men**

are **satisfied** with their friendships—according to a 2015 US study, suggesting that the sexes are more aligned than we might think.

FRIENDS BY NUMBERS

A 2015 study published in the *Journal of Social and Personal Relationships* found that men and women were very similar in their number of friends. They had:

4 friends they could talk to **about their sex lives**,

5–6 friends they could call when they were **in trouble**, and

5–6 friends who would celebrate **birthdays** with them.

DIMENSIONS OF FRIENDSHIP

What are the most fundamental friend-like behaviors? Psychologist Beverley Fehr found the following statements were most "prototypical," or essentially friend-like. Use them to assess your own friendships.

- ✔ **If I need to talk**, my friend will listen. (Women rated this higher than men, but men still put it at the top of the list.)
- ✔ **If I'm in trouble**, my friend will help me.
- ✔ **If I need my friend**, she or he will be there for me.
- ✔ **If I have a problem**, my friend will listen.
- ✔ **If someone was insulting me** or saying negative things behind my back, my friend would stick up for me.
- ✔ **If I need food, clothing, or a place to stay**, my friend will help.
- ✔ **If I have a problem or need support**, my friend will help.
- ✔ **No matter who I am or what I do**, my friend will accept me.
- ✔ **If we have a fight or an argument**, we'll work it out.
- ✔ **Even if it feels as though no one cares**, I know my friend does.
- ✔ **If my friend has upset me,** I feel I can let him or her know.
- ✔ **If I have a secret**, I can trust my friend not to tell anyone else.

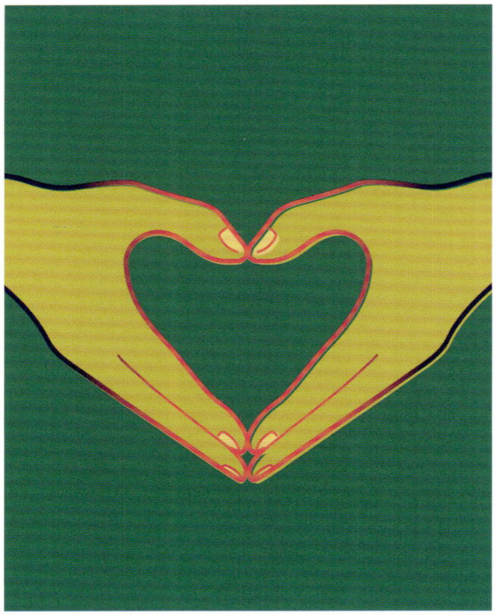

SUCCESSFUL IN LOVE?

MAKING ROMANCE WORK FOR YOU

A loving relationship does not just happen: it is grown, with attention and work from both partners. Communication skills play a big part, alongside patient acceptance of personal differences.

A key concept in the psychology of romance was developed in the mid-20th century by psychologist John Bowlby. According to his "attachment theory," our childhood relationships and subsequent experiences combine to create different attachment styles, or ways of relating to a partner (see "Attachment styles and your relationship," opposite). People with different styles can want very different things—and if we are looking for success in our romantic partnerships, it's important to understand these differences and be prepared to work around them.

Emotional security

Secure people tend to have the most secure relationships, but it's also true that a bond needs only one secure partner to obtain the necessary stability. If the secure partner is content to give reassurance and is not threatened by the idea of being needed, an anxious person can relax, and is often devoted and loving. An avoidant type will often want to spend time alone, and the secret of success here is in the other partner not taking that personally.

Communication

Constant communication gives built-in protection to any relationship, providing a healthy basis for any compromises needed. Sacrifices silently endured tend to fester, whereas a willingness to talk often leads to solutions even to issues that may initially have seemed impossible to resolve. Emotional security also requires acceptance of your partner's own personality, needs, and feelings, and a willingness to find welcoming space for all of these in your life.

Companionship

It is important to share activities, and to keep outside pressures from limiting the time available for these. Constant nurture of a relationship, mutual enjoyment, and affection contribute to a loving future.

3–6%

OF HAPPINESS

Haven't found Mr. or Ms. Right? Don't be too downhearted. According to a 2007 report for the *Journal of Happiness Studies*, **romantic relationship quality** only accounted for 3–6 percent of **people's total happiness**.

ATTACHMENT STYLES AND YOUR RELATIONSHIP

Psychologist John Bowlby identified three attachment styles, or ways that you relate in a relationship: secure, anxious, and avoidant. It is possible for any permutation of these styles to work in a romantic partnership, but certain combinations are particularly well matched and others will tend to be successful only if certain pitfalls are avoided, and each partner deals patiently with the other's tendencies. The chart below characterizes each style in terms of typical thought patterns. At the bottom of the page is guidance on how to get the best out of all six possible matches.

Style	Life has taught them ...	Feelings about intimacy	Views of partner's feelings	Reaction to conflict
Secure	Other people can probably be relied upon, and I'm worthy of love.	Intimacy is natural, comfortable, and right.	My partner's feelings are my responsibility. We take care of each other.	We talk through issues and find a solution that addresses the needs of both partners.
Anxious	I really want love, but I probably don't deserve it. I must be careful not to drive my partner away.	I want intimacy, but if my partner sees I'm too needy they won't want me.	I'm hypersensitive to any signs of rejection. If my partner reassures me quickly, though, I'll calm down.	If I say anything direct, I'm worried I might lose my partner. I tend to worry silently, though sometimes I might explode in anger.
Avoidant	I can't rely on anyone but myself. I have no time for sentimentality and all that nonsense.	I need my independence. Pushed too far, I yearn to get away.	My partner's feelings are not my responsibility. I can't be blamed for them.	I want nothing more than to be left in peace. I don't feel the need to talk in detail through every little issue.

How can your "atttachment style" combination work well?

Anxious + Anxious

Both partners have to work on communication skills, and being empathetic but direct with each other.

Anxious + Avoidant

One fears rejection and needs to cultivate strength; the other fears intimacy and needs to learn to be more giving.

Anxious + Secure

The secure partner assumes it's normal to soothe anxieties. Both partners want intimacy—a good basis for ironing out any issues.

Avoidant + Avoidant

Both partners need to work at communication skills. Trial separations can help each to reevaluate.

Avoidant + Secure

Secure people aren't threatened by an avoidant person's desire for "space." Avoidant people feel less stress as a result.

Secure + Secure

Both partners treat intimacy as a given, and communicate clearly. The main threat might be falling for another.

CREATING A BALANCE

WORK, HOME, AND A WHOLE SELF

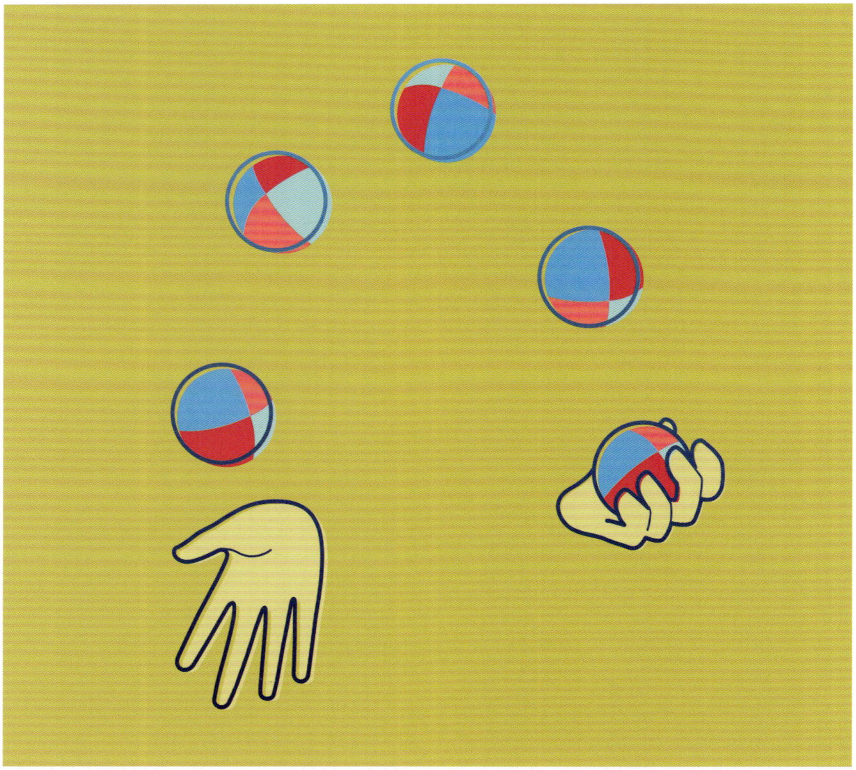

Can we ever achieve the perfect "work-life balance"? Maybe, but only with compromises. In any case, your priorities will shift as time goes by, so you need to keep reviewing your needs as your circumstances change.

Many people find themselves struggling to balance earning a living, being part of a family, and following their dreams. The ideal is for these things to support each other, but this can be hard to achieve.

Work and life

A concept psychologists have studied in recent years is that of "role accumulation"—that is, how we have to manage being different selves in different situations, such as home and work. Depending on how we handle things, this mix can be either a blessing or a burden.

On the positive side, family can support work and vice versa. Studies confirm that if we're happy in one area, we can carry a good mood into the other; likewise, skills can be transferred—parenting can make us more comfortable with responsibility, work can teach us time-management skills that help with the family calendar, and so on. At the same time, these factors can buffer each other—if work is going badly, a good social life can support us, while pride in our job can keep our self-esteem high if things aren't going so well at home.

How can we attain a good balance? A 2007 study for the *Journal of Vocational Behavior* argues that we need a high "CSE," or Core Self-Evaluation. This means having:

- High self-esteem
- Low neuroticism—not seeing ourselves as vulnerable
- A high internal locus of control (see p.152–153)
- High self-efficacy (see pp.102–103).

If our CSE is positive, we are better able to use our work to help in our home life, and vice versa. A negative CSE, on the other hand, leaves us feeling that each interferes with the other. It's worth noting that people with a high CSE may seek greater challenges and put themselves under more pressure, so the ideal state of mind is to rate ourselves well but beware of overcommitting. Understanding ourselves and our goals throughout our lives helps us to make choices and take actions to maintain balance and avoid burnout.

Pain or gain?

A 2012 study for the College of Business in Florida points out that, while role accumulation can be beneficial, it also has its negative side. If we're deeply committed to both work and home, it can be hard to avoid exhaustion. The answer is to seek authenticity: what matters to you most? If you're reaching for your dreams, juggling roles tends to seem more worthwhile.

PLOT WHAT MATTERS TO YOU MOST

To identify which areas of your life matter to you most, American psychologists Farid Muna and Ned Mansour suggest that you draw your life as a series of interlocking circles, like in the example below. Vary the size of the circles depending on how important each area is to you, and show where areas of your life overlap.

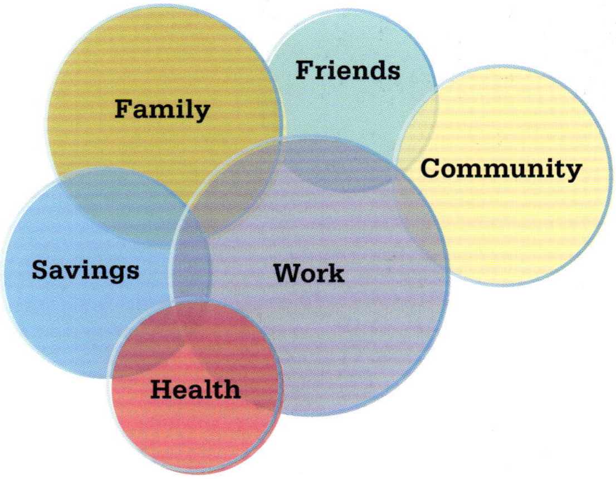

When you've mapped out your life and aspirations, talk over the following questions with your partner, trusted friends, mentors, and family. If you prefer, substitute "I" for "We."

- Do I have a long-term wish list?
- What will make me happy 10, 20, or 40 years from now?
- What do I imagine are my future goals?
- What threats, opportunities, strengths, and weaknesses do I face?
- How will these impact my success?
- What do I want to accomplish with the rest of my life?

RETRO-PLOTTING

Psychologists Farid Muna and Ned Mansour suggest a technique for analyzing what matters to you based on reflecting on past experiences. On a graph, plot events that made you happy or sad in relation to the high-to-low happiness axis. Don't dwell in the past, but try to understand what it was that made events either happy or sad, so you can learn the lessons and apply them to your current situation.

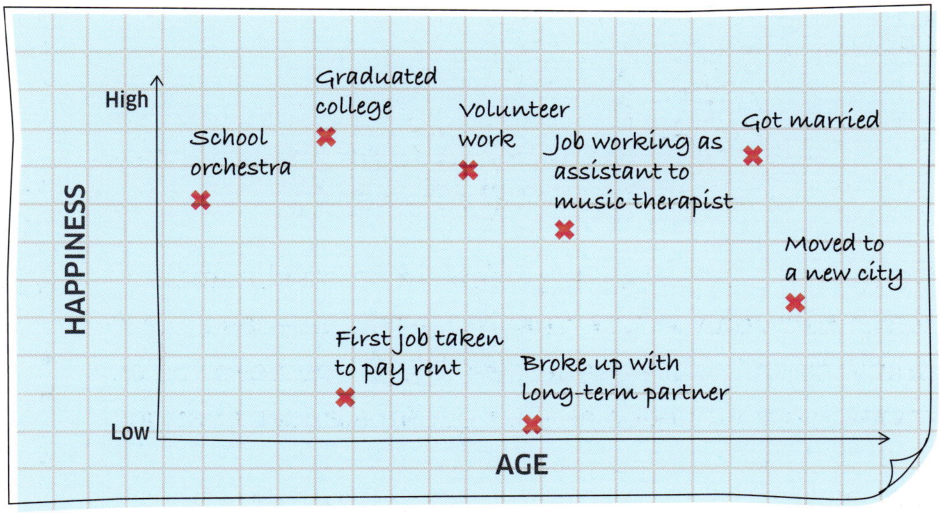

SUCCESS FOR LIFE

HOW WELL-BEING HELPS US

Well-being is not just a matter of luck: it can also, to some extent, be an attitude. If we can find ways to be open, friendly, giving, optimistic, and calm, we may tap into a mood that makes success more achievable.

Success, according to one convincing perspective on the subject, is not a finishing line we cross, but a way of living. We cannot usefully separate success from the rest of our lives, as it connects in complex ways with our happiness, our self-image, and the people we care about. In fact, it's healthy to treat success as a process, so that we're not so much reaching a pinnacle as walking a path. When working on our ambitions, it's good to think of our lives as a whole. Focusing on our well-being, as well as on our individual goals, can enlarge us as individuals and make success both more meaningful to us and more reachable.

Which comes first?

Successes make us happy, we might think, but the research suggests that in fact happiness tends to precede success. In one study, American psychologists Julia K. Boehm and Sonja Lyubomirsky found that people who regularly

STEPS TO WELL-BEING

According to American psychologists Lisa Mainiero and Sherry Sullivan, as we develop we go through specific stages (see below). How we handle each stage impacts our well-being and what we deem to be important.

- **Challenge**—the key factor at the beginning of our career
- **Balance**—our priority in midlife
- **Authenticity**—the driving force in our late career

experienced positive emotions—the "P" in positive psychology's PERMA scheme of well-being (see p.49)—were more likely to do well in life. These emotions didn't have to be dramatic: in fact, the best predictor of happiness was low-level but regular experiences of positive feeling. For these people, happiness, either by nature or by cultivated mental practice, was a habit. The result? They met with more success. People assessed as happy were found to be more likely to earn bigger salaries a few years after the assessement. Their careers were demonstrated to be measurably more successful, as the following indicators suggest:

- If interviewed, they were more likely to get a callback
- They were less likely to lose their jobs or become unemployed
- If they did find themselves out of work, they were more likely to find another job
- Their colleagues were more supportive toward them.

The reason for their success was, basically, that happiness made these people engage in success-attracting behaviors. They had more energy and were friendlier. They cooperated better with others and were less confrontational. Their problem-solving was more creative, and they set themselves higher goals, persisted longer, and were more optimistic. Happiness naturally inclines us to behave in ways that make other people more willing to work with us and that improve our own performance. Taking care of well-being is, in fact, one of the soundest investments for your future that you're likely to be able to make.

Lifelong well-being

What's the basis for long-term well-being? It's partly what American psychologists Sonja Lyubomirsky and Kennon M. Sheldon call our "chronic happiness" capacity. This is created by a mix of factors:

- Our genetically determined setpoint, which may be relatively happy or relatively sad
- Our life circumstances
- The activities we engage in.

While we may not be able to do much about our genes, the pursuit of success is very much about changing our circumstances and activities for the better. As we do this, it's wise to remember that well-being is a lifelong project. When planning our success, we can help ourselves by building the resources that we anticipate may satisfy our *future* needs. You can't anticipate everything, of course, but if you treat success as a lifelong process, you can look beyond narrow forms of achievement and truly experience a successful and fulfilling life.

WHY HAPPIER PEOPLE ARE MORE EFFECTIVE

American psychologists Julia K. Boehm and Sonja Lyubomirsky, in an article entitled "The Promise of Sustainable Happiness," have summarized some of the reasons why happy people tend to be more effective in pursuit of their goals. Below are four chains of cause and effect based on these findings, showing how happiness tends to lead to enhanced effectiveness. Unhappy people, conversely, follow negative chains, leading to diminished effectiveness.

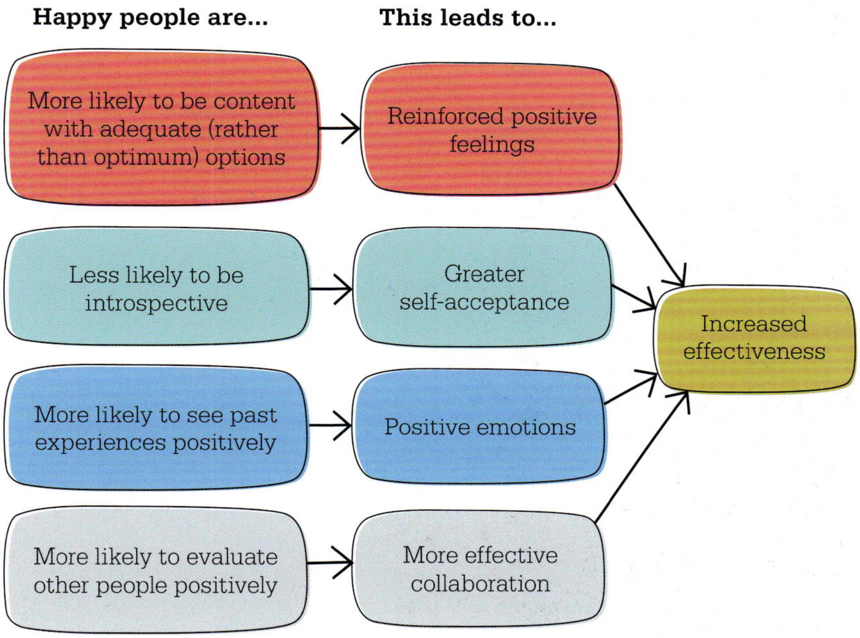

SOURCES AND BIBLIOGRAPHY

Web links accessed 12–31 Aug 2016.
HBR = *Harvard Business Review*

CHAPTER 1

12–13 H. Kimsey-House, K. Kimsey-House, P. Sandahl, and L. Whitworth, *Co-Active Coaching*, 3rd ed., Boston, Nicholas Brealey Publishing, 2011, http://www.coactive.com. **16–17** E. Diener and M. Seligman, "Beyond Money," *Psychological Science in the Public Interest* 5, no. 1 (2004), 1–31; P. Chen, P. C. Ellsworth, and N. Schwarz, "Finding a Fit or Developing It," *Personality and Social Psychology Bulletin* 41, no. 10 (2015), 1411–1424; D. De Clercq, B. Honig, and B. Martin, "The roles of learning orientation and passion for work in the formation of entrepreneurial intention," *International Small Business Journal* 31, no. 6 (Sep 2013), 652–676. **18–19** B. George, P. Sims, A. N. McLean, and D. Mayer, "Discovering Your Authentic Leadership," *HBR* (Feb 2007), 129–138; K. Cherry, "The Big Five Personality Traits," Verywell.com, updated 10 Jan 2016; D. McClelland, *Human Motivation*, Cambridge, Cambridge University Press, 1987. **20–21** R. St. John, "8 Secrets of Success," TED Talk, Feb 2005; E. Andersen, "Learning to Learn," *HBR* (Mar 2016), 98–101; K. P. Cross, "Not can, but *will* college teaching be improved?," *New Directions for Higher Education* 17 (Mar 1977), 1–15. **22–23** F. Cury, A. J. Elliot, D. Da Fonseca, and A. C. Moller, "The Social–Cognitive Model of Achievement Motivation and the 2 × 2 Achievement Goal Framework," *Journal of Personality and Social Psychology* 90, no. 4 (2006), 666–679; S. DeRue and K. M. Workman, "Driving Leadership Development with Positivity," Center for Positive Organizations; B. Johnson, "The Goal-Setting Process Warren Buffett Uses To Say 'No' And Achieve More," GoalsOnTrack.com, 10 Feb 2016. **24–25** M. Strode, "Wind-Wafted Wild Flowers." **26–27** F. Nickols, "The Goals Grid," 2003, http://www.nickols.us; C. Dweck, "The power of believing that you can improve," TED Talk, Nov 2014. **28–29** B. Tracy, *Eat that frog!* London, Hodder & Stoughton, 2016; "How many people have mental health problems?," Mind, http://www.mind.org.uk; "Work-life balance," Mental Health Foundation, https://www.mentalhealth.org.uk; S. Friedman, *Total Leadership*, Boston, Harvard Business Review Press, 2014; "Kenexa Research Institute Finds That When It Comes To Work/Life Balance, Men and Women Are Not Created Equal," 25 Jul 2007. **30–31** A. Brown, J. Bimrose, S-A. Barnes, S. Kirpal, T. Grønning, and M. Dæhlen, "Changing patterns of working, learning and career development across Europe," Brussels: Education, Audiovisual & Culture Executive Agency, 2010; W. Johnson, "Disrupt Yourself," *HBR* (Jul–Aug 2012), 147–150; A. Brown, J. Bimrose, S-A. Barnes, and D. Hughes, "The role of career adaptabilities for mid-career changers," *Journal of Vocational Behavior* 80 (2012), 754–761; E. L. Goldberg, "The Changing Tides of Careers," *People & Strategy* 35, no. 4 (2012), 52–58; C. Copeland, "Employee Tenure Trends, 1983–2014," Employee Benefit Research Institute's *Notes* 36, no. 2 (Feb 2015). **32–33** P. Reuell, "Positive Peer Pressure More Effective Than Cash Incentives, Study Finds," UC San Diego News Center, 11 Jun 2013; A. Mueller, "Goal keepers: The power of positive peer pressure," *St. Louis Business Journal*, 12 Sep 2014; T. L. Webb and P. Sheeran, "Integrating concepts from goal theories to understand the achievement of personal goals," *European Journal of Social Psychology* 35 (2005), 69–96; "Why Peer Pressure Doesn't Add Up To Retirement Savings," NPR, 31 Jul 2015; S. Bharatam, "Three ways to overcome peer pressure and excel in business world," Business Daily Africa, 11 May 2015. **34–35** L. Nash and H. Stevenson, "Success That Lasts," *HBR* (Feb 2004), 102–109; W. Wood and D. T. Neal, "A New Look at Habits and the Habit-Goal Interface," *Psychological Review* 114, no. 4 (Oct 2007), 843–863; B. Verplanken and S. Faes, "Good intentions, bad habits, and effects of forming implementation intentions on healthy eating," *European Journal of Social Psychology* 29, no. 5–6 (Aug–Sep 1999), 591–604. **36–37** M. McMahon, M. Watson, and J. Bimrose, "Career adaptability," *Journal of Vocational Behavior* 80 (2012), 762–768; "Language Myth #6: Women Talk Too Much," PBS, http://www.pbs.org/speak/speech/prejudice/women/; W. D. A. Fernando and L. Cohen, "Exploring the interplay between gender, organizational context and career," *Career Development International* 16, no. 6 (2011), 553–571. **38–39** T. Amabile and S. Kramer, "The Power of Small Wins," *HBR* 89, no. 5 (May 2011), 70–80; T. Amabile and S. Kramer, "Do Happier People Work Harder?," *The New York Times*, 3 Sep 2011; "Research & Articles," Teresa Amabile, http://progressprinciple.com/research. **40–41** C. Johnson, "Four Tips for How to Become More Consistent," http://www.chalenejohnson.com; A. Wrzesniewski and B. Schwartz, "The Secret of Effective Motivation,"

The New York Times, 4 Jul 2014. **42–43** R. F. Baumeister, E. Bratslavsky, M. Muraven, and D. M. Tice, "Ego Depletion: Is the Active Self a Limited Resource?," *Journal of Personality and Social Psychology* 74, no. 5 (1998), 1252–1265; M. Inzlicht and B. J. Schmeichel, "What Is Ego Depletion? Toward a Mechanistic Revision of the Resource Model of Self-Control," *Perspectives on Psychological Science* 7, no. 5 (Sep 2012), 450–463; D. McGinn, "Being More Productive," *HBR* (May 2011), 83–87; A. Salis, "The science of 'hangry'," *The Conversation*, 20 Jul 2015; "How Much Sleep Do We Really Need?," National Sleep Foundation. **44–45** K. Schulz, "On being wrong," TED Talk, Mar 2011; S. Lewis, "Embrace the near win," TED Talk, Mar 2014; C. Chabris and D. Simons, *The Invisible Gorilla*, London, HarperCollins, 2010.

CHAPTER 2

48–51 M. Seligman, *Building the State of Wellbeing*, South Australia, Government of South Australia, 2013; "The A in PERMA," The Positive Psychology Foundation, 8 Aug 2011, http://www.positivepsyc.com; R. Waldinger, "What makes a good life?," TED Talk, Jan 2016; A. Adler, M. L. Kern, L. E. Waters, and M. A. White, "A multidimensional approach to measuring well-being in students," *The Journal of Positive Psychology* 10, no. 3 (2015), 262–271; P. O'Grady, "Achievement vs Accomplishment," *Psychology Today*, 11 Nov 2012. **52–53** T. Bradberry, "Why You Should Spend Your Money on Experiences, Not Things," http://www.talentsmart.com; M. E. P. Seligman, T. A. Steen, N. Park, and C. Peterson, "Positive Psychology Progress," *American Psychologist* 60, no. 5 (2005), 410–421; S. Achor, "Positive Intelligence," *HBR* (Jan–Feb 2012), 100–102. **54–57** R. Biswas-Diener, T. B. Kashdan, and G. Minhas, "A dynamic approach to psychological strength development and intervention," *The Journal of Positive Psychology* 6, no. 2 (2011), 106–118; D. R. Vago and D. A. Silbersweig, "Self-awareness, self-regulation, and self-transcendence (S-ART)," *Frontiers in Human Neuroscience*, 25 Oct 2012, http://journal.frontiersin.org. **58–59** R. Habib, "Emotional Intelligence," TEDx Talk, Feb 2015; D. Goleman, *Emotional Intelligence*, 10th anniversary ed., New York, Bantam, 2006. **60–61** H. Armson, K. Eva, E. Holmboe, J. Lockyer, E. Loney, K. Mann, and J. Sargeant, "Factors influencing responsiveness to feedback," *Advances in Health Sciences Education* 17, no. 1 (2012), 15–26; T. Bradberry, "9 Habits of Profoundly Influential People". **62–63** D. Dunning and J. Kruger, "Unskilled and Unaware of It," *Journal of Personality and Social Psychology* 77, no. 6 (1999), 1121–1134; B. Barker, J. Dutton, E. Heaphy, L. M. Roberts, G. Spreitzer, and R. Quinn, "How To Play To Your Strengths," *HBR* (Jan 2005), 74–80. **64–65** C. S. Dweck and D. S. Yeager, "Mindsets That Promote Resilience," *Educational Psychologist* 47, no. 4 (2012), 301–314; D. Perkins-Gough, "The Significance of Grit," *Educational Leadership* 71, no. 1 (2013), 14–20; T. Bradberry, "8 Ways Smart People Use Failure to Their Advantage". **66–67** A. Bandura, "Self-efficacy: Toward a unifying theory of behavioral change," *Psychological Review* 84, no. 2 (1977), 191–215. **68–71** T. Lomas, D. Ridge, T. Cartwright, and T. Edginton, "Engagement with meditation as a positive health trajectory," *Psychology & Health* 29, no. 2 (2014), 218–236; P. J. Davis, A. O'Donovan, and C. A. Pepping, "The positive effects of mindfulness on self-esteem," *The Journal of Positive Psychology* 8, no. 5 (2013), 376–386; J. Hunter and D. W. McCormick, "Mindfulness in the Workplace," paper presented at the Academy of Management Annual Meeting, Anaheim, 2008; L. Wasmer Andrews, "Four Good Times of Day to Meditate (And One to Avoid)," *Psychology Today*, 6 Mar 2012; T. Bradberry, "5 Ways Mindfulness Will Turbocharge Your Career"; J. Dixon, R. McCorkle, P. H. Van Ness, and A. Williams, "Determinants of Meditation Practice Inventory," *Alternative Therapies* 17, no. 5 (Sep–Oct 2011), 16–23. **72–73** D. Pink, "The puzzle of motivation," TED Talk, Aug 2009; S. Dinsmore, "How to find work you love," TED Talk, Sep 2015; J. M. Berg, J. E. Dutton, and A. Wrzesniewski, "Managing Yourself," *HBR* (Jun 2010), 114–117. **74–75** M. Heffernan, "Dare to disagree," TED Talk, Aug 2012. **76–77** "What is character?," Via Institute on Character, www.viacharacter.org; N. Mayerson, "'Characterizing the Workplace,'" Via Institute on Character, 2015, www.viacharacter.org; C. Peterson and M. Seligman, *Character Strengths and Virtues*, Oxford, New York, Oxford University Press, 2004; "The Via Survey," Via Institute on Character, www.viacharacter.org; *The Science of Character (8min "Cloud Film")* [online video], 2014, https://www.youtube.com; "The VIA classification of character strengths," © Copyright 2004–2016, VIA Institute on Character. All rights reserved. Used with permission. www.viacharacter.org. **78–79** D. Bradley, "Why Gladwell's 10,000-hour rule is wrong," BBC, 14 Nov 2012, http://www.bbc.com; K. Anders Ericsson, "Training history, deliberate practise and elite sports performance," *British Journal of Sports Medicine*, 29 Oct 2014, http://bjsm.bmj.com; R. Nuwer, "The 10,000 Hour Rule Is Not Real," Smithsonian Magazine, 20 Aug 2014, http://www.smithsonianmag.com; J. R. Lim, "Is Musical Talent Rooted in Genes?," Live Science, 5 Aug 2014, http://www.livescience.com; K. R. Von Culin, E. Tsukayama, and A. L. Duckworth, "Unpacking grit," *The Journal of Positive Psychology* 9, no. 4 (2014), 306–312; M. Seligman, *Authentic Happiness*, New York, Free Press, 2002.

CHAPTER 3

82–83 D. D. Burns, *Feeling Good*, New York, Avon Books, HarperCollins, 1980. **84–85** I. Joseph, "4 Ways to Build

Self-Confidence and Boost Your Performance," Huffington Post, 7 Dec 2015, http://www.huffingtonpost.ca; A. Cuddy, "Your body language shapes who you are," TED Talk, Jun 2012. **86–87** A. D. Joudrey and J. E. Wallace, "Leisure as a coping resource," *Human Relations* 62, no. 2 (2009), 195–217; M. Wang and M. C. Sunny Wong, "Happiness and Leisure Across Countries," *Journal of Happiness Studies* 15, no. 1 (2014), 85–118; R. Hunicke, M. LeBlanc, and R. Zubek, "MDA: A Formal Approach to Game Design and Game Research," paper presented at the Challenges in Games AI Workshop, Nineteenth National Conference of Artificial Intelligence, 2004; *Aesthetics of Play – Redefining Genres in Gaming – Extra Credits* [online video], 2012, https://www.youtube.com. **88–89** H. Adam and A. D. Galinsky, "Enclothed cognition," *Journal of Experimental Social Psychology* 48, no. 4 (2012), 918–925; T. Shafir, "How Your Body Affects Your Happiness," TEDx Talk, Nov 2013; K. Hefferon, "The Body 2.0," paper presented at Canadian Positive Psychology Conference, 2014. **90–91** L. Deschene, "How to Deal with Uncomfortable Feelings & Create Positive Ones," Tiny Buddha, http://tinybuddha.com; J. T. Cacioppo, J. M. Ernst, M. H. Burleson, M. K. McClintock, W. B. Malarkey, L. C. Hawkley, R. B. Kowalewski, A. Paulsen, J. A. Hobson, K. Hugdahl, D. Spiegel, and G. G. Berntson, "Lonely traits and concomitant physiological processes," *International Journal of Psychophysiology* 35, no. 2–3 (2000), 143–154; M. Tartakovsky, "How to Manage Emotions More Effectively," Psych Central, 3 Jul 2012, http://psychcentral.com; K. Dahlgren, "Don't Go Wasting Your Emotion," Emotion on the Brain, 10 Oct 2012, https://sites.tufts.edu; A. Bechara, "The role of emotion in decision-making," *Brain and Cognition* 55 (2004), 30–40. **92–93** A. Maslow, *The Psychology of Science*, London, Harper & Row, 1966. **94–95** A. Duckworth and J. J. Gross, "Self-Control and Grit," *Current Directions in Psychological Science* 23, no. 5 (2014), 319–325; J. Urist, "What the Marshmallow Test Really Teaches About Self-Control," The Atlantic, 24 Sep 2014, http://www.theatlantic.com; M. Severns, "Reconsidering the Marshmallow Test," Slate, 16 Oct 2012, http://www.slate.com; "The Marshmallow Study Revisited," University of Rochester, 11 Oct 2012, http://www.rochester.edu; "Emotional Intelligence," Mind Tools, https://www.mindtools.com. **96–97** Team of experts at American Psychological Association, "Stress in America: Paying With Our Health," American Psychological Association, 4 Feb 2015, https://www.apa.org; "Stressed Out By Work? You're Not Alone," Wharton, University of Pennsylvania, 30 Oct 2014, http://knowledge.wharton.upenn.edu. **98–99** V. I. Lohr, C. H. Pearson-Mims, and G. K. Goodwin, "Interior plants may improve worker productivity and reduce stress in a windowless environment," *Journal of Environmental Horticulture* 14, no. 2 (1996), 97–100; "Stress and wellbeing," Australian Psychological Society, 2015, https://www.psychology.org.au; Team of experts at American Psychological Association, "Stress in America: Paying With Our Health," American Psychological Association, 4 Feb 2015, https://www.apa.org. **100–101** K. McGonigal, "How to make stress your friend," TED Talk, Sep 2013; A. W. Brooks, "Get Excited," *Journal of Experimental Psychology* 143, no. 3 (2014), 1144–1158; L. Bambrick, "The Yerkes-whatzy law of who now?," Secret Geek, 17 May 2007, http://www.secretgeek.net; D. Levitin, "How to stay calm when you know you'll be stressed," TEDGlobal, Sep 2015; D. G. Dutton and A. P. Aron, "Some evidence for heightened sexual attraction under conditions of high anxiety," *Journal of Personality and Social Psychology* 30, no. 4 (Oct 1974), 510–517. **102–103** L. Babauta, "A Roadmap to Overcoming Insecurities," *Zen Habits*, 14 Mar 2016, http://zenhabits.net. **104–105** K. Bahn, "Women, Academe, and Imposter Syndrome," *Chronicle of Higher Education* 60, no. 30 (2014), A51–A51; J. Nelson, "What's behind the imposter syndrome," *Canadian Business* 84, no. 18 (2011), p.129; M. Price, "'Imposters' Downshift Career Goals," *Science Magazine*, 4 Sep 2013, http://www.sciencemag.org. **106–107** J. Morgan and D. Sisak, "Aspiring to succeed," *Journal of Business Venturing* 31 (2016), 1–21; T. A. Pychyl, "Fear of Failure," *Psychology Today*, 13 Feb 2009; G. Cacciotti, J. C. Hayton, J. R. Mitchell, and A. Giazitzoglu, "A reconceptualization of fear of failure in entrepreneurship," *Journal of Business Venturing* 31 (2016), 302–325. **108–109** A. Ledgerwood, "Getting stuck in the negatives (and how to get unstuck)," TEDx Talk, Jun 2013; B. Brown, "The power of vulnerability," TED Talk, Dec 2010; B. Brown, "Listening to shame," TED Talk, Mar 2012; C. Cadwalladr, "Brené Brown: 'People will find a million reasons to tear your work down,'" *The Guardian*, 22 Nov 2015. **110–111** J. Wooden, "The difference between winning and succeeding," TED Talk, Mar 2009; D. R. Deeter-Schmelz and R. P. Ramsey, "Fear of Success in Salespeople," paper presented at American Marketing Association, 2001, 248–255; S. Babbel, "Fear of Success," *Psychology Today*, 3 Jan 2011.

CHAPTER 4

114–115 "Adaptability and Flexibility," University of Bradford, http://www.bradford.ac.uk; C. Bergland, "New Paradigm of Thought Demystifies Cognitive Flexibility," *Psychology Today*, 7 Sep 2015; S. Beilock, "Want to Successfully Manage Your Emotions? Be Flexible," *Psychology Today*, 2 Nov 2011. **116–119** "Be Happy: How to Make Your Own Luck," *Women's Health*, 28 Mar 2014; R. Wiseman, "The Luck Factor," *Skeptical Inquirer* 27, no. 3 (2003); C. N. Lazarus, "Four Simple Ways to Increase Your Psychological Flexibility," *Psychology Today*, 20 Mar 2014; H. Sohn and E. Lee, *Integrated Korean: Advanced Intermediate 2*, University of Hawai'i Press, Honolulu, 2003, p.22; R. Smith, "It Takes Patience to Know Bad Luck From Good Luck," *Psychology Today*, 19 Mar 2015; D. Collinson, "Go Luck Yourself!" *Psychology Today*, 27 Apr 2016. **120–121** L. Babauta, "Why We Struggle With Change," *Zen Habits*, 19 Feb 2016, http://zenhabits.net; C. McHugh, "The art of being yourself," TEDx Talk, Feb 2013; K. Hall, "Got a Problem? The Good News Is You Only Have Four Options," *Psychology Today*, 7 Feb 2012; K. Hall, "Three Blocks to Radical Acceptance," *Psychology Today*, 15 Dec 2013; S. A. Diamond, "Essential Secrets of Psychotherapy," *Psychology Today*, 26 Jun 2008. **122–123** D. A. Olson, J. Liu, and K. S. Shultz, "The Influence of Facebook Usage on Perceptions of Social Support, Personal Efficacy, and Life Satisfaction," *Journal of Organizational Psychology* 12, no. 3/4 (2012), 133–144; S. Duică, R. Balázsi, R. Ciulei, and A. Bivolaru, "The mediating role of coping strategies between achievement goals and competitive anxiety in elite sport," *Cognition, Brain, Behavior* 18, no. 2 (2014), 109–124; "The Cost of Coping," *Psychology Today*, 1 Nov 1998; J. C. Weitlauf, R. E. Smith, and D. Cervone, "Generalization Effects of Coping-Skills Training," *Journal of Applied Psychology* 85, no. 4 (2000), 625–633; G. A. Bonanno, A. Papa, K. Lalande, M. Westphal, and K. Coifman, "The Importance of Being Flexible," *Psychological Science* 15, no. 7 (2004), 482–487. **124–125** B. J. C. Claessens, W. van Eerde, C. G. Rutte, and R. A. Roe, "A review of the time management literature," *Personnel Review* 36, no. 2 (2007), 255–276; L. Evans, "The Exact Amount Of Time You Should Work Every Day," Fast Company, 15 Sep 2014, http://www.fastcompany.com; H. E. Elsabahy, W. F. Sleem, and H. G. El Atroush, "Effect of Time Management Program on Job Satisfaction for Head Nurses," *Journal of Education and Practice* 6, no. 32 (2015), 36–44; "Easy time-management tips," NHS, reviewed 6 Jan 2016, http://www.nhs.uk. **126–127** P. F. Drucker, *The Effective Executive*, New York, HarperCollins, 2006. **128–129** R. Rugulies, M. H. T. Martin, A. H. Garde, R. Persson, and K. Albertsen, "Deadlines at Work and Sleep Quality," *American Journal of Industrial Medicine* 55, (2012) 260–269; Y. Tu and D. Soman, "The Categorization of Time and Its Impact on Task Initiation," *Journal of Consumer Research* 41, no. 3 (2014), 810–822; M. Blake Hargrove, D. L. Nelson, and C. L. Cooper, "Generating eustress by challenging employees," *Organizational Dynamics* 42, no. 1 (2013), 61–69. **130–131** K. Ching Hei, "Moves in Refusal," *China Media Research* 5, no. 3 (2009), 31–44; C. Freshman, "Don't *Just* Say No," *Negotiation Journal* 24, no. 1 (2008), 89–100; V. M. Patrick and H. Hagtvedt, "How to say 'no'," *International Journal of Research in Marketing* 29, no. 4 (2012), 390–394. **132–133** B. Kane. "The Science of Analysis Paralysis," Todoist, 8 Jul 2015, https://blog.todoist.com; E. Jones, "Analysis paralysis? 4 tips for making better decisions," *The HR Specialist,* Nov 2015; R. Hertwig, and I. Erev, "The description–experience gap in risky choice," *Trends in Cognitive Sciences* 13, no. 12 (2009), 517–523; "New Survey Reveals Extent, Impact of Information Overload on Workers," Lexis Nexis, 20 Oct 2010, http://www.lexisnexis.com; C. K. Hsee, Y. Yang, X. Zheng, and H. Wang, "Lay Rationalism," *Journal of Marketing Research* 52, no. 1 (2015), 134–146. **134–135** W. D. Gray, C. R. Sims, W. T. Fu, and M. J. Schoelles, "The Soft Constraints Hypothesis," *Psychological Review* 113, no. 3 (2006), 461–482; L. R. Weingart, "Impact of group goals, task component complexity, effort, and planning on group performance," *Journal of Applied Psychology* 77, no. 5 (1992), 682–693; A. C. Montoya, D. R. Carter, J. Martin, and L. A. DeChurch, "The Five Perils of Team Planning" in M. D. Mumford, and M. Frese (eds.), *The Psychology of Planning in Organizations*, New York, London, Routledge, 2015. **136–137** P. Ni, "5 Tips to Reduce the Fear of Public Speaking," *Psychology Today*, 6 Nov 2013; B. Richmond, "The Brain Takes Rejection Like Physical Pain," Motherboard, 14 Oct 2013, http://motherboard.vice.com; B. D. Flaxington, "Overcoming Fear of Public Speaking," *Psychology Today*, 16 Mar 2015; J. Treasure, "How to speak so that people want to listen," TED Talk, Jun 2014. **138–139** P. Fripp, "Selling Yourself and Your Ideas to Senior Management," *Contract Management* 50, no. 4 (2010), 12–15; M. Owen, "Three statistics that can make or break your sales pitch," *TheBusiness*, DueDil, 20 Oct 2015; K. D. Elsbach, "How to Pitch a Brilliant Idea," *HBR* 81, no. 9 (Sep 2003), 117–123. **140–141** O. Zwikael, R. Dutt Pathak, G. Singh, and S. Ahmed, "The moderating effect of risk on the relationship between planning and success," *International Journal of Project Management* 32, no. 3 (2014), 435–441; K. A. Brown, N. Lea Hyer, and R. Ettenson, "The Question Every Project Team Should Answer," *MIT Sloan Management Review* 55, no. 1 (2013), 49–57; D. Dvir and A. J. Shenhar, "What Great Projects Have in Common," *MIT Sloan Management Review* 52, no. 3 (2011), 19–21. **142–143** "The Tannenbaum-Schmidt Leadership Continuum," Mind Tools, https://www.mindtools.com; A. Lebedeva, "Five Essential Project Management Skills," *Information Management* 49, no. 5 (2015), 28–33; P. Ellis and J. Abbott, "Leadership and management skills in health care," *British Journal of Cardiac Nursing* 8, no. 2 (2013), 96–99. **144–145** J. S. Nairne, M. Vasconcelos, and J. N. S. Pandeirada, "Adaptive Memory and Learning," in N. M. Seel (ed.) *Encyclopedia of the Sciences of Learning*, New York, Springer, 2012, 118–121; J. S. Nairne and J. N. S. Pandeirada, "Adaptive Memory: Remembering With a Stone-Age Brain," *Current Directions in Psychological Science* 17, no. 4 (2008), 239–243; D. Kahneman and J. Riis, "Living, and Thinking about it" in N. Baylis, F. A. Huppert, and B. Keverne (eds.), *The Science of Well-Being*, Oxford, Oxford University Press, 2005, 285–301.

146–147 J. E. Van Loon, and H. L. Lai, "Information Literacy Skills as a Critical Thinking Framework in the Undergraduate Engineering Curriculum," *Library Scholarly Publications,* Paper 80, 1–8; D. McRaney, "Survivorship Bias," You Are Not So Smart, 23 May 2013, https://youarenotsosmart.com. **148–149** M. Stange, M. Grau, S. Osazuwa, C. Graydon, and M. J. Dixon, "Reinforcing Small Wins and Frustrating Near-Misses," *Journal of Gambling Studies* (2016), 1–17, http://link.springer.com; V. Denes-Raj and S. Epstein, "Conflict Between Intuitive and Rational Processing," *Journal of Personality and Social Psychology* 66, no. 5 (1994), 819–829.

CHAPTER 5

152–153 "Locus of Control," Changing Minds, http://changingminds.org; T. W. H. Ng, K. L. Sorenson, and L. T. Eby, "Locus of control at work," *Journal of Organizational Behavior* 27, no. 8 (2006), 1057–1087; D. D. Burns MD, *Feeling Good*, New York, HarperCollins, 1992 and 1999, p.125; A. Van den Broeck, W. Lens, H. De Witte, and H. Van Coillie, "Unraveling the importance of the quantity and the quality of workers' motivation for well-being," *Journal of Vocational Behavior* 82, no. 1 (2013), 69–78; T. Willner, I. Gati, and Y. Guan, "Career decision-making profiles and career decision-making difficulties," *Journal of Vocational Behavior* 88 (2015), 143–153. **154–155** B. Gaille, "17 Employee Motivation Statistics and Trends," 10 Nov 2013, http://brandongaille.com; A. Adkins, "Majority of U.S. Employees Not Engaged Despite Gains in 2014," Gallup, 28 Jan 2015, http://www.gallup.com. **156–159** P. Steel, "The Nature of Procrastination," *Psychological Bulletin* 133, no. 1 (2007), 65–94; D. Thompson, "The Procrastination Doom Loop—and How to Break It," *The Atlantic*, 26 Aug 2014, http://www.theatlantic.com; E. Jaffe, "Why Wait? The Science Behind Procrastination," *Observer* 26, no. 4 (2013); A. L. Wichman, P. Briñol, R. E. Petty, D. D. Rucker, Z. L. Tormala, and G. Weary, "Doubting one's doubt," *Journal of Experimental Social Psychology* 46, no. 2 (2010), 350–355; "10 Foolproof Tips for Overcoming Procrastination," PsyBlog, 31 Mar 2014, http://www.spring.org.uk; "How to Avoid Procrastination," PsyBlog, 29 Jan 2009, http://www.spring.org.uk; M. E. Beutel, E. M. Klein, S. Aufenanger, E. Brähler, M. Dreier, K. W. Müller, O. Ouiring, L. Reinecke, G. Schmutzer, B. Stark, and K. Wölfling, "Procrastination, Distress and Life Satisfaction across the Age Range," *PLoS ONE* 11, no. 2 (2016). **160–161** X. Gong, K. L. Fletcher, and J. H. Bolin, "Dimensions of Perfectionism Mediate the Relationship Between Parenting Styles and Coping," *Journal of Counseling & Development* 93, no. 3 (2015), 259–268; P. Gaudreau, "Self-assessment of the four subtypes of perfectionism in the 2 × 2 model of perfectionism," *Personality and Individual Differences* 84 (2015), 52–62. **162–163** D. DiSalvo, "Visualize Success if You Want to Fail," Forbes, 8 Jun 2011, http://www.forbes.com; M. A. Conway, K. Meares, and S. Standart, "Images and goals," *Memory* 12, no. 4 (2004), 525–531; C. K. Y. Chan and L. D. Cameron, "Promoting physical activity with goal-oriented mental imagery," *Journal of Behavioral Medicine* 35, no. 3 (2011), 347–363; S. E. Taylor, L. B. Pham, I. D. Rivkin, and D. A. Armor, "Harnessing the Imagination," *American Psychologist* 53, no. 4 (1998), 429–439. **164–165** J. Du, X. Fan, and T. Feng, "Multiple emotional contagions in service encounters," *Journal of the Academy of Marketing Sciences* 39, no. 3 (2011), 449–466; B. M. Staw, R. I. Sutton, and L. H. Pelled, "Employee Positive Emotion and Favorable Outcomes at the Workplace," *Organization Science* 5, no. 1 (1994), 51–71; C. A. Bartel and R. Saavedra, "The Collective Construction of Work Group Moods," *Administrative Science Quarterly,* 45, no. 2 (2000), 197–231. **166–167** S. Moss, "The dualistic model of passion," http://www.sicotests.com; V. T. Ho, S. Wong, and C. Hoon Lee, "A Tale of Passion," *Journal of Management Studies* 48, no. 1 (2011), 26–47; W. Davies, "Some Thoughts And Questions On Csikszentmihalyi's Flow," Science 2.0, 26 Sep 2010, http://www.science20.com; P. Dubreuil, J. Forest, and F. Courcy, "From strengths use to work performance," *The Journal of Positive Psychology* 9, no. 4 (2014), 335–349. **168–169** M. Csikszentmihalyi, *Flow*, Harper Perennial, New York, 1990. **170–171** S. McNerney, "Rethinking the Endowment Effect," Big Think, http://bigthink.com; A. J. Elliot and K. M. Sheldon, "Avoidance Achievement Motivation," *Journal of Personality and Social Psychology* 73, no. 1 (1997), 171–185. **172–173** R. Yong Joo Chua, P. Ingram, and M. W. Morris, "From the head and the heart," *Academy of Management Journal* 51, no. 3 (2008), 436–452; R. Hoffman and B. Casnocha, "The science of networking," *The Guardian*, 13 Apr 2012; G. Soda, A. Usai, and A. Zaheer, "Network Memory," *Academy of Management Journal* 47, no. 6 (2004), 893–906; M. Simmons, "The Surprising Science Behind How Super Connectors Scale Their Networks," Forbes, 4 Sep 2013, http://www.forbes.com; S. Vozza, "The Science Behind Successful Networking," Fast Company, 3 Oct 2015, http://www.fastcompany.com. **174–175** M. K. Smith, "Social Capital," *The encylopaedia of informal education*, 2000–2009, http://infed.org/mobi/social-capital; M. K. Smith, "Robert Putnam," *The encyclopaedia of informal education*, 2001, 2007, www.infed.org/thinkers/putnam.htm; The World Bank, "The Initiative on Defining, Monitoring and Measuring Social Capital," Social Capital Initiative Working Paper No. 2, 1998, p.5; M. K. Smith, "Social capital," *The encyclopaedia of informal education*, 2000–2009, http://infed.org/mobi/social-capital; S. E. Seibert and M. L. Kraimer, "A social capital theory of career success," *Academy of Management Journal* 44, no. 4 (2001), 291–237. **176–179** C. J. Neumann, "Fostering creativity," *EMBO Reports* 8, no. 3 (2007), 202–206; E. Hulme, B. Thomas, and H. DeLaRosby, "Developing Creativity Ecosystems," *About Campus* 19, no. 1 (2014), 14–23; S. Hebron, "John Keats and 'negative capability'," British Library, http://www.bl.uk; E. Grossman, "Why Science Needs People Who Cry," TEDx Talk, Jan 2016; A. Massey, "Developing creativity for the world of work," *Art, Design & Communication in Higher Education* 4, no. 1 (2005), 17–30; A. VanGundy, *101 Activities for Teaching Creativity and Problem Solving*, San Francisco, Pfeiffer, 2005, p.325. **180–181** J. P. Eggers and L. Song, "Dealing with failure," *Academy of Management Journal* 58, no. 6 (2015), 1785–1803; C. Argyris, "Teaching Smart People How to Learn," *HBR* (May–June 1991), 99–109. **182–183** S. L. Parker, N. L. Jimmieson, and C. E. Amiot, "Self-determination as a moderator of demands and control," *Journal of Vocational Behavior* 76, no. 1 (2010), 52–67. **184–185** A. Spiers and G. J. Walker, "The Effects of Ethnicity and Leisure Satisfaction on Happiness, Peacefulness, and Quality of Life," *Leisure Sciences* 31, no. 1 (2008), 84–89; G. M. Schwartz and J. Campagna, "New meaning for the emotional state of the elderly, from a leisure standpoint," *Leisure Studies* 27, no. 2 (2008), 207–211; W. Wang, C. Kao, T. Huan, and C. Wu, "Free Time Management Contributes to Better Quality of Life," *Journal of Happiness Studies* 12, no. 4 (2011), 561–573; M. G. Ragheb and J. G. Beard, "Measuring Leisure Attitude," *Journal of Leisure Research* 14, no. 2 (1982), 155–167; L. Grodzki, *Building Your Ideal Private Practice*, New York, W. W. Norton & Company, 2000.

CHAPTER 6

188–189 M. M. Tugade and B. L. Fredrickson, "Regulation of positive emotions," *Journal of Happiness Studies* 8, no. 3 (2007), 311–333; R. A. Cummins and M. Wooden, "Personal Resilience in Times of Crisis," *Journal of Happiness Studies* 15, no. 1 (2014), 223–235; *Debunking the 4 most dangerous self help myths* [online video], 2015, https://www.youtube.com; J. V. Wood, W. Q. E. Perunovic, and J. W. Lee, "Positive Self-Statements," *Psychological Science* 20, no. 7 (2009), 860–866. **190–191** H. Knipprath and K. De Rick, "How Social and Human Capital Predict Participation in Lifelong Learning," *Adult Education Quarterly* 65, no. 1 (2015), 50–66; K. Steffens, "Competences, Learning Theories and MOOCs," *European Journal of Education* 50, no. 1 (2015), 41–59; "Contemporary theories of learning," National College for Teaching & Leadership, https://www.nationalcollege.org.uk. **192–193** With thanks to Mario Andretti, and his publicist Patty Reid, for permission to use this quote. **194–195** L. Li, X. Liu, and A. L. Steckelberg, "Assessor or assessee," *British Journal of Educational Technology* 41, no. 3 (2010), 525–536; P. L. Harms, and D. B. Roebuck, "Teaching the art and craft of giving and receiving feedback," *Business Communication Quarterly* 73, no. 4 (2010), 413–431. **196–197** G. D. Bodie, D. Worthington, M. Imhof, and L. O. Cooper, "What Would a Unified Field of Listening Look Like?," *International Journal of Listening* 22, no. 2 (2008), 103–122. **198–199** D. A. Olson and J. Jackson, "Expanding Leadership Diversity Through Formal Mentoring Programs," *Journal of Leadership Studies* 3, no. 1 (2009), 47–60; W. Gentry, S. Stawiski, G. Eckert, and M. Ruderman, "Crafting Your Career," *Center for Creative Leadership* (2013), www.ccl.org. **200–201** S. Chaiken and D. Maheswaran, "Heuristic Processing Can Bias Systematic Processing," *Journal of Personality and Social Psychology* 66, no. 3 (1994), 460–473; W. P. Bottom, K. Gibson, S. E. Daniels, and J. K. Murnighan, "When Talk Is Not Cheap," *Organization Science* 13, no. 5 (2002), 497–513; T. Simons, "Behavioral Integrity," *Organization Science* 13, no. 1 (2002), 18–35. **202–203** L. Uziel, "Look at Me, I'm Happy and Creative," *Personality and Social Psychology Bulletin* 36, no. 12 (2010), 1591–1602; D. Graeber, *Debt: The First 5,000 Years*, New York, Melville House, 2011, p.110. **204–205** K. T. Yamauchi and D. I. Templer, "The Development of a Money Attitude Scale," *Journal of Personality Assessment* 46, no. 5 (1982) 522–528; T. Li-Ping Tang, "The Development of a Short Money Ethic Scale," *Personality and Individual Differences* 19, no. 6 (1995), 809–816. **206–207** B. J. Gillespie, J. Lever, D. Frederick, and T. Royce, "Close adult friendships, gender, and the life cycle," *Journal of Social and Personal Relationships* 32, no. 6 (2014), 709–736; B. Fehr, "Intimacy Expectations in Same-Sex Friendships," *Journal of Personality and Social Psychology* 86, no. 2 (2004), 265–284. **208–209** I. Schindler, C. P. Fagundes, and K. W. Murdock, "Predictors of romantic relationship formation," *Personal Relationships* 17 (2012), 97–105; M. Demir, "Sweetheart, you really make me happy," *Journal of Happiness Studies* 9, no. 2 (2008), 257–277. **210–211** S. L. Boyar and D. C. Mosley Jr., "The relationship between core self-evaluations and work and family satisfaction," *Journal of Vocational Behavior* 71, no. 2 (2007), 265–281; Z. Chen and G. N. Powell, "No pain, no gain? A resource-based model of work-to-family enrichment and conflict," *Journal of Vocational Behavior* 81 (2012), 89–98; F. A. Muna and N. Mansour, "Balancing work and personal life," *Journal of Management Development* 28, no. 2 (2009), 121–133. **212–213** J. K. Boehm and S. Lyubomirksy, "Does Happiness Promote Career Success?," *Journal of Career Assessment* 16, no. 1 (2008), 101–116; S. Lyubomirsky, K. M. Sheldon, and D. Schkade, "Pursuing Happiness," *Review of General Psychology* 9, no. 2 (2005), 111–131; C. D. Ryff and S. M. Heidrich, "Experience and Well-being," *International Journal of Behavioral Development* 20, no. 2 (1997), 193–206; D. A. Olson and K. S. Shultz, "Employability and Career Success," *Industrial and Organizational Psychology* 6, no. 1 (2013), 17–20.

INDEX

Page numbers in **bold** refer to main entries.

A

B

C

D

O

P

R

S